Unity 3 Game Development HOTSH⊕T

Eight projects specifically designed to exploit Unity's full potential

Jate Wittayabundit

[PACKT]
PUBLISHING

BIRMINGHAM - MUMBAI

Unity 3 Game Development HOTSHOT

First published: August 2011

Production Reference: 1180811

Published by Packt Publishing Ltd.
Livery Place
35 Livery Street
Birmingham B3 2PB, UK

ISBN 978-1-849691-12-3

www.packtpub.com

Cover Image by Jate Wittayabundit (jatewit@jatewit.com)

Credits

Author

Jate Wittayabundit

Reviewers

Jaap Kreijkamp

Fraser McCormick

Brad McGinn

Clifford Peters

Acquisition Editor

Steven Wilding

Development Editor

Maitreya Bhakal

Technical Editor

Manasi Poonthottam

Project Coordinator

Zainab Bagasrawala

Copy Editor

Laxmi Subramanian

Proofreader

Aaron Nash

Indexer

Monica Ajmera Mehta

Production Coordinator

Arvindkumar Gupta

Cover Work

Arvindkumar Gupta

About the Author

Jate Wittayabundit was born in Bangkok, Thailand in 1980 and has a passion for both Arts and Mathematics. He received a bachelor's degree in Architecture in 2003 and was an interior architect for several companies. Then, he came to Ottawa, Canada in 2005 and graduated in the Game Development program at Algonquin College in 2008.

Since he graduated in the Game Development program, he started working at Launchfire Interactive Inc. (www.launchfire.com) as a Flash ActionScript programmer and developed many games and interactive content (for clients such as Dell, Alaska Airline, and so on). In 2009, he decided to move to Toronto, which is a bigger city, to get more chances to work in the game industry. He started a new position as a Game Developer and 3D Artist at Splashworks.com Inc. (www.splashworks.com). At Splashworks, he got a chance to work with many different games and clients (such as Shockwave, Swiss Chalet, and so on). It also gave him a chance to get to know Unity and to work with it.

The first video game he played was Super Mario Bros. and he has loved playing games ever since. He believes that being an architect is also his strength; it supports his concepts and ideas of how the real world could apply in the virtual world.

In his spare time, he loves to work on 3D software, such as Zbrush or 3D Studio Max. He also loves painting and drawing. Currently, he's trying to marry his architectural and 3D skills with his game development skills to create the next innovation game.

You can go to www.jatewit.com to check out some of his works.

About the Reviewers

Jaap Kreijkamp completed his master's degree in Computer Science at Vrije Universiteit, Amsterdam. He started his career as a software developer at the university. After four years, he moved into developing embedded software and large payment servers before ending up as a game developer. Jaap has worked on several educational computer programs as a lead developer, and recently published the iOS title *Revolt* together with Kristopher Peterson using Unity as the main development tool.

Fraser McCormick has been programming professionally for over a decade, building online applications, tools, and games with a combination of server-side code and frontend technologies, such as Flash and Unity. He likes biscuits, playing Capoeira, and trying to take over the world with indie games.

Clifford Peters first started using Unity back in 2008 and has enjoyed using it ever since. He has made a few games in his spare time, including the one submitted to a Unity programming contest. He is currently attending college, pursuing a degree in Computer Science.

www.PacktPub.com

Support files, eBooks, discount offers, and more

You might want to visit www.PacktPub.com for support files and downloads related to your book.

Did you know that Packt offers eBook versions of every book published, with PDF and ePub files available? You can upgrade to the eBook version at www.PacktPub.com and as a print book customer, you are entitled to a discount on the eBook copy. Get in touch with us at service@packtpub.com for more details.

At www.PacktPub.com, you can also read a collection of free technical articles, sign up for a range of free newsletters and receive exclusive discounts and offers on Packt books and eBooks.

http://PacktLib.PacktPub.com

Do you need instant solutions to your IT questions? PacktLib is Packt's online digital book library. Here, you can access, read and search across Packt's entire library of books.

Why Subscribe?

- ▸ Fully searchable across every book published by Packt
- ▸ Copy and paste, print and bookmark content
- ▸ On demand and accessible via web browser

Free Access for Packt account holders

If you have an account with Packt at www.PacktPub.com, you can use this to access PacktLib today and view nine entirely free books. Simply use your login credentials for immediate access.

Table of Contents

Preface

Only Unity fits the bill of being a game engine that allows you to create a full 3D game for free, and with phenomenal community support. This book will equip you with the skills to create professional looking games at no cost.

Unity 3 Game Development Hotshot will teach you how to exploit the full array of Unity 3D's technology in order to create an advanced gaming experience for the user, with eight exciting and challenging projects that provide a step-by-step explanation, diagrams, and screenshots to help you achieve that goal.

Every project is designed to push your Unity skills to the very limits and beyond. You will create a hero/heroine which will be used in an RPG game. You will create a menu for the RPG game allowing you to customize your character with powerups, armor, and weapons. You will shade, model, rig, and animate your hero/heroine, so that they start to look more like a character from Final Fantasy than a simple sprite.

Now for some damage—rocket launchers! Typically the most powerful weapon in any first-person shooter, you will create a rocket launcher that has fire and smoke particles and most importantly causes splash damage for that all-important area effect. You will create AI-controlled enemies for your hero/heroine to eliminate the rocket launcher. We will create an interactive world that is destructible, so if the rocket launchers miss their target they will damage the surrounding environment. Finally, you learn to save and load so you can take a break from the action for life's necessities like going to the bathroom. The final touch will be for you to upload your scores online so everyone can see the carnage.

What this book covers

Project 1, Develop a Sprite and Platform Game: This project will show the user how to create a sprite animation for a 2D platform game. There will be an explanation of the difference between a perspective and orthographic camera, how to set up a background camera and the character camera, how to create a 2D sprite from your texture (using `mainTexture` and `mainTextureOffset` function in Unity), how to set up a sprite sheet, as well as the jumping and gravity animations.

Project 2, Create a Menu for an RPG Game- Add Powerups, Weapons, and Armor: This project will use the first project to create a cool and complex UI that is mostly used in the RPG game. The project starts by creating the menu window with `OnGUI()`, which will include the tab button for the user to go to different menus, and be able to manage the items, change the armor or weapon for the character, and choose the items and skills.

Project 3, Model and Shade your Hero/Heroine: We will start by exporting the 3D character model from 3D Studio MAX with the right unit scale and rotation by using the FBX exporter from 3D Studio Max and import it to Unity. Then, we will write a custom shader by using the new surface shader, which will be available from version 3.0.

Project 4, Add Character Control and Animation to your Hero/Heroine: Beginning with setting up the walk, run, idle, jump, and fall animations, we will adapt the built-in third-person controller in Unity to create a custom third-person controller. We will also use the character controller, cross fade animation, and the camera to follow our character.

Project 5, Build a Rocket Launcher!: In this project, we will create a first-person controller similar to the Resident Evil Style with the character animation. We will create a rocket launcher, rocket, and the particle effect by using the prefab and instantiate function to clone the object.

Project 6, Create Smart AI: This project will continue from the last project, and we will create an AI enemy and make it smart enough to follow our character, shoot at us, and follow the way point. We will also use the Gizmo class to help us show the direction of the AI.

Project 7, Forge a Destructible and Interactive Virtual World: We will use the new unity built-in beast lightmap to create a lightmap to make the world more realistic. Then, we will create the Physics object in the scene that will react with our character by walking through it or shooting at it.

Project 8, Let the World See the Carnage! Save, Load, and Post High Scores: This project will show you how to load, save, and post your high score by using `playerPref`. We will also learn to make the web game load faster and not let the user wait too long by using streaming when we publish from Unity.

Appendix A, Important Functions: This appendix includes the details of some important functions such as, Awake(), Start(), and so on, sourced from Unity scripting reference.

Appendix B, Coroutines and Yield: This appendix includes the explanation of Coroutines/Yield and how to use them, sourced from Unity scripting reference.

Appendix C, Major Differences between C# and Unity JavaScript: This appendix shows the differences between C# and Unity JavaScript by using examples sourced from the Unity answer website and Unity scripting reference.

Appendix D, Shaders and Cg/HLSL Programming: This appendix explains the structure of the Shaders and Cg/HLSL language, basic function in CG/HLSL, and so on, sourced from Unity scripting reference and NVIDIA website.

What you need for this book

You will need Unity 3.x that you can download from `http://www.unity3d.com/download/` and 3D Studio Max (Optional), which can be downloaded from `http://usa.autodesk.com/3ds-max/trial/`.

Who this book is for

This book is for users who already have some basic knowledge of how to use the Unity game engine and intermediate users who want to explore Unity above and beyond the basic techniques.

Conventions

In this book, you will find several headings appearing frequently.

To give clear instructions of how to complete a procedure or task, we use:

Mission briefing

This section explains what you will build, with a screenshot of the completed project.

Why Is It Awesome?

This section explains why the project is cool, unique, exciting, and interesting. It describes what advantage the project will give you.

Your Hotshot Objectives

This section explains the major tasks required to complete your project.

- ▶ Task 1
- ▶ Task 2
- ▶ Task 3
- ▶ Task 4, and so on

Mission Checklist

This section explains any pre-requisites for the project, such as resources or libraries that need to be downloaded, and so on.

Task 1

This section explains the task that you will perform.

Prepare for Lift Off

This section explains any preliminary work that you may need to do before beginning work on the task.

Engage Thrusters

This section lists the steps required in order to complete the task.

Objective Complete - Mini Debriefing

This section explains how the steps performed in the previous section allow us to complete the task. This section is mandatory.

Classified Intel

The extra information in this section is relevant to the task.

You will also find a number of styles of text that distinguish between different kinds of information. Here are some examples of these styles, and an explanation of their meaning.

Code words in text are shown as follows: " We can change the **Tiling** by calling the `material.mainTextureScale` function to set the X tile and Y tile."

A block of code is set as follows:

```
public var f_speed : float = 5.0;
public var loopSprites : SpriteManager[];
private var in_direction : int;
```

When we wish to draw your attention to a particular part of a code block, the relevant lines or items are set in bold:

```
if (hit.collider.tag == "Key") {
    if (!b_hasKey) {
        //We hit our Key
        audio.volume = 1.0;
        audio.PlayOneShot(getKeySound);
        b_hasKey = true;
        Destroy (hit.gameObject);
    }
}
```

New terms and **important words** are shown in bold. Words that you see on the screen, in menus or dialog boxes for example, appear in the text like this: "Click on the **Continue** button to break the prefab."

 Warnings or important notes appear in a box like this.

 Tips and tricks appear like this.

Reader feedback

Feedback from our readers is always welcome. Let us know what you think about this book—what you liked or may have disliked. Reader feedback is important for us to develop titles that you really get the most out of.

To send us general feedback, simply send an e-mail to feedback@packtpub.com, and mention the book title via the subject of your message.

If there is a book that you need and would like to see us publish, please send us a note in the **SUGGEST A TITLE** form on www.packtpub.com or e-mail suggest@packtpub.com.

If there is a topic that you have expertise in and you are interested in either writing or contributing to a book, see our author guide on www.packtpub.com/authors.

Customer support

Now that you are the proud owner of a Packt book, we have a number of things to help you to get the most from your purchase.

Downloading the example code

You can download the example code files for all Packt books you have purchased from your account at http://www.PacktPub.com. If you purchased this book elsewhere, you can visit http://www.PacktPub.com/support and register to have the files e-mailed directly to you.

Downloading the color images of this book

We also provide you a PDF file that has color images of the screenshots used in this book. The color images will help you better understand the changes in the output. You can download this file from https://www.packtpub.com/sites/default/files/Images.pdf.

Errata

Although we have taken every care to ensure the accuracy of our content, mistakes do happen. If you find a mistake in one of our books—maybe a mistake in the text or the code—we would be grateful if you would report this to us. By doing so, you can save other readers from frustration and help us improve subsequent versions of this book. If you find any errata, please report them by visiting http://www.packtpub.com/support, selecting your book, clicking on the **errata submission form** link, and entering the details of your errata. Once your errata are verified, your submission will be accepted and the errata will be uploaded on our website, or added to any list of existing errata, under the Errata section of that title. Any existing errata can be viewed by selecting your title from http://www.packtpub.com/support.

Piracy

Piracy of copyright material on the Internet is an ongoing problem across all media. At Packt, we take the protection of our copyright and licenses very seriously. If you come across any illegal copies of our works, in any form, on the Internet, please provide us with the location address or website name immediately so that we can pursue a remedy.

Please contact us at copyright@packtpub.com with a link to the suspected pirated material.

We appreciate your help in protecting our authors, and our ability to bring you valuable content.

Questions

You can contact us at questions@packtpub.com if you are having a problem with any aspect of the book, and we will do our best to address it.

Project 1
Develop a Sprite and Platform Game

Even in today's world, people remember Mario, Sonic, and Mega Man. Of course, Mario was first introduced in the Eighties, followed by Mega Man and Sonic, but even now the new generation love these games. Yes, we are talking about the old style 2D platform games, which still exist.

In this book, we will start the first chapter with a 2D platform game because there are some basic tricks for a 2D platform game, which will help you—those who haven't got into the 3D world yet—to understand more before jumping into the 3D world for the project in later chapters.

Mission briefing

We'll be creating a 2D platform or side-scrolling game, which is similar to Mario or other games that we have mentioned previously; it will have a simple character that the player will be able to move, jump, and collect a key item to be able to pass the level, and a **Restart** button for the player to play the game again.

We will use the 2D character sprite sheet (as shown in the previous image), and create the sprite manager class to control it instead of the 3D character model. Some of you might have a few questions: *Why are we doing this? Why don't we just use the 3D model, which should be easier to do, instead of creating the sprite manager class?*

Well, there are some advantages of using a sprite manager class. Firstly, creating a 3D model and animation takes time. It takes more time to create a simple 3D character with animation than to create a 2D character with a sprite sheet because you don't have to deal with the polygon count, rigging the character, unwarping the textures, and animating it. You just draw it. Since the 2D sprite object only shows one view, we can use the plane object to save the number of polygons instead of using the 3D character object. It is also an advantage to learn this sprite technique to create an animated texture in your game.

The purpose of this chapter is to familiarize you with all the tools and language syntax in Unity, which is very important to create a playable game. We will also see how to use MonoDevelop for a JavaScript user (sometimes called UnityScript; in the rest of the book, we will call it Unity JavaScript) and what is good about MonoDevelop when compared to Unitron (or UniSciTE in PC).

What does it do?

In this project, we will start with creating a camera for our game, and adding light and level to the scene. Next, we want to create our character object as a plane, apply the transparent material, and use the 2D graphic sprite sheet for its texture. We will also create the script, which will control the sprite sheet to show the right graphic on our character object. This script will allow us to be able to control our character to walk and jump by pressing the arrow key. Also, we will learn how to set up the custom input manager. Then, we will have the right animation for the character idle, walking, or jumping.

For the level, we will create it by using a Unity built-in cube and give it a collision which will react with the character by using a Unity built-in physics. To end the game, we will create a trigger event by creating a door and a key. The player needs to collect the key to open the door and end the game. We will also add sound to make our game seem alive, but we are not finishing it yet. The game needs to be replayable. Lastly, we will add a **Replay** or **Play again** button to replay our game by using destroy and instantiate to reset our character position and key item.

Why Is It Awesome?

When we are done with this chapter, we will get a good understanding of how to create a sprite and 2D platform game by using a 3D game engine such as Unity. Also, we will be able to create our own 2D platform style game like Sonic, Mario, Mega Man, and so on, and reuse some of our techniques, scripts, and concepts to create a 3D game at a later stage.

Your Hotshot Objectives

This project will be split into six tasks. Since we are not creating any enemies in our game, we don't have to deal with any complex scripting. It will be a simple step-by-step process from beginning to end. Here is the outline of the tasks:

- ▸ Creating a camera and a level
- ▸ Creating a 2D character
- ▸ Creating `CharacterController` and `SpriteManager` classes
- ▸ Jumping and physics
- ▸ Creating key and door
- ▸ Adding **Sound** and **Replay** button

Mission Checklist

Before we start, we will need to get the latest Unity version `http://unity3d.com/unity/download/` which includes MonoDevelop that we will use for our scripting editor. We will also need a few graphics for our character, key, and door as well as a collection of sound FX. These could be downloaded as ZIP files from Packt's website: `http://www.packtpub.com/support?nid=8267`.

Browse to the preceding URL and download `Chapter1.zip` package and unzip it. Inside the `Chapter1` folder, there are five subfolders, which are `Buttons`, `Characters`, `FBX`, `Level`, and `Sound`.

Creating a camera and a level

This part is just about creating a camera and a level to use in our platform game. We will be creating a camera that will show all the objects in the scene and follow our character movement.

Prepare for Lift Off

Before we start creating this project, we will create the project in Unity by following
these steps:

1. Create a new project by going to **File | New Project** to bring up the **Project Wizard**
    window. Next, click on the **Create new Project** tab and set the **Project Directory** as
    you want, as we can see in the following screenshot:

 As we can see from the preceding screenshot, we won't
import any Unity assets packages because we won't be using
any in this chapter.

2. Import the Chapter1 package folder that you downloaded into the project assets
    folder, by copying it into the project's **Assets** folder or drag-and-dropping it into the
    Unity window, as we can see in the following screenshot:

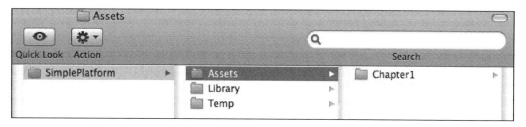

3. Go back to Unity and make sure that you have `Plane` and `background.png` in your `Project` folder, as shown in the following screenshot:

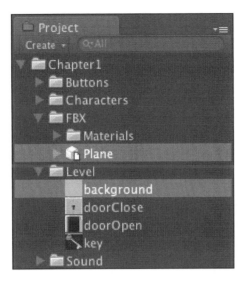

4. Click on the `Plane` object in the **Project** view to bring up its **Inspector** view. Next, we go to the **FBXImporter | Meshes** component, and set the **Scale Factor** to **1**, as shown in the following screenshot, and click on the **Apply** button:

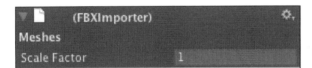

Engage Thrusters

We are now ready to start, so let's get on with it!

1. Let's start by creating the background with the `Plane` prefab object in the `FBX` folder—go to the **Project** view, click on the **Plane** prefab object, and drag it into the **Hierarchy** view.

There is also the Unity built-in `Plane` object that you can use, but you don't really want to use it, because the Unity built-in `Plane` object will have way too many triangles for our 2D objects. As we can see from the following screenshot, our prefab `Plane` only has two triangles, but the Unity built-in `Plane` object will have around 200 triangles.

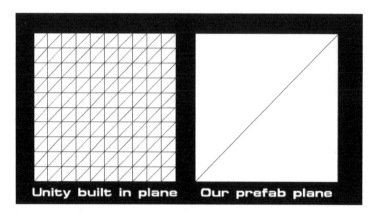

Unity built in plane   Our prefab plane

2. In the **Hierarchy** view, right-click on the **Plane** prefab object, and choose **Rename** to change the name to **Background**.

3. Then, click on this object and go to its **Inspector** view, and set its transform **Position** to **X: 0, Y: 0, Z: 24**, **Rotation** to **X: 0, Y: 180, Z: 0**, **Scale** to **X: 200, Y: 200, Z: 1**.

4. Right-click on the **Animation** component in the **Inspector** view and choose the **Remove Component** option to remove it, as shown in the following screenshot:

This will bring up the pop-up window, as shown in the following screenshot. Click on the **Continue** button to break the prefab:

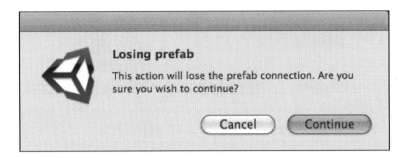

5. Now, to create the background material, go to **Assets | Create | Material**, and name it whatever you want; here we will call it **M_Background**. Then, we assign our background texture to this material, in the project window click on **M_Background**. We will see the **Inspector** view of the background material, as shown in the following screenshot:

 If you don't see the detail as seen in the preceding screenshot, you can click anywhere that isn't a button on the banner (the lighter gray area that says **M_Background**) to show the details.

6. Next, drag the background.png file from the Chapter1/Level folder in the **Project** view and drop it in the texture thumbnail, and then set the following:

   ❑ **Shader: Diffuse**

   ❑ **Main Color:R:164, G:219, B:225, A: 255**

   ❑ **Base (RGB): x-Tiling: 2, Offset: 0; y-Tiling: 2, Offset: 0**

Now, we are adding our material to the background object, click on `Background` object in the **Hierarchy** view to open the **Inspector** view, and in **Mesh Renderer | Materials**, set the parameters as follows:

❑ **Size: 1**

❑ **Element 0**: **M_Background**

7. Next, we will create a new `Tag` and `Layer` for our `Background` object; go to **Edit | Project Settings | Tags** and click on the arrow next to the **Tags** option to open it, as shown in the following screenshot:

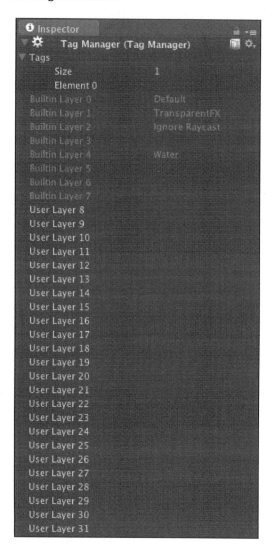

8. Enter the parameters as follows:

   For **Element 0** type **Background**, for **Element 1** type **Floor**, for **Element 2** type **Wall**, and then for **User Layer 8** type **Background**, for **User Layer 9** type **Level**; we select our Background object, and then go back to the Background object's **Inspector** view setup as follows:

   - **Tag**: **Background**
   - **Layer**: **Background**

9. Set the **Main Camera**, which is already in our scene when we first create the project, as follows:

   - **Position**: **x: 0, y: 0, z: -20**
   - **Projection**: **Perspective**

10. To light up our scene by adding sound light into it, go to **GameObject | Create Other | Directional Light** and set its parameters as follows:

    - **Rotation**: **x:20, y:0, z:0**

11. For the last step, we will create our quick, easy, and simple level:

    - First, we need to create our container to contain all the objects for the level. Go to **GameObject | Create Empty** or use *Command + Shift + N* in Mac and *Ctrl + Shift + N* in Windows, and change the name to **Level**, and reset the transform position to **X: 0, Y:0, Z: 0)**, rotation to **X: 0, Y: 0, Z: 0**, and scale to **X: 1, Y: 1, Z: 1**.

    - For creating our floor, let's go to **GameObject | Create Other | Cube**, change the name of this object to **Floor**, and change the tag and layer as follows:

      - **Tag**: **Floor**
      - **Layer**: **Level**
        - Same thing for creating a wall; just repeat the same step and change the name to **Wall**, and set the tag and layer as follows:
      - **Tag**: **Wall**
      - **Layer**: **Level**

So, now we have our **Floor** cube and **Wall** cube.

- ❑ Next, we want to apply the material to our cubes. We will have only one material for both the floor and wall to make it simple. Go to **Assets | Create | Material**, name it **M_Level**, adjust the color to **R: 150, G: 230, B: 225, A: 255**, and apply this material to the `Floor` and `Wall` objects by dragging the material `Floor` and `Wall` objects in the **Hierarchy** view. Then we drag-and-drop `Floor` and `Wall` inside our `Level` object, as shown in the following screenshot:

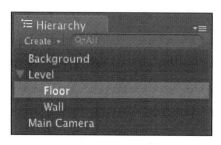

- ❑ Now, we will click on the `floor` object in the hierarchy, and press *Command + D* for Mac users or *Ctrl + D* for Windows users to copy it six times, and click on the `wall` object in the hierarchy and copy it twice. So now we have seven `floor` objects and three `wall` objects.

- ❑ Next we create our level by setting up the position and scale of our `floor` and `wall` objects. Let's set them up as follows:

  - ▸ 1st Floor object: Position: x: -4, y: -9, z: 0   Scale: x: 125, y: 15, z: 1
  - ▸ 2nd Floor object: Position: x: -6, y: 5, z: 0   Scale: x: 32, y: 1, z: 1
  - ▸ 3rd Floor object: Position: x: -25, y: 12, z: 0 Scale: x: 19.5, y: 1, z: 1
  - ▸ 4th Floor object: Position: x: 14, y: 12, z: 0 Scale: x: 20, y: 1, z: 1
  - ▸ 5th Floor object: Position: x: -7, y: 9, z: 0   Scale: x: 9, y: 1, z: 1
  - ▸ 6th Floor object: Position: x: -31, y: 1, z: 0 Scale: x: 6, y: 1, z: 1
  - ▸ 7th Floor object: Position: x: 21, y: 2, z: 0   Scale: x: 10, y: 1, z: 1
  - ▸ 1st Wall object: Position: x: -49, y: 17, z: 0 Scale: x: 36, y: 40, z: 1
  - ▸ 2nd Wall object: Position: x: 42, y: 17, z: 0 Scale: x: 38, y: 39, z: 1
  - ▸ 3rd Wall object: Position: x: -7, y: 23, z: 0 Scale: x: 1, y: 36, z: 1

- ❑ Finally, we will save the scene by pressing *Command + s* in Mac or *Control + s* in Windows. Since it is our first save, we will be asked to name this scene, so let's name it **SimplePlatform**.

Objective Complete - Mini Debriefing

Basically, what we have done here is create a `Background` object behind the `Level` object, and set the `Main Camera` in front of the `Level` object. Our `Main Camera` will also follow our character while he is moving. This way we can make sure that the player will always see our character and background image. We can set our scene and level, as shown in the following diagram:

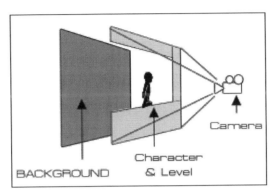

In our `Main Camera`, we set the **Projection** to **Perspective** because we want to show the thickness of our level and the depth of the object, which will give a nice view for the player.

Classified Intel

We can set the **Camera Projection** in our scene to be either **Orthographic** or **Perspective**. The difference between both projections is that with the **Orthographic Projection**, the object won't scale by the distance of the camera. So in our scene, we will see only one side of the object that faces the camera. On the other hand, in **Perspective Projection** we will see the depth of the object that will scale down by the distance of the camera, which is very similar to real life.

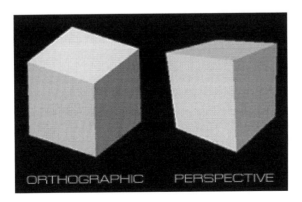

In our scene, we won't see any significant difference on our background object because our background object is a plane and doesn't have any thickness on it, but if we are trying to adjust the **Projection** of our camera, we will see the difference between the two projections. We can do this by going to the **Hierarchy** view, clicking on **Main Camera**, changing **Projection** to **Orthographic**, and **Size** to **8.5**, and then changing **Projection** back to **Perspective**. The difference is shown in the following screenshot:

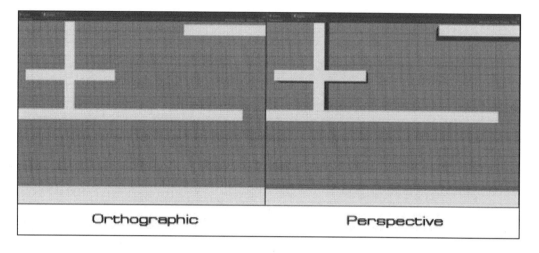

Creating a 2D character

In this step, we will create our 2D character and material, which will contain our 2D character sprite sheet from our Chapter1 package folder. We will have our character act out three different types of animation: staying, walking, and jumping.

Prepare for Lift Off

Let's make sure that we have all the sprites we need in the project folder:

1. Go to Chapter1/Characters where you will see three subfolders, Jump, Stay, and Walk.

2. Open the jump folder. We will see the files J_Frame1.png, J_Frame2.png, and J_Frame3.png. Next, open the Stay folder, we will see the s_set.png file. Then, open the last folder Walk, we will see the w_set.png file as shown in the following screenshot:

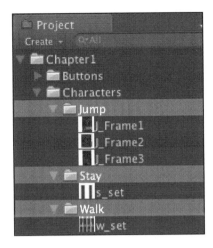

Now, we are ready to get started.

Engage Thrusters

Since our character is a 2D sprite animation, we only need to have a plane object to contain it. Let's do it as the follows:

1. Go to the `Plane` prefab object in the `FBX` folder and drag it into the **Hierarchy** view.

2. Next, right-click on the **Animation** component in the **Inspector** view and choose the **Remove Component** option to remove it. We will see the pop-up window, so just click on the **Continue** button, similar to the one we did for our `Background` object.

3. Then, we click on this object and go to its **Inspector** view, and set it as follows:

   □ **Tag: Player**

   □ **Position: x: -25, y: 16, z: 0**

   □ **Rotation: x: 0, y: 180, z: 0**

   □ **Scale: x: 5, y: 5, z: 1**

4. We will call our character `Player`. Go to the **Hierarchy** view, right-click on the `Plane` prefab object, and choose **Rename** to change the name to **Player**.

5. Next, go to **Assets | Create | Material** and name it **M_Character**.

6. Go to material's **Inspector** view and set it up as follows:

   □ **Shader: Transparent | Cutout | Soft Edge Unlit**

   □ Base (RGB) Alpha (A)

   □ Drag-and-drop our `s_set.png` from the `Characters/Stay` folder to the texture thumbnail in material inspector

- ❑ **X: Tiling: 0.5, Offset: 0**
- ❑ **Y: Tiling: 1, Offset: 0**
- ❑ **Base Alpha cutoff**: Drag the dragger to the very right end

We have now got the material for our `Player`.

7. Next, we go back to the `Player` and assign this material to him by dragging and dropping `M_Character` from the **Project** view to the `Player` object in the **Hierarchy** view. Finally, add the **Box Collider** and add a **RigidBody** to the `Player`. We will use the **Box Collider** because our `Player` is basically a plane and doesn't need any complex collider to detect his collision.

8. Let's click on the `Player` and go to **Component | Physics | Box Collider** set **Size: x: 0.4, y: 0.875, z: 1** and **Center: x: 0, y: -0.06275, z: 0**.

9. Then, we will add the **RigidBody**, which is used to calculate our walking speed, jumping, and collision detection with the level; go to **Component | Physics | RigidBody** and make sure that **Use Gravity** is **On** and the **Kinematic** option is **Off**.

10. Set the freeze the rotation of the object (**Freeze Rotation**) by clicking on the arrow in front of **Constraints**. In **Freeze Rotation**, check each box **X**, **Y**, and **Z** to freeze rotation. We will also check the **Z** box to freeze the character movement in the Z-axis, as shown in the following screenshot:

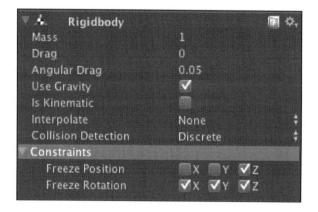

Objective Complete - Mini Debriefing

We just created a plane that will act as our main character, our `Player`. We also created a material for our `Player` by using **Transparent | Cutout | Soft Edge Unlit Shader**. This **Shader** will cut out the Alpha channel and make it transparent. In addition, it will also soften the edge, not to the shape of the object it is on, but instead it will soften the edges of the image itself. We can control which portion of the image will be cut out, and how much the edge will soften by adjusting the **Base Alpha Cutoff** slider.

We also set the tiling for the X-axis to 0.5 because our image contains two frames, but we want to use only one image at a time. We used the **Box Collider** instead of **Mesh Collider**. We were also adding a **RigidBody** for our character and setting it to enable **Freeze Rotation**, which will ignore all the rotation on our character that will be calculated by Physics Engine in Unity. This will cause our `Player` not to rotate.

The **RigidBody** will also give our character the ability to activate the Physics Engine in Unity, such as gravity or velocity, and act as real-life physics. We will see this in the next step.

Classified Intel

Why do we need to freeze the rotation and position of the **Rigidbody** in our character?

 We freeze the rotation of the **Rigidbody** because we are using the sprite texture to present the character movement. So, we don't want our character to rotate when it moves. We also freeze the position on the Z-axis because our character will only move on the X and Y axes. In this way, we can also save the CPU cycles because Unity will ignore the unnecessary calculation and only calculate the one it needs.

Box Collider **and** Mesh Collider

So why are we using **Box Collider** instead of **Mesh Collider**? Both the colliders are basically similar. Think about it this way: each surface of the mesh will have its own normal that will be perpendicular to each vertices and check if it hits any object. So, if we think about our plane object, we will see that it has only one face that has the normal pointing towards the camera. So, it means that if we apply the **Mesh Collider** to the plane object, we won't get any collision detection from the top, bottom, left, right, and back side of the plane. This is basically because there is no surface at the top, bottom, left, right, and back side of this object to create the collision detection with the other objects.

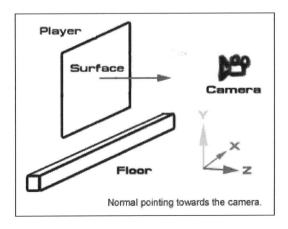

On the other hand, **Box Collider** uses the volume that it represents to check for the collision detection. This result will be a lot faster than the **Mesh Collider**. In this case, we are checking the volume of the character **Box Collider** with the the Floor **Box Collider** to see whether there is any part of the Floor collider without Player or not, as we can see in the following diagram:

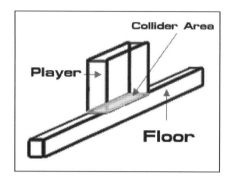

 The **Box Collider** can save a lot of memory and CPU cycles in real-time rendering compared to the **Mesh Collider**.

Next, we will talk about **Tiling** in **Material**, which is very similar to many 3D programs. Every texture that we applied to the material there will be stretched to fit in the square space, which we can see in the 1x1 cube.

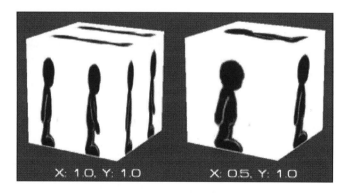

Tiling is very much similar to scaling, and it's basically repeating the texture on X and Y axes. So, if we set the **Tiling X: 0.5, Y: 1.0**, we see the result as shown in the previous figure with the texture on X-axis that scales half size, but it still looks the same in Y. We also see that the second image will show only the first left side of the texture (the first frame of our character). Now, if we want to show the right side of our texture what will we do? We will use **Offset** in **Material**, which will give a different result from **Tiling**. The **Offset** basically tells us the starting position of our texture. So, if we set the **Offset X: 0.0, Y: 0.0**, this means that our texture will display from the top-left corner of the original texture. On the other hand, if we set **Offset X: 0.5, Y: 0.0**, we will see the result that our texture's start point is at the middle of the original texture image, and we will see our material show the right side of our texture (the second frame of our character, as we can see in the following figure):

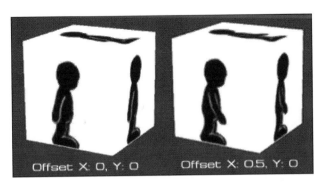

We can change the **Tiling** by calling the `material.mainTextureScale` function to set the X tile and Y tile, and use calling `material.mainTextureOffset` to set the X and Y **Offset**.

After learning this technique, we can manage our sprite image by just changing the number of **Tiling** and **Offset** of our character **Material** in the next step.

Creating CharacterControl class and SpriteManager class

In this section, we will create new Unity JavaScript code to control the movement of our character, and a sprite animation for each action of our character. We have a choice to use Unitron (Mac), UniSciTE (Windows), or MonoDevelop, but in this book we will use MonoDevelop as our scripting editor instead of Unitron or UniSciTE. MonoDevelop is mainly designed for C# and .NET environment, so if you are comfortable with C#, you will probably love it. However, we will still use it to edit our JavaScript because it has a lot of functions that will help us to write the script faster and debug better, such as finding and replacing words in the whole project by pressing *Command + Shift + F* in Mac or *Control + Shift + F* in Windows, and autocomplete, to name a few. Moving from Unity JavaScript to C# is also a comparatively smooth transition.

Prepare for Lift Off

Now, we are just about to start coding, but first let's make it organized:

1. Create a new folder in your project window and name it `Scripting`. This folder will contain our script for this chapter.

2. Next, we want to set up our Unity to use MonoDevelop as our main Scripting editor (**Unity | Preferences** in Mac or **Edit | Preferences** in Windows).

3. We will see a Unity preferences window. In the **General** tab, go to the **External Script Editor** and change **Use build-in editor (Unitron/UniSciTE)** to **MonoDevlop** by clicking on **Browse...** and choose **Applications | Unity** | `MonoDevelop.app` in Mac or **{unity install path} | Unity | MonoDevelop** | `MonoDevelop.exe` in Windows, and we are done.

> The default Unity script editor is set to **Unitron/UniSciTE** because they are the built-in editors that are included in Unity from the beginning. MonoDevelop is basically the IDE that is just included in Unity 3.X, which has a better scripting and debugging environment. We can see more information about how to set up the MonoDevelop on this website: `http://unity3d.com/support/documentation/Manual/HOWTO-MonoDevelop.html`.

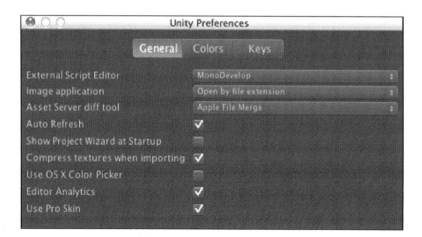

Engage Thrusters

1. First, go to **Assets | Create | Javascript** and name our script as `CharacterController_2D`.

2. Double-click on the script; it will open the **MonoDevelop** window.

3. Now, we will see three windows in the **MonoDevelop** screen:

    ❑ On the top-left is **Solution**; we can see our project folder here, but it will only show the folder that contains a script.

    ❑ On the bottom-left, we will see a **Document Outline**; this window will show all the functions, classes, and parameters in the file.

    ❑ The last window on the right will be used to type our code.

4. Let's get our hands dirty with some code—first create the `CharacterController_2D` class. At present, we are creating parameters:

    ```
    public var f_speed : float = 5.0;
    public var loopSprites : SpriteManager[];
    private var in_direction : int;
    ```

    `f_speed` is the speed of our character, and we set it to `public` so we can adjust it inside the Unity editor. The array `loopSprites` of the `SpriteManager` class will control the update of our sprite animation texture, which we will create later. `in_direction` tracks the direction of our character, which will return only 1 (right direction) or `-1` (left direction).

5. Next, we will include the script in the `Start()` function, which is already created by default:

    ```
    public function Start() : void {
        in_direction = 1;
    //Initialization Sprite Manager
        for (var i : int = 0; i<loopSprites.length; i++) {
            loopSprites[i].init();
        }
    //Update Main Camera to the character position
        Camera.main.transform.position = new Vector3(transform.
    position.x, transform.position.y, Camera.main.transform.
    position.z);
    }
    ```

6. Next, we will include the script in the `Update()` function, which is already created by default similar to the `Start()` function:

    ```
    // Update is called once per frame
    public function Update () : void {
        if (Input.GetButton("Horizontal")) {
            //Walking
            in_direction = Input.GetAxis("Horizontal") < 0 ? -1: 1;
            rigidbody.velocity = new Vector3((in_direction*f_speed),
    rigidbody.velocity.y, 0);
            //Reset Stay animation frame back to the first frame
            loopSprites[0].resetFrame();
    ```

```
    //Update Walking animation while the character is walking
        loopSprites[1].updateAnimation(in_direction, renderer.
material);
    } else {
        //Stay
        //Reset Walking animation frame back to the first frame
        loopSprites[1].resetFrame();
        //Update Stay animation while the character is not walking
        loopSprites[0].updateAnimation(in_direction, renderer.
material);
    }
}
```

7. Then, we create a `LateUpdate()` function, which is called after all the `Update()` functions have been called. We will use this function to update our camera position after our character movement by setting its transform to follow our character:

```
public function LateUpdate() : void {
//Update Main Camera
    Camera.main.transform.position = new Vector3(transform.
position.x, transform.position.y, Camera.main.transform.
position.z);


}
```

8. Next, we create the `SpriteManager` class to manage our sprite texture in the `CharacterController_2D.js` file; continue from our preceding script, and add the following:

```
class SpriteManager {
    public var spriteTexture : Texture2D; //Set Texture use for a
loop animation such as walking, stay, etc.
    public var in_framePerSec : int; //Get frame per sec to
calculate time
    public var in_gridX : int; //Get max number of Horizontal images
    public var in_gridY : int; //Get max number of Vertical images

    private var f_timePercent : float;
    private var f_nextTime : float; //Update time by using frame
persecond
    private var f_gridX : float;
    private var f_gridY : float;
    private var in_curFrame : int;

    public function init () : void {
        f_timePercent = 1.0/in_framePerSec;
```

```
      f_nextTime = f_timePercent; //Update time by using frame
persecond
      f_gridX = 1.0/in_gridX;
      f_gridY = 1.0/in_gridY;
      in_curFrame = 1;
   }

   public function updateAnimation (_direction : int, _material :
Material) : void {
      //Update material
      _material.mainTexture = spriteTexture;
      //Update frame by time
      if (Time.time>f_nextTime) {
        f_nextTime = Time.time + f_timePercent;
        in_curFrame++;
        if (in_curFrame>in_framePerSec) {
          in_curFrame = 1;
        }
      }
      _material.mainTextureScale = new Vector2 (_direction * f_
gridX, f_gridY);
      var in_col : int = 0;
      if (in_gridY>1) {
        //If there is more than one grid on the y-axis update the
texture
        in_col= Mathf.Ceil(in_curFrame/in_gridX);
      }
      if (_direction == 1) { //Right
      _material.mainTextureOffset = new Vector2(((in_curFrame)%in_
gridX) * f_gridX, in_col*f_gridY);
      } else { //Left
        //Flip Texture
        _material.mainTextureOffset = new Vector2(((in_gridX + (in_
curFrame)%in_gridX)) * f_gridX, in_col*f_gridY);
      }
   }

   public function resetFrame () :void {
      in_curFrame = 1;
   }
}
```

9. Now, save it and go back to Unity; drag-and-drop our script to our `Player`, then click on `Player` and go to the **Inspector** window. Click on the **Loop Sprites**, and set **Size** to **2**, then set the following:

    - **Element 0**:

        ▸ **Sprite Texture: s_set**

        ▸ **In_frame Per Sec: 2**

        ▸ **In_grid X: 2**

        ▸ **In_grid Y: 1**

    - **Element 1**:

        ▸ **Sprite Texture: w_set**

        ▸ **In_frame Per Sec: 8**

        ▸ **In_grid X: 4**

        ▸ **In_grid Y: 2**

We are done. Let's click on the **play** button to play the game. We will see our `Player` moving his hand back and forth. Next, press the *A* key or ¬ key, *D* key or ® key to move the `Player` to the left or to the right; now we see that he is walking. Isn't that cool?

Objective Complete - Mini Debriefing

We just created a script that controls the movement of our character, and his animation. First, we set `in_direction` to 1 because we want our character To start by facing the right-hand side. Then, we are looping through the array and initializing the `SpriteManager` class from its length. We will get the main camera from the current scene by using `Camera.main`. This syntax allows us to access the `Main Camera` object from anywhere we want, and then we assign the main camera position point to our character. Next, we will put the script in the `Update()` function, which is already created by default —similar to the `Start()` function. This function will be used to control our character movement from walking to jumping, and for updating the animation.

Then, we used the `Input` class to detect when the player presses a key on the keyboard. We do all the character control in the `update()` function. First, we use `if (Input.GetButton("Horizontal")) { }` to check if the player pressed a `Horizontal` key, (for which the default in Unity is *A, D*, left arrow, or right arrow key), and we move our character if he/she did. The first line in this `if` statement checks the direction, which we are using, `in_direction =Input.GetAxis("Horizontal") < 0 ? -1: 1;`, which means that if the player presses a `Horizontal` key, we will get the axis number from the `Input.GetAxis("Horizontal")` function. The `Input.GetAxis` function will return the range from -1 to 1 depending on the pressure of the player pressing. Then, we check if the number is lower than 0 or not, if it's then the function returns -1 (move to left), if not it returns 1 (move to right). Then in the line `rigidbody.velocity = new Vector3((in_direction*f_speed), rigidbody.velocity.y, 0);`, we applied the direction and speed to the `rigidbody` velocity. We don't apply any velocity in the Z-axis because we are not moving our character in that direction.

Lastly, we included the `SpriteManager` class in our `CharacterController_2D.js` file to control our sprite texture to play loop animation by using the maximum of frame we had calculated with the time to play each frame. Let's take a look at our `SpriteManager` class. `spriteTexture` is basically a set of sprite texture that get held in this class. This textures will get a call and apply to the main material texture when the character is changing their movement, such as from walk to stay, stay to walk, or walk to jump, and so on. `in_framePerSec` is the total frames of the sprite texture, which will be used to calculate when the next frame will be showed. `in_gridX` is the number of the row in our sprite texture, and `in_gridY` is the number of the column in our sprite texture, which will be used to calculate the **Tiling** and **Offset** of the texture that we have already seen in the last step. We also have private parameters `f_timePercent`, `f_nextTime`, `f_gridX`, `f_gridY`, and `in_curFrame`, which are used to calculate in the `updateAnimation()` function. Next, we have the `init()` function. This function is basically for setting up our parameters. Then, the `updateAnimation()` function will get the material and direction from our main character to calculate and update our sprite animation. Lastly, we have a `resetFrame()` function to reset our animation frame back to one.

Classified Intel

There are a few more things that we need to know:

Input Manager

In Unity, we can set a custom **Input Manager** by going to **Edit | Project Settings | Input**. In the **Inspector**, click on **Axes** and you will see **Size: 17**, which is the array length of all the inputs. If we want more than 17 inputs, we can put the number here (the default is 17). Next, we will see all 17 names from **Horizontal** to **Jump** as a default setting. Each one will have its own parameters, which we can set up, as follows:

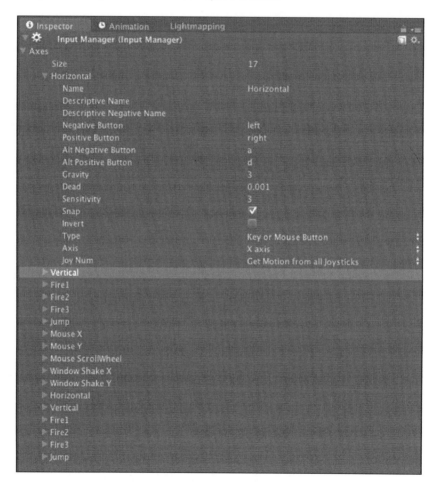

We can see the information of each parameter on the Unity website:

http://unity3d.com/support/documentation/Components/class-InputManager.html.

In our code, we use the `Input.GetButton("Horizontal")` function. `GetButton` means we are checking if the `Horizontal` button is being held down. The `Horizontal` is the name of the first input button, as we can see in the preceding screenshot. We can also use `Input.GetKey("left")` to control our character. It will have the same result with `Input.GetButton`, but the difference is `GetKey` will only detect the specific key in our code. It isn't flexible for the user to adjust the key configuration during the game play. The **Negative Button** and **Positive Button** here will send the negative and positive value, which in most cases is used for controlling direction such as left, right, up, and down. There is a **Dead** parameter, which will set any number that is lower than this parameter to **0**, which is very useful when we use a joystick. Also, setting the **Type** to **key/mouse button** and enabling the **Snap** parameter will reset axis values to zero after it receives opposite inputs.

Jumping and physics

Now, we are making our character jump by using `Physics.Raycast` in Unity. We can also use the `OnCollisionEnter`, `OnCollisionExit`, or `OnCollisionStay` functions to check the collision detection between our character and the floor, but in this case we will use `Raycast` because it's more flexible to adjust.

However, because the `Raycast` is only a line with no thickness, there is a chance that if we have a very thin platform, the `Raycast` can miss it. And it will cause the problem that we might not be able to jump. So, we should make sure that the platform should have the thickness of least 0.1 units.

Engage Thrusters

Continuing from the last step, let's get on with it as follows:

1. Let's open our `CharacterController_2D.js` file and add this code to it; first our parameters:

```
private var b_isJumping : boolean;
private var f_height : float;
private var f_lastY : float;
public var jumpSprite : JumpSpriteManager;
public var layerMask : LayerMask; //to check for the raycast
```

2. Then, we go to the `public function Start ()` function and add the following code inside this function:

```
    //Get mesh from the character MeshFilter
   mesh = GetComponent(MeshFilter).sharedMesh;
    //Get hight from the top of our character to the bottom of our
box collider
    f_height = mesh.bounds.size.y* transform.localScale.y;
```

```
//Set up the last y-axis position of our character
f_lastY = transform.position.y;
b_isJumping = false;
```

3. Next, we go to the `public function Update ()` function and add some code as follows (the highlighted part is our new code):

```
//If our character isn't jumping
if (!b_isJumping) {
if (Input.GetButton("Horizontal")) {
        //Walking
        in_direction = Input.GetAxis("Horizontal") < 0 ? -1 : 1;
        rigidbody.velocity = new Vector3((in_direction*f_speed),
rigidbody.velocity.y, 0);
        loopSprites[0].resetFrame();
        loopSprites[1].updateAnimation(in_direction, renderer.
material);
    } else {
        loopSprites[1].resetFrame();
        loopSprites[0].updateAnimation(in_direction, renderer.
material);
    }
    if (Input.GetButton("Jump")) { //Jump
      b_isJumping = true;
      //Then make it Jump
      loopSprites[0].resetFrame();
      loopSprites[1].resetFrame();
      rigidbody.velocity = new Vector3(rigidbody.velocity.x,
-Physics.gravity.y, 0);
    }
  } else {
    //update animation while it Jump
    jumpSprite.updateJumpAnimation(in_direction, rigidbody.
velocity.y, renderer.material);
  }
```

So, we basically add the statement to check if our character is jumping or not.

4. Next, we add the highlighted code in the `LateUpdate()` function, in which we already had our camera update position:

```
public function LateUpdate() : void {
  //Checking Jumping by using Raycast
  var hit : RaycastHit;
  var v3_hit : Vector3 = transform.TransformDirection (-Vector3.
up) * (f_height * 0.5);
  var v3_right : Vector3 = new Vector3(transform.position.x +
(collider.bounds.size.x*0.45), transform.position.y, transform.
position.z);
```

```
    var v3_left : Vector3 = new Vector3(transform.position.x -
(collider.bounds.size.x*0.45), transform.position.y, transform.
position.z);
if (Physics.Raycast (transform.position, v3_hit, hit, 2.5,
layerMask.value)) {
b_isJumping = false;
        } else if (Physics.Raycast (v3_right, v3_hit, hit, 2.5,
layerMask.value)) {
    if (b_isJumping) {
  b_isJumping = false;
        }
        } else if (Physics.Raycast (v3_left, v3_hit, hit, 2.5,
layerMask.value)) {
if (b_isJumping) {
  b_isJumping = false;
        }
    } else {
    if (!b_isJumping) {
    if (Mathf.Floor(transform.position.y) == f_lastY) {
      b_isJumping = false;
    } else {
      b_isJumping = true;
    }
        }
    }
f_lastY = Mathf.Floor(transform.position.y);
//Update Main Camera
    mainCamera.transform.position = new Vector3(transform.
position.x, transform.position.y, mainCamera.transform.
position.z);

}
```

5. This is a very nice function that will allow us to debug our game, the result of which we won't see in the real game. Let's add the following block of code:

```
public function OnDrawGizmos() : void {
  mesh = GetComponent(MeshFilter).sharedMesh;
  f_height = mesh.bounds.size.y* transform.localScale.y;
    var v3_right : Vector3 = new Vector3(transform.position.x +
(collider.bounds.size.x*0.45), transform.position.y, transform.
position.z);
    var v3_left : Vector3 = new Vector3(transform.position.x -
(collider.bounds.size.x*0.45), transform.position.y, transform.
position.z);
  Gizmos.color = Color.red;
  Gizmos.DrawRay(transform.position, transform.TransformDirection
(-Vector3.up) * (f_height * 0.5));
  Gizmos.DrawRay(v3_right, transform.TransformDirection (-Vector3.
up) * (f_height * 0.5));
```

```
Gizmos.DrawRay(v3_left, transform.TransformDirection (-Vector3.
up) * (f_height * 0.5));
}
```

6. Finally , we add another `SpriteManager` class, which is a little different from our first sprite class. This `SpriteManager` is for our jumping animation. Since our jumping animation is quite unique and not a loop animation, we need another sprite class to control it. Let's add this code underneath our `SpriteManager` class and call it `JumpSpriteManager`:

```
class JumpSpriteManager {
   public var t_jumpStartTexture : Texture2D; //Alternative Jump
Texture play after t_jumpReadyTextures
   public var t_jumpAirTexture : Texture2D; //Alternative Jump
Texture play when the player in the air at the top position of
projectile
   public var t_jumpDownTexture : Texture2D; //Alternative Jump
Texture play when the player fall to the ground

   public function updateJumpAnimation (_direction : int, _
velocityY : float, _material : Material) : void {
      //Checking for the player position in the air
      if ((_velocityY>= -2.0) && (_velocityY<= 2.0)) { //Top of the
projectile
        _material.mainTexture =t_jumpAirTexture;
      } else if (_velocityY> 2.0) { //Start Jump
        _material.mainTexture = t_jumpStartTexture;
      } else {   //Fall
        _material.mainTexture = t_jumpDownTexture;
      }
      _material.mainTextureScale = new Vector2 (_direction * 1, 1);
      _material.mainTextureOffset = new Vector2 (_direction * 1, 1);
   }
}
```

7. Now we are done with coding, go back to Unity, go to `Hierarchy`, and click on our `Player`, then go to the **Inspector** view. Now, we will see a new parameter **Jump Sprite**; click on it to get the parameters, then set the following:

    ❏ **T_jump Start Texture: J_Frame1**

    ❏ **T_jump Air Texture: J_Frame2**

    ❏ **T_jump Down Texture: J_Frame3**

    ❏ **Layer Mask: Level**

We have now finished this step. Let's click plays the game and *Space* on the keyboard. Now, you will see your `Player` Jumping.

Objective Complete - Mini Debriefing

First, we attached the jumping ability to our character. `b_isJumping` is for checking if the character is already jumping in the air or not. `f_height` is the height from top to bottom of our character, which we will use to calculate physics later. `f_lastY` is the last position of our character in the Y-axis. `jumpSprite` is the `SpriteJumpManager` class, which will be a bit different from our `SpriteManager` class because our `jumpsprite` is not loop animation, so we need to create a new class to control this.

Then, in the start function we had a code that sets up and gets the information that we need as soon as our character is created. The `mesh = GetComponent(MeshFilter).sharedMesh;` line will basically get the mesh information from the **GameObject** that our `CharacterController_2D` script attached, which is our `Player`. Next, we get the height of this mesh by its size multiplied by the local scale of this object. Then, we set up `f_lastY` to the object's current position and set the `b_isJumping` parameter to false.

Next, if it is jumping, it will update the jumping Sprite animation. If it isn't jumping, it will go to our old code to check for walking or staying. We also added a new `Input.GetButton("Jump")`, which will check if the player pressed **jump**; in that case it will reset all the loop sprites and change the Y-velocity to negative gravity. This will basically make our character jump after the player presses the **jump** button.

We also added a `Physics.Raycast` to make our character move better and bug free. Then, we used the `OnDrawGizmos()` function to see and check if our ray from `Physics.Raycast` is from the right position or not. We can also use this to test or debug our game without taking the code out because it won't be shown on the real game. As we can see from the following figure, the red arrows represent where the raycast is, but we don't actually see them in the game:

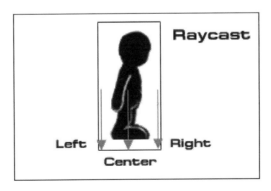

The `Physics.Raycast` is used to check if our character is on the floor or not. If it isn't, it will tell the game that now our character isn't on the floor, making its state equal to the jumping state (or we can say that it is in the air). By using this checking statement, we will be able to play a jumping animation when our character is falling down, but the player doesn't press the **jump** button.

We also draw three rays:

1. We draw the ray from the middle of our character to the bottom.

2. We draw the ray at the very right bound of the object to the bottom; we won't draw the ray at exactly the right bound position because we don't want it to hit the edge thickness of the floor.

3. Then, we do the same thing as with the right bound to the left bound.

Next, we check to make sure that the ray didn't hit anything and our character isn't jumping. We check the last Y-position for our character—whether it is equal to the current Y-position or not. If it is, it means the character is on the floor, so we set `b_isJumping = false`. If it doesn't, the character will fall down and we set `b_isJumping = true`. Finally, we update our character's last position on the Y-axis.

Next, we want the `OnDrawGizmos()` function to show our `Physics Raycast` in our editor scene which will give us a nice visual to see our `Ray` pointing to the right direction. In this function, we will use `Gizmos`, which is the class that basically allows us to draw the visual debugging or set-up aids in the scene view. We can get more information on how to use `Gizmos` from the following website:

`http://unity3d.com/support/documentation/ScriptReference/Gizmos.html`

Lastly, we create another Sprite class to manage our jumping texture to show the jumping animation by checking its velocity in the Y-axis. In the `JumpSpriteManager`, we almost have everything similar to our `SpriteManager`. Since we don't need a loop animation in this Jumping Sprite, but we still need to change the texture. First, we will change the main texture to `t_jumpAirTextures`, which will show the sprite while the character is at the top in the air. So, we check the velocity in the Y-axis, to see if it is between -2 to 2. Next, we check if the `velocityY` is greater than 2. This means that the player has just started jumping, but anything other than that means our character has fallen. Finally, we update our character's **Tiling** and **Offset**.

Classified Intel

There is something else we must look at in this chapter—the `Physics.Raycast`.

Physics.Raycast

Why do we need to shift a little bit from the collider edge by multiple **0.45** instead of **0.5**?

```
var hit : RaycastHit;
  var v3_hit : Vector3 = transform.TransformDirection (Vector3.
forward) * (f_height * 0.5);
  var v3_right : Vector3 = new Vector3(transform.position.x + (collider.
bounds.size.x*0.45), transform.position.y, transform.position.z);
```

From the line of code `if (Physics.Raycast (v3_right, v3_hit, hit, 2.5))`, we will see that the `Raycast` is drawing from the middle of our character on the right bound downward by `2.5` units. Now we can take a look at the `Gizmos` that we drew in the editor:

As we can see in the preceding figure, our gizmo (the red line) is basically shifting from the boundary of the box collider (green box) a little bit. This will only check at the bottom of our character because our box collider covers the line. On the other hand, if we draw the `Raycast` at the edge of the box collider, it will cause the problem that our character will be able to walk on air while the edge of the floor hits the `Raycast`, as shown in the previous figure.

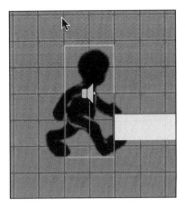

One last thing for the `Gizmos`: if we want to see our gizmos in the game scene, we can click on the **Gizmos** tab on the top-right corner of the game scene:

Creating a key and door

In this step, we will create the finish point, which is the door in this case. We will also create a `Trigger Collider`, which makes it so that the player can't end the game if he/she didn't collect our item; of course it's the key to our door.

Prepare for Lift Off

Let's prepare and make sure that we have all the graphics that we need; go to the `Graphics` folder in the `Project` window, and make sure in our subfolder `Level`, we have `doorClose.png`, `doorOpen.png`, and `key.png`. Let's get start.

Engage Thrusters

Here, we will create the object's `Key` and `Door`. Let's do this as follows:

1. Let's create the new material for our key, so go to **Assets | Create | Material**, name it `M_Key`, and set the following:

   - **Shader: Transparent | Cutout | Specular**
   - **Main Color: R: 255, G: 166, B: 0, A: 255**
   - **Specular Color: R: 236, G: 224, B: 26, A: 0**
   - **Shininess: Drag the dragger almost to the right side**
   - **Base (RGB) TransGloss (A)**
   - Drag-and-drop our `key.png` in the `Graphics/Level` to the texture thumbnail in the material inspector:

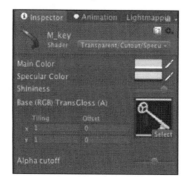

2. Next, we create another material for our door; go to **Assets | Create | Material**, name it **M_Door**, and set the following:

    ❑ **Shader**: **Diffuse**

    ❑ **Main Color**: **R: 219, G: 255, B: 255, A: 255**

    ❑ **Base (RGB)**

    ❑ Drag-and-drop our `doorClose.png` in the `Graphics/Level` to the texture thumbnail in the material inspector

3. Before we create our mesh object, we have to create a new `Tag` for our `Door` and `Key`, so go to **Edit | Project Settings | Tags**.

4. Under the **Element 3** type **Door**, and under **Element 4** type **Key**. Now, we will create a key object by using a plane in Unity; it's very similar to our `Player`. So, go to the `Plane` prefab object in the `FBX` folder and drag it into the **Hierarchy** view.

5. In the **Hierarchy** view, right-click on the `Plane` prefab object, and choose **Rename** to change the name to **Key**.

6. Next, right-click on the **Animation** component in the **Inspector** view and choose the **Remove Component** option to remove it. We will see the pop-up window, so just click on the **Continue** button similar to how we did for our `Player` object.

7. Click on this object and go to its **Inspector** view, and set the following:

    ❑ **Tag**: **Key**

    ❑ **Position**: **x: 21, y: 7.5, z: 0**

    ❑ **Rotation**: **x: 0, y: 180, z: 0**

    ❑ **Scale**: **x: 2.75, y: 2.75, z: 2.75**

8. Assign our `M_Key` to this material. Then add the `Box Collider` to the `Key` as we did for our `Player`; go to **Component | Physics | Box Collider** set **Size: x: 1, y: 1, z: 1** and **Center: x: 0, y: 0, z: 0**, and toggle **Is Trigger** to **true**.

9. Copy the `Key` by pressing *Command + D* or *Control + D* to create the `Door` object. Then, we name it `Door`, assign material `M_Door` to it, and set the following:

    ❑ **Tag**: **Door**

    ❑ **Position**: **x: 19.5, y: 16, z: 0**

    ❑ **Rotation**: **x: 0, y: 180, z: 0**

    ❑ **Scale**: **x: 7.5, y: 7.5, z: 1**

10. We have finished creating our Door and Key. Next, we will go back to our code and add some scripting to make our Door and Key work. Double-click our `CharacterController_2D.js`, and add these parameters to it:

```
public var doorOpenTexture : Texture2D;
public var doorCloseTexture : Texture2D;
private var b_hasKey : boolean;
```

11. Then, we add these lines of code to the `Start()` function:

```
    //Start with no Key
  b_hasKey = false;
```

This will set the character to start without a key.

12. Next, we add the `OnTriggerEnter()` function to our code; this function will check if our character hit Key or Door:

```
public function OnTriggerEnter (hit : Collider) : IEnumerator {
  if (hit.collider.tag == "Key") {
    if (!b_hasKey) {
      //We hit our Key
      b_hasKey = true;
      Destroy (hit.gameObject);
    }
  }

  if (hit.collider.tag == "Door") {
    if (b_hasKey) {
      //If we had Key and hit door the door will open
      hit.gameObject.renderer.material.mainTexture =
doorOpenTexture;
      //wait for 1 second and destroy our character
      yieldWaitForSeconds(1);
      Destroy (gameObject);
      //We close the door
      hit.gameObject.renderer.material.mainTexture =
doorCloseTexture;
    }
  }
}
```

In this function, we are checking if our character hit the key or door by checking their tag. When the player hits the key, the key will destroy itself and we set our character to have a key by setting b_hasKey = true. Also, when we hit the door, we are checking if our character has the key or not. If the character has the key, it will change the door texture to doorOpen texture. Then, we wait for one second to remove our character and we change the door texture back to doorClose texture to close the door.

13. Before we are done, we need to add `doorOpen.png` and `doorClose.png` to the `Player`. Go back to Unity, and click on the `Player`; in the **Inspector** view now, we will see two new parameters, **Door Open Texture** and **Door Close Texture**; drag-and-drop `doorOpen.png` to **Door Open Texture** and `doorClose.png` to **Door Close Texture**. Now we are done.

Click **play** and try out your game, collecting the key and going to the door. Behold the door opening and closing!

Objective Complete - Mini Debriefing

We just created a `key` and `door` object, and placed them at our level. We also created the function that will trigger when the character hits the `key` and `door` objects. Then, we changed the texture of our `door` object when our character had a `key` object and hit the door. Lastly, we waited for one second to remove our character from the scene and changed the `door` texture back to closed state by using `yield` and `Destroy`.

Classified Intel

We can pause or wait for the next action by using `coroutines`.

Coroutines

In our script, we need to wait for a second between opening the door and ending the game. We could do this by looping or performing some other task for a second, but that would stop the animations, the sound, and everything else. We get around this by using the `yield` command; this tells Unity to stop running our function and come back later (in our game, 1 second later as we call `yield WaitForSecond(1)`). By using the `yield` command our function becomes `Coroutines` and now it must return `IEnumerator` (Unity needs this so that it can tell when to start our function again). This means `Coroutines` can't return a value like a normal function. We can change most functions in our `MonoBehaviours` script into `Coroutines`, apart from the ones which already run in every frame, such as `Update()`, `FixedUpdate()`, `OnGUI()`, and so on. We can get more information about `coroutines` from the following Unity script reference:

`http://unity3d.com/support/documentation/ScriptReference/Coroutine.html`.

Next, we will talk about the return type. Sometimes, when we use JavaScript, we don't really care about what type to return or what type of parameters we will pass to the function, because it is really convenient to type only `var myParams = 0` or `function DoSomething(var)`. This isn't a bad thing to do, but if we are working with a team of people, it is very important to have code that is readable for others. So, it is better to have this habit. It also makes the code run faster, since it doesn't have to go and do type lookups. On the other hand, if we use C#, we will be forced by the language itself to type the return type of this function or the type of this parameter. So, it's a good thing to know because you will be able to read C# code easily if you have to and it is readable for everyone, even the person using C#.

Adding a sound and replay button

Finally, we are in the last step of this chapter. We will add sound effects and a simple replay button for us to be able play this again.

Prepare for Lift Off

Let's make sure that we have all the graphics that we need for the **replay** button; go to the `Chapter1` folder in the **Project** window, and make sure we have `restartButtonOut.png` and `restartButtonOver.png` in our subfolder `Buttons`. We also need some sound effects to use for our character, go to our `Sound` subfolder. We will see `button_click.aiff`, `doorOpen.wav`, `getKey.aiff`, and `Jump.wav`. Unity, by default, translates every sound that we import in our project to 3D, but we don't really need it as we are creating a 2D game. So, we will click on each sound in the `Sound` folder in the **Project** view and go to their **Inspector** window and uncheck **3D Sound** and then click on the **Apply** button:

Engage Thrusters

In this section, we will create the button and script for the restart button:

1. First, we need to create a simple `TextureButton` class to control our restart button (**Assets | Create | Javascript**) and name our script to `TextureButton`. Double-click to open `MonoDevelop` and add the following code:

```
public var normalTexture : Texture2D;
public var rollOverTexture : Texture2D;
public var clickSound : AudioClip;
public var key : GameObject;
public var Player : GameObject;
```

From the preceding code, we have two `Texture2D` parameters, `normalTexture` and `rollOverTexture`, for the **restart** button when it's in the rollout and rollover state. We also have an audio to play a click sound FX.

2. Next, we have `key` and `Player GameObject`, which we will assign the prefab of `key` and `Player` to use when the game is at an end. We are creating a function to change our restart button texture when the user performs rollover and rollout. Add the following script:

```
public function OnMouseEnter () : void {  //Mouse Roll over
function
   guiTexture.texture = rollOverTexture;
}


public function OnMouseExit() : void { //Mouse Roll out function
   guiTexture.texture = normalTexture;
}
```

3. Now, we will create the function that will reset our character back to the start position, and the key will appear in the scene again by using `Instatiate` to clone our object from our prefab object in the projects, which we will create at a later state.

4. Finally, we have `@script RequireComponent (AudioSource)` to basically force the script to add an `AudioSource` script to our `restartButton`, and to prevent the error when we are running this script without the `AudioSource` script. Let's add the following script:

```
public function OnMouseUp() : IEnumerator{ // Mouse up function
   audio.PlayOneShot(clickSound);
   yield new WaitForSeconds (1.0); //Wait for 0.5 secs. until do
the next function
   //Create a new Player at the start position by cloning from our
prefab
   Instantiate(Player, new Vector3(Player.transform.position.x,
Player.transform.position.y, 0.0), Player.transform.rotation);
```

```
   //Create a new key at the start position by cloning from our
prefab
   Instantiate(key, new Vector3(key.transform.position.x, key.
transform.position.y, 0.0), key.transform.rotation);
   //Hide restart button
   guiTexture.enabled = false;
}


@scriptRequireComponent(AudioSource)
```

5. Then, we go back to our `CharacterController_2D.js` to add sound code for playing the sound effect and a **restart** button. Add these parameters to the top of this class:

```
private var restartButton : GUITexture;
public var doorOpenSound : AudioClip;
public var getKeySound : AudioClip;
public var jumpSound : AudioClip;
```

6. Add code to get the `restartButton` from our game scene; put this code in the `Start()` function:

```
//Get restartButton from the Game Scene
   restartButton = GameObject.FindWithTag("RestartButton").
guiTexture;
   //make restart Button disabled
   restartButton.enabled = false;
```

7. Add a jump sound, inside the `Update()` function and inside `if (Input.GetButton("Jump")) {}` as follows:

```
if (Input.GetButton("Jump")) { //Jump
       b_isJumping = true;
   //Then make it Jump
   audio.volume = 0.3;
   audio.PlayOneShot(jumpSound);
       loopSprites[0].resetFrame();
       loopSprites[1].resetFrame();
       rigidbody.velocity = new Vector3(rigidbody.velocity.x,
-Physics.gravity.y, 0);
       }
```

8. Next, we add the `getKey` sound, `doorOpen` sound, and enable our `restartButton`. Go to `OnTriggerEnter()` and update the code. First, inside `if (hit.collider.tag == "Key") {}` add the highlighted code:

```
if (hit.collider.tag == "Key") {
    if (!b_hasKey) {
        //We hit our Key
```

```
    audio.volume = 1.0;
    audio.PlayOneShot(getKeySound);
        b_hasKey = true;
        Destroy (hit.gameObject);
    }
}
```

9. Inside `if (hit.collider.tag == "Door") {}`, add the highlighted code:

```
if (hit.collider.tag == "Door") {
    if (b_hasKey) {
    audio.volume = 1.0;
    audio.PlayOneShot(doorOpenSound);
        //If we had Key and hit door the door will open
        hit.gameObject.renderer.material.mainTexture =
doorOpenTexture;
        //wait for 1 second and destroy our character
        yieldWaitForSeconds(1);
        Destroy (gameObject);
        //We close the door
        hit.gameObject.renderer.material.mainTexture =
doorCloseTexture;
      //Show Restart Button
      restartButton.enabled = true;
      }
    }
```

And for the last thing before we go back to Unity, put this line at the end of the code to basically force the script to add an `AudioSource` script to `CharacterController_2D.js`:

```
@scriptRequireComponent (AudioSource)
```

10. Then, we go back to Unity, and click on the `Player` to open the **Inspector**. We will see **Door Open Sound**, **Get Key Sound**, and **Jump Sound**. Then, we assign the sounds to these as follows:

    - **Door Open Sound**: `doorOpen.wav`

    - **Get Key Sound**: `getKey.aiff`

    - **Jump Sound:** `Jump.wav`

11. Next, we need to add an `Audio Source` script to be able to use our sound for the `Player`. This is because we already attached this script to the game object, so Unity doesn't add it for us.

12. Go to **Component | Audio | AudioSource**. There, create three prefabs for the `key`, `Player`, and `restartButton`. Go to **Assets | Create | Prefab** three times, and name all of them as follows: **Key**, **Player**, and **restartButton**.

13. Next, we drag our `Player` in **Hierarchy** to the **Player Prefab** in the **Project** window. We will also do the same with `Key`; drag our `Key` in **Hierarchy** to the **Key Prefab** in the **Project** window.

14. For the `restartButton`, we need to create a new tag; go to **Edit | Project Settings | Tags**. Under **Element 5** type **RestartButton**.

15. Next, create a new `GUI Texture` object, which is for our replay button **GameObject | Create Other | GUI Texture** and name it `restartButton`, and in the object inspector set it as follows:

    ❑ **Tag: RestartButton**

    ❑ **Position**: **x: 0.5, y: 0.5, z: 0**

    ❑ **Rotation**: **x: 0, y: 0, z: 0**

    ❑ **Scale**: **x: 0, y: 0, z: 1**

    ❑ **GUITexture:**

    ❑ **Texture**: Drag-and-drop `restartButtonOut.png` here

    ❑ **Color**: Leave it as default

    ❑ **Pixel Inset**:

    ▸ **X: -64, Y: -16, Width: 128, Height: 32**

16. Drag `restartButton` in **Hierarchy** and drop to the **restartButtonPrefab** in the **Project** Window, click on the **restartButtonPrefab** in the **Project** window, and drag our `TextureButton.js` script to **restartButtonPrefab**. In the **Inspector**, we add all objects needed for **Texture Button (Script)** as follows:

    ❑ **Normal Texture**: Drag-and-drop `restartButtonOut.png` in here

    ❑ **Roll Over Texture**: Drag-and-drop `restartButtonOver.png` in here

    ❑ **Click Sound**: Drag-and-drop `button_click.aiff` here

    ❑ **Key**: Drag-and-drop `Key Prefab` here

    ❑ **Player**: Drag-and-drop `Player Prefab` here

Ok, now we are done; click **play** to see what we have. Now, when we collect the key and go inside the door, we will see a **restart** button appear; click on this button and the game will restart.

Objective Complete - Mini Debriefing

We just finished creating a **restart** button for our platform game. We used `Destroy` and `Instantiate` to remove and create a new clone of the object from the prefab. We also added a sound effect to our restart button and character. Then, we set `audio.volume` to `1.0;` to set the volume of our sound effect and used `audio.PlayOneShot(AudioClip);` to play a sound effect once it is triggered.

Classified Intel

In `restartButton`, we can also add `Application.LoadLevel(LevelName)` to reset our game, which is much easier than using `instantiate`, but the `Application.LoadLevel` will destroy all the game objects in the scene and reload again. In this case, we use `instantiate` in our game because we only have one scene and don't want to load the whole game level again. However, we can also put `DontDestroyOnLoad()` in the `Awake()` function of the object that we don't want to destroy, but it needs a bit of setup. So, there is no right or wrong. It depends on what we want to use or where we want the project to go.

Game over-Wrapping it up

We just created a simple 2D platform game, and it is our first piece to get started with Unity. In this chapter, we have learnt how to manage a sprite animation by adjusting the `Tiling` and `Offset` of the material. We have gone through the `MonoDevelop` scripting editor and created a JavaScript class. Also, we have learnt the basics of how to use **Input Manager**, **Physics Raycast**, **Gizmos**, and **Collider**. Finally, we have attached the sound effect and a **restart** button to our game. Let's take a look at what we have:

Are you ready to go gung ho? A Hotshot challenge

Now we have a game that looks good, but it's not complete, yet. So, why don't you try to do something by using the knowledge gained from this chapter to add more fun to your game and make it look better? Let's try the following:

- Add a background music and more sound effects
- Make more challenges in our level, such as create a movable platform, collect more items to open the door, or even have a longer level
- Add obstacles that can make your character dead, lose Hit Points, or restart to another position
- Add Hit Point for our character
- Create an animated background or level by using the concept from our `SpriteManager` class swapping the texture
- Create a parallax background by adding more layers for the background or foreground object

Project 2

Create a Menu for an RPG Game—Add Powerups, Weapons, and Armor

Here we are in the second chapter. When we talk about traditional role-playing games, we will probably be thinking about the development of the character, such as the attributes, skills, powers, levels or experience, and so on. When we are playing an RPG, we typically have to open the menu or UI to adjust and manage our main character, such as increase the character attribute, change the weapon, or choose skills. The menu is very important in an RPG game. So, in this chapter, we will make the menu in an RPG game by using the GUI class in Unity.

Mission briefing

We'll create a simple menu, yet complex enough for the RPG game. In this chapter, we will continue using some assets from the first chapter. So, we won't have to recreate the character again. This menu will include a **STATUS** tab, which will show the current attributes, skills, and equipment of our character. Next is an **INVENTORY** tab that will contain all the items that our character has as well as the information for each item when the user rolls over.

The last tab is the **EQUIPMENT** tab with which the user will be able to change the weapon, armor, accessory, and skill, as shown in the following screenshot:

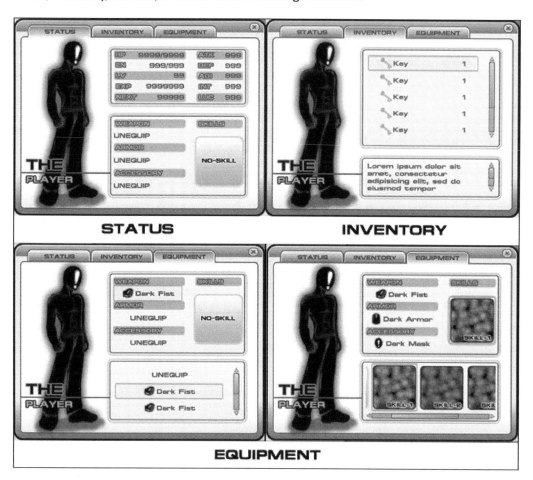

The purpose of this chapter is to understand the GUI class in Unity and create our custom user interface, which is different from GUITexture that we used to create our **restart** button in the first chapter. There is also GUIText, which we will use to display the text of any font we import in the screen coordinate. Both are the type of rendering component that can be used once per object. So, if we try to create a complete menu, we will need many GUITexture/GUIText objects and the scripts to handle them. On the other hand, GUI class is operating inside one function OnGUI, and we only deal with one object and only create a script that will display all buttons in the **menu** tab.

What does it do?

In this project, we will apply the custom GUI graphics to Unity by using GUI Skin. We can have multiple styles of our GUI graphics in Unity. Let's say that we have multiple types of fonts that we want to use in our menu; Unity has a way to do this. We can create a GUI Skin and apply our custom skin to the area that we want to show the font in. That is the great thing about Unity.

Now, we want to create a menu scripting class that will bring up a new menu window in the game scene when the player presses *M*. Next, we create a script to make three tab buttons, which will take the player to each tab, **STATUS**, **INVENTORY**, and **EQUIPMENT**.

In the **STATUS** tab, we will create a script that will show the image of our character, hit points, magic points, skill, and all the attributes of this character. Next, we will create an **INVENTORY** tab, which will contain all the items that the player can scroll up and down to choose an item. Finally, we will create the tab that the player can use to manage and change the equipment and skills of the character by clicking it.

Next, we will create a menu game object and apply the script to this game object. Lastly, we will add the parameter and textures to our menu and start playing.

Why Is It Awesome?

When we complete this chapter, we will be able to create our custom UI for our RPG game, not only RPG, but we will also be able to create the user interface for every genre. Also, we will get a good understanding of the GUI class in Unity, which is very powerful, if we want to create an awesome user interface such as with Dragon Age, Final Fantasy, and so on.

Your Hotshot Objectives

Since we are creating a menu for an RPG style game, we need a menu that is a little more complex than the usual menu. So, it will be split into five tasks. Here is the outline of the tasks:

- ► Custom skin with GUI Skin
- ► Creating a menu object
- ► Creating a status tab
- ► Creating an inventory tab
- ► Creating an equipment tab

Mission Checklist

Before we start, we will need to get the project folder and assets from this book's website: `http://www.packtpub.com/support?nid=8267`, which includes the finished project from the first chapter and the assets that we need to use in this chapter. Browse to the URL and download the `Chapter2.zip` package; unzip it, and we will see `Chapter2.unitypackage`, which we will use to import to our second project in Unity.

Custom skin with GUI Skin

Those of you who are familiar with HTML will probably have a good understanding of using a repeating image for a background to reduce memory usage. Unity uses the same idea to create a graphic for the user interface, which will save a lot of memory and size for our game. In this section, we will take a look at the GUI Skin, which is the main key to creating a custom skin in Unity.

Prepare for Lift Off

We will begin by creating the new project in Unity. Let's start:

1. First, create a new project and name it **MenuInRPG**, similar to what we did in the first chapter. Click on the **Create Project** button, as shown in the following screenshot:

2. Next, import the assets package by going to **Assets | Import Package | Custom Package...**); choose the `Chapter2.unityPackage`, which we just downloaded, and then click on the **Import** button in the pop-up window link, as shown in the following screenshot:

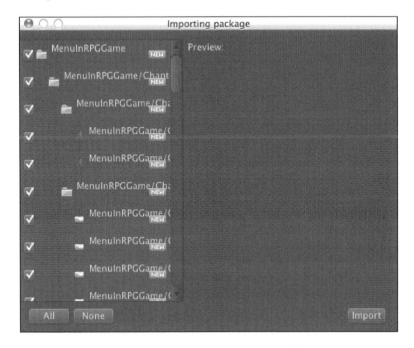

3. Wait until it's done, and you will see the **MenuInRPGGame** and **SimplePlatform** folders in the **Window** view. Next, click on the arrow in front of the **MenuInRPGGame** folder to bring up the drop-down and you will see the **Chapter2** folder and the **MenuInRPG** scene, as shown in the following screenshot:

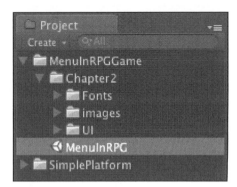

4. Next, double-click on the **MenuInRPG** scene, as shown in the preceding screenshot, to open the scene that we will work on in this chapter.

5. When you double-click on the **MenuInRPG** scene, Unity will display a pop-up asking whether we want to save the current scene or not. As we want to use the **MenuInRPG** scene, just click on the **Don't save** button to open up the **MenuInRPG** scene, as shown in the following screenshot:

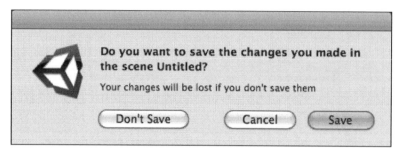

6. Then, go to `Chapter2/UI` folder and click on the `arrowDHover.png` to bring up its **Inspector** view. In the **Inspector** view, make sure that **GUI** is selected in the **Texture Type** properties, and **Truecolor** is selected in **Format**. Then, we will click on the **Apply** button, as shown in the following screenshot:

So why do we set it up in this way? It is because we want to have a UI graphic to look as close to the source image as possible. However, we set the **Format** to **Truecolor**, which will make the size of the image larger than **Compress**, but will show the right color of the UI graphics.

7. At last, we will edit the layers' name by going to the **Layer Inspector** and set the **User Layer 8** to **Background** and **User Layer 9** to **Level**.

Engage Thrusters

Now, we are ready to create the GUI Skin:

1. Let's create a new GUI Skin by going to **Assets | Create | GUI Skin**, and we will see **New GUISkin** in our project window. Name the GUI Skin as **MenuSkin**. Then, we click on our **MenuSkin** and go to its **Inspector**. We will see something similar to the following screenshot:

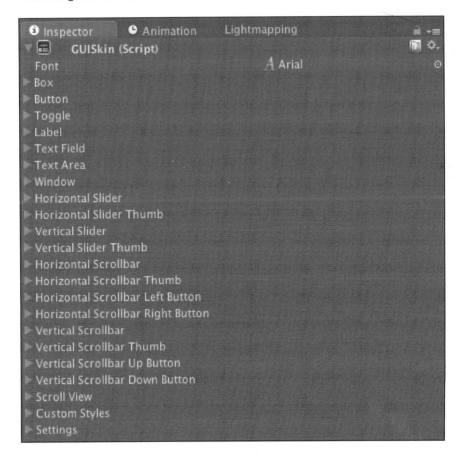

2. You will see many properties, but don't be afraid, because this is the main key to creating a custom graphics for our UI. **Font** is the base font for the GUI Skin. From **Box** to **Scroll View**, each property is a **GUIStyle**, which we will be able to use for creating our custom UI. The **Custom Styles** property is the array of **GUIStyle** that we can set up for the extra style. **Settings** are the setup for the entire **GUI**.

3. Next, we will set up the new font style for our menu UI; go to **Font** line in this **Inspector** view, click the circle icon, and select the font **Federation Kalin**.

4. Now you have set up the base font for our GUI Skin. Next, click on the arrow in front of the **Box** line to bring up a drop-down. We will see all the properties. We can see more information and learn more about these properties on the Unity website: `http://unity3d.com/support/documentation/Components/class-GUISkin.html`.

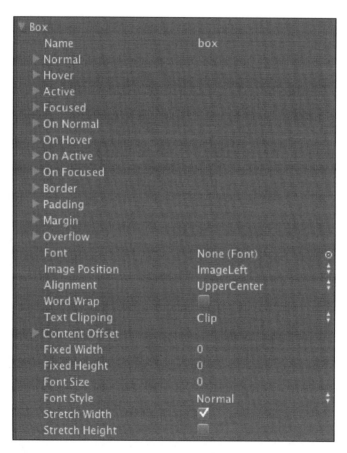

5. **Name** is basically the name of this style, which the box is the default style of the GUI.Box. Next, we will start by setting our custom UI to this GUI Skin; click on the arrow in front of **Normal** to bring up the drop-down, and you will see two parameters **Background** and **Text Color**.

6. Click on the circle icon at the right of the **Background** line to bring up the **Select Texture2D** window and choose the `boxNormal.png` texture, or you can drag the `boxNormal.png` texture from our `Chapter2/UI` folder and drop it to the **Background** space.

 We can also use the search bar to find our texture by going to the **Project** view and typing **boxNormal** in the search bar, as shown in the following screenshot:

7. Then under the **Text Color** line, we leave the color as the default color—because we will not have any text shown in this style—and repeat the previous step with **On Normal** by using the `boxNormal.png` texture.

8. Next, click on the arrow in front of **Hover** under the **Background**. Choose `boxActive.png` texture, and repeat this step for **Active** and **On Active**.

9. Then, go to each property in the **Box** style and set the following:

   □ **Border: Left: 14, Right: 14, Top: 14, Bottom: 14**

   □ **Padding: Left: 6, Right: 6, Top: 6, Bottom: 6**

   For the other properties in this style, we will leave them as default.

10. Next, we go to the following properties in **GUISkin inspector** and set them as follows:

    □ **Label**

       □ **Normal | Text Color: R: 27, G: 95, B: 104, A: 255**

    □ **Window**

       □ **Normal | Background**: `myWindow.png`

       □ **On Normal | Background**: `myWindow.png`

       □ **Border: Left: 27, Right: 27, Top: 55, Bottom: 96**

       □ **Padding: Left: 30, Right: 30, Top: 60, Bottom: 30**

- ❑ **Horizontal Scrollbar**
  - ▸ **Normal | Background**: `horScrollBar.png`
  - ▸ **Border: Left: 4, Right: 4, Top: 4, Bottom: 4**
- ❑ **Horizontal Scrollbar Thumb**
  - ▸ **Normal | Background**: `horScrollBarThumbNormal.png`
- ❑ **Hover | Background**: `horScrollBarThumbHover.png`
  - ▸ **Border: Left: 4, Right: 4, Top: 4, Bottom: 4**
- ❑ **Horizontal Scrollbar Left Button**
  - ▸ **Normal | Background**: `arrowLNormal.png`
  - ▸ **Hover | Background**: `arrowLHover.png`
  - ▸ **Fixed Width**: 14
  - ▸ **Fixed Height**: 15
- ❑ **Horizontal Scrollbar Right Button**
  - ▸ **Normal | Background**: `arrowRNormal.png`
  - ▸ **Hover | Background**: `arrowRHover.png`
  - ▸ **Fixed Width**: 14
  - ▸ **Fixed Height**: 15
- ❑ **Vertical Scrollbar**
  - ▸ **Normal | Background**: `verScrollBar.png`
  - ▸ **Border: Left: 4, Right: 4, Top: 4, Bottom: 4**
  - ▸ **Padding: Left: 0, Right: 0, Top: 0, Bottom: 0**
- ❑ **Vertical Scrollbar Thumb**
  - ▸ **Normal | Background**: `verScrollBarThumbNormal.png`
  - ▸ **Hover | Background**: `verScrollBarThumbHover.png`
  - ▸ **Border: Left: 4, Right: 4, Top: 4, Bottom: 4**

- ❑ **Vertical Scrollbar Up Button**
  - ▶ **Normal | Background**: `arrowUNormal.png`
  - ▶ **Hover | Background**: `arrowUHover.png`
  - ▶ **Fixed Width**: **16**
  - ▶ **Fixed Height**: **14**
- ❑ **Vertical Scrollbar Down Button**
  - ▶ **Normal | Background**: `arrowDNormal.png`
  - ▶ **Hover | Background**: `arrowDHover.png`
  - ▶ **Fixed Width**: **16**
  - ▶ **Fixed Height**: **14**

We have finished the setup of the default style.

11. Now we will go to the **Custom Styles** property and create our custom **GUIStyle** to use for this menu; go to **Custom Styles** and under **Size** change the number to **6**. Then, we will see **Element 0** to **Element 5**.

12. Next, we go to the first element or **Element 0**; under **Name** type **Tab Button**, and we will see **Element 0** change to **Tab Button**. Set it as follows:
    - ▶ **Tab Button** (or **Element 0**)
      - ❑ **Name**: **Tab Button**
      - ❑ **Normal**
        - ❑ **Background**: `tabButtonNormal.png`
        - ❑ **Text Color**: **R: 27, G: 62, B: 67, A: 255**
    - ▶ **Hover**
      - ❑ **Background**: `tabButtonHover.png`
      - ❑ **Text Color**: **R: 211, G: 166, B: 9, A: 255**
    - ▶ **Active**
      - ❑ **Background**: `tabButtonActive.png`
      - ❑ **Text Color**: **R: 27, G: 62, B: 67, A: 255**
    - ▶ **On Normal:**
      - ❑ **Background**: `tabButtonActive.png`
      - ❑ **Text Color**: **R: 27, G: 62, B: 67, A: 255**

- ▸ **Border**: Left: 12, Right: 12, Top: 12, Bottom: 4

- ▸ **Padding**: Left: 6, Right: 6, Top: 6, Bottom: 4

- ▸ **Alignment**: Middle Center

- ▸ **Fixed Height**: 31

- ▸ **Font Size**: 14

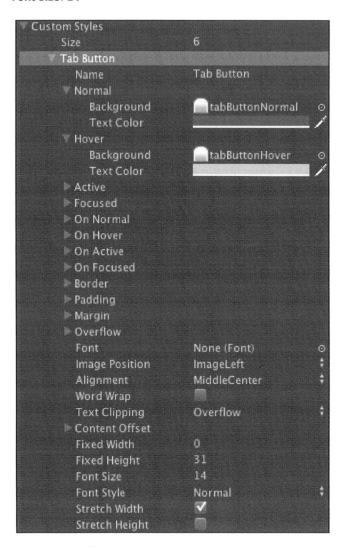

For the **Text Color**, we can also use the Eyedropper tool next to the color box to copy the same color, as we can see in the following screenshot:

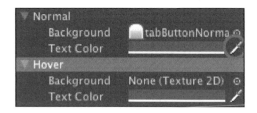

13. We have finished our first style, but we still have five left, so let's carry on:

   ▸ **Exit Button** (or **Element 1**)

      ❑ **Name**: **Exit Button**

      ❑ **Normal** | **Background**: buttonCloseNormal.png

      ❑ **Hover** | **Background**: buttonCloseHover.png

      ❑ **Fixed Width**: **26**

      ❑ **Fixed Height**: **22**

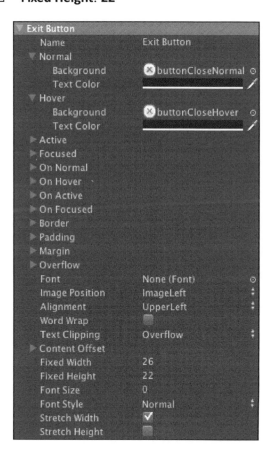

- ▸ **Text Item** (or **Element 2**)
    - ❏ **Name**: **Text Item**
    - ❏ **Normal | Text Color**: **R: 27, G: 95, B: 104, A: 255**
    - ❏ **Alignment**: **Middle Left**
    - ❏ **Word Wrap**: **Check**

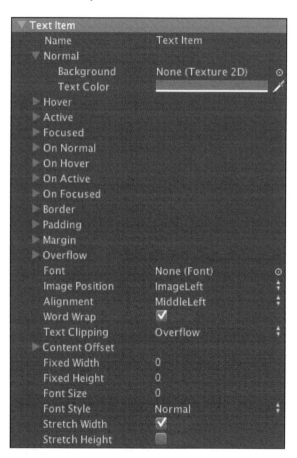

- ▸ **Text Amount** (or **Element 3**)
    - ❏ **Name**: **Text Amount**
    - ❏ **Normal | Text Color**: **R: 27, G: 95, B: 104, A: 255**
    - ❏ **Alignment**: **Middle Right**
    - ❏ **Word Wrap**: **Check**

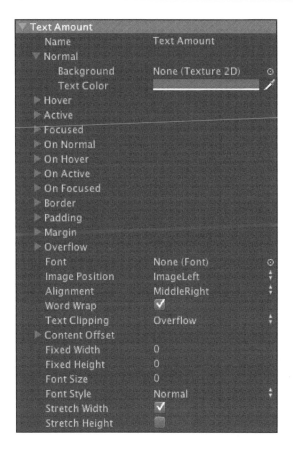

- **Selected Item** (or **Element 4**)

  - ❑ **Name: Selected Item**

  - ❑ **Normal | Text Color**: R: 27, G: 95, B: 104, A: 255

  - ❑ **Hover**

      - ❑ **Background**: `itemSelectNormal.png`

      - ❑ **Text Color**: R: 27, G: 95, B: 104, A: 255

- **Active**

  - ❑ **Background**: `itemSelectNormal.png`

  - ❑ **Text Color**: R: 27, G: 95, B: 104, A: 255

- **On Normal**

  - ❑ **Background**: `itemSelectActive.png`

  - ❑ **Text Color**: R: 27, G: 95, B: 104, A: 255

- ❑ **Border**: **Left: 6**, **Right: 6**, **Top: 6**, **Bottom: 6**
- ❑ **Padding**: **Left: 4**, **Right: 4**, **Top: 4**, **Bottom: 4**
- ❑ **Margin**: **Left: 2**, **Right: 2**, **Top: 2**, **Bottom: 2**
- ❑ **Alignment**: **Middle Center**
- ❑ **Word Wrap**: **Check**

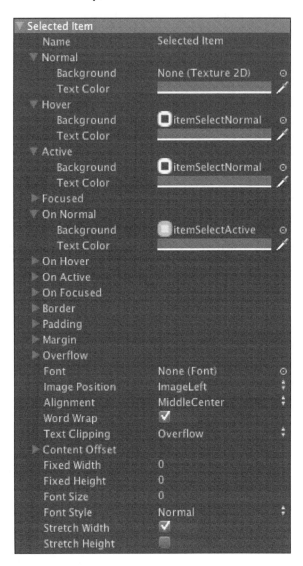

- ▸ **Disabled Click** (or **Element 5**)
  - ❑ **Name**: **Disabled Click**
  - ❑ **Normal**
    - ❑ **Background**: `itemSelectActive.png`
    - ❑ **Text Color**: R: 27, G: 95, B: 104, A: 255
  - ❑ **Border**: **Left: 6, Right: 6, Top: 6, Bottom: 6**
  - ❑ **Padding**: **Left: 4, Right: 4, Top: 4, Bottom: 4**
  - ❑ **Margin**: **Left: 2, Right: 2, Top: 2, Bottom: 2**
  - ❑ **Alignment**: **Middle Center**
  - ❑ **Word Wrap**: **Check**

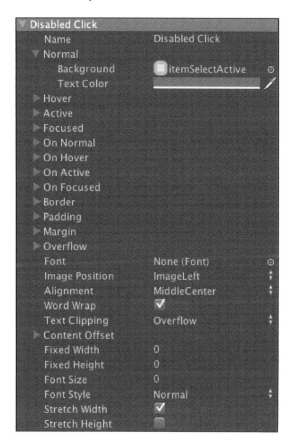

And we have now finished this step.

Objective Complete - Mini Debriefing

Basically, what we have done here is create the **GUISkin** asset as the skin for our menu. First, we tell the GUI that we will use the font name Federation Kalin as our main font for this GUI Skin by setting up the Font in the first line in this skin inspector. Then, we changed all the default skin textures to use our UI graphics from our UI folder by setting all the necessary properties and parameters in **Box**, **Label**, **Window**, **Horizontal Scrollbar**, **Horizontal Scrollbar Thumb**, **Horizontal Scrollbar Left Button**, **Horizontal Scrollbar Right Button**, **Vertical Scrollbar**, **Vertical Scrollbar Thumb**, **Vertical Scrollbar Up Button**, **Vertical Scrollbar Down Button** style. Then, we created six **Custom Styles**, **Tab Button**, **Exit Button**, **Text Item**, **Text Amount**, **Selected Item**, and **Disabled Click**, which will be used in our script in the next section.

> The **Custom Style** is basically the **GUIStyle** that we can add into our **GUISkin**. This **Style** allows us to create a custom **Style** that will act differently from the default style (**Box**, **Label**, **Window**, and so on) in this **GUISkin**.

Classified Intel

In this section, we applied UI graphics to **GUISkin.** You might have a question here—how does it work? Here, we will go through the basic concept of how to create a custom UI in Photoshop and get the right texture to use in our **GUISkin**.

First, let's take a look at the myWindow.png in our Chapter2/UI folder. We will see the capsule shape. You might be curious—how are we going to create a window graphics with this capsule shape? Well, the trick is the properties **Border** on which we set the parameters **Left**, **Right**, **Top**, and **Bottom**. As we already mentioned, use the repeating image in the background of the HTML code.

Here is how the Unity **GUIStyle** works. Take a look at the following figure:

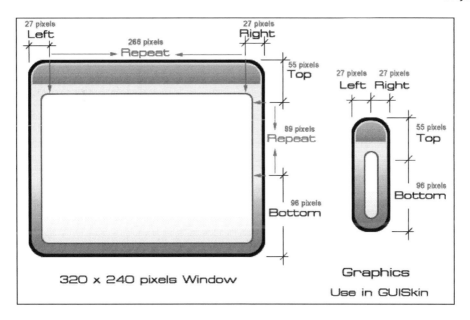

First, we set the parameters for the **Border**. These parameters will offset the pixels of the current UI graphics from 0 to the number that we assigned. For example, if we want to draw a rectangular window, which is 320 pixels in width and 240 pixels in height, and we set the **Left** Border to 27, **Right** to 27, **Top** to 55, and **Bottom** to 96, this will tell Unity **GUIStyle** to always draw the graphics from pixel 0 to pixel 27 on the left side with the same scale as the source texture. What will happen from pixel 28? Basically, it will repeat pixel 27 until it hits the right **Border**, which is also set to 27 pixels from the right. So, this means that we tell the **GUIStyle** to draw graphics from the source texture from pixel 0 to pixel 27, and repeat the texture from pixel 28 to pixel 293, then switch back and draw pixel 294 to pixel 320 from the source texture, which is the offset of 27 pixels from the right. This also applies to the top and bottom **Borders**, as we can see on the left side of the preceding figure.

From this concept, we can save a lot of memory because instead of using a 320 x 240 pixel image, we just use 54 x 151 pixels. However, in some cases we don't want any repeating pixels for our UI such as fixed button graphics—for example, our `Exit Button` style—or any fixed texture, and so on, as we can see in the following figure:

We can just set the **Fixed Width** and **Fixed Height** properties in **GUIStyle** to match our image size. For instance, we have our exit button image, which is 26 pixels wide and 22 pixels high. We just set the **Fixed Width** to 26 and **Fixed Height** to 22. We can also set only **Fixed Width** or **Fixed Height** in **GUIStyle**—as we already did in our **Custom Styles** Tab Button—as we can see in the following figure:

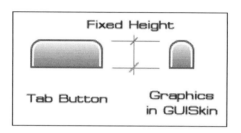

We set the **Fixed Height** to **31**, and we leave the **Fixed Width** at **0**, which means that the height of the style will always be 31 pixels but the width can vary from zero to infinity.

Creating a menu object

Continuing from the first step, we will now create our menu game object in the scene, with which we will be able to open and close the menu window. Pressing the *M* key will open the menu window, and clicking on the **close** button in the window will close the menu window. We will also create three tab buttons for the player to be able to see through the different pages, **STATUS**, **INVENTORY**, and **EQUIPMENT**, as we can see in the following screenshot:

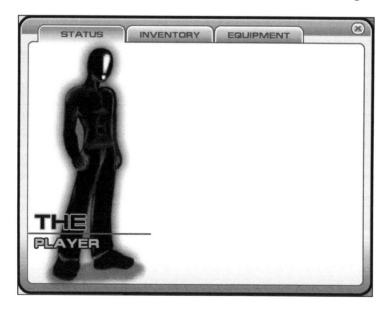

Prepare for Lift Off

Just make sure that we have our `Player.png` texture in the `Chapter2/images` folder. Now, we are ready.

Engage Thrusters

We will begin by creating the menu:

1. First, we want to create an empty game object in our scene and name it `menu`; go to **GameObject | Create Empty** and name it `MenuObject`. We will use this object for our menu.

2. Next, we will create the menu JavaScript that will control our entire menu; go to **Assets | Create | Javascript**, name it `Menu`, double-click on it to launch `MonoDevelop`, and we will get our hands dirty with the code.

3. Open the `Menu.js` file, and type these variables as follows:

```
//For toggle the open and close our menu window
//We made it static so that we can access this variable from
everywhere.
public static var b_openMenu : boolean;

public var customSkin : GUISkin; //We assign our MenuSkin here
public var t_hero : Texture;   //Character background texture
public var t_statusBox1 : Texture; //First Info box background
texture
public var t_statusBox2 : Texture; //Second Info box background
texture
public var t_skillBox : Texture; //Skill box background texture

private var in_toolbar : int = 0;
private var s_toolbars : String[] = ["STATUS", "INVENTORY",
"EQUIPMENT"];
private var r_hero : Rect = new Rect (19, 35, 225, 441);
private var r_window : Rect = new Rect (10, 10, 640, 480);
private var r_closeBtn : Rect = new Rect (598, 8, 26, 22);
private var r_tabButton : Rect = new Rect (35, 15, 480, 40);
```

Here, we just created the necessary variables for our Menu window, as shown in the following screenshot:

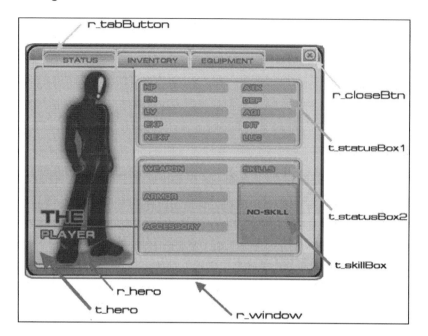

 The result of t_statusBox1, t_statusBox2, and t_skillBox will be shown in the *Creating the Status tab* section.

4. Next, we will set b_openMenu to false in the Start function, because we don't want our menu to show until the player presses the *M* key, so type the code as follows:

```
public function Start () : void {
  b_openMenu = false; //Set our menu disabled at the first run
}
```

5. Then, we go to the Update function and set it as follows:

```
// Update is called once per frame
public function Update () : void {
  //When the user press M key show the menu window
  if (Input.GetKey(KeyCode.M)) {
    if (b_openMenu == false) {
      b_openMenu = true;
    }
  }
}
```

6. Next, we will use the `OnGUI` function to create our window.

 OnGUI function acts similar to an `Update` function, but `OnGUI` gets called more than once, for rendering and handling **GUI** events, meaning that `OnGUI` implementation might be called several times per frame (one call per event).

7. In the `OnGUI` function, we will assign our `customSkin`, create a window menu, make it draggable, and check to make sure that the window is always on the screen; so add this code after the `Update` function:

```
//All GUI Class will create in this function
public function OnGUI () : void {
  GUI.skin = customSkin; //Assign our MenuSkin to the Gui Skin
  if (b_openMenu) {  //If open menu == true create a menu window
    r_window = GUI.Window (0, r_window, DoMyWindow, ""); //create
a new window by the size of rect
    //This whole code is to make sure that our window can't be
dragged outside of the screen area
    ///////////////////////////////////////////////////////////////
/////////////////
    r_window.x = Mathf.Clamp(r_window.x, 0.0, Screen.width - r_
window.width);
    r_window.y = Mathf.Clamp(r_window.y, 0.0, Screen.height - r_
window.height);       ////////////////////////////////////////////
//////////////////////////////
  }
}


//Our window function operates here
private function DoMyWindow (windowID : int) : void {
  //We create tab button here.
  in_toolbar = GUI.Toolbar (r_tabButton, in_toolbar, s_toolbars,
GUI.skin.GetStyle("Tab Button"));

  switch (in_toolbar) {
    case 0 : //Status
      //Create a status page
      break;
    case 1 : //Items
      //Create an item page
      break;
    case 2 : //Equip
      //Create an equipment page
      break;
```

```
      }
      //Draw our background character texture
      GUI.DrawTexture(r_hero, t_hero);

      //We create a close button here
      if (GUI.Button (r_closeBtn, "", GUI.skin.GetStyle("Exit
Button"))) {
         b_openMenu = false;
      }

      //Make our window dragable in whole area
      GUI.DragWindow();
   }
```

Since we want everything inside our menu window, we used the DoMyWindow function to take a GUI.Window as one parameter. Inside the DoMyWindow function, we create all the buttons and textures. Then, we make our window draggable by adding GUI.DragWindow(). With that we are done with coding for this step.

8. Next, go back to **Unity**, click on Menu.js, and drag-and-drop it to the Menu game object in the **Hierarchy**. Next, click on the Menu game object in the **Hierarchy**, open the **Menu (Script)**, and set the parameters as follows:

   - **Custom Skin**: Drag-and-drop our MenuSkin (GUISkin) here

   - **T_hero**: Drag-and-drop blackDude.png from the Chapter2/images folder here

   - **T_status Box 1**: Drag-and-drop stat1.png from the Chapter2/images folder here

   - **T_status Box 2**: Drag-and-drop stat2.png from the Chapter2/images folder here

   - **T_skill Box**: Drag-and-drop skill0.png from the Chapter2/images folder here

9. Then, we can click on the **play** button to see the result. In the game scene, we can press the *M* key to bring up our window and click the **x** button at the top-right corner to close it.

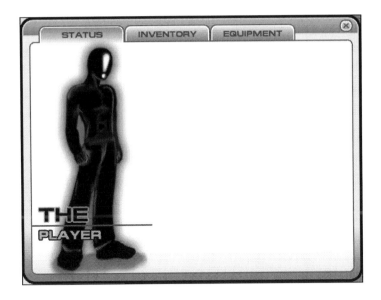

Objective Complete - Mini Debriefing

We just created a menu window, which can be opened by pressing the *M* key and closed by clicking on the **x** button at the top-right corner of the menu window. We also have our character texture nicely placed inside our menu window. Next, we made this window draggable and made sure it is always on the screen by using the following code:

```
r_window.x = Mathf.Clamp(r_window.x, 0.0, Screen.width - r_window.
width);
r_window.y = Mathf.Clamp(r_window.y, 0.0, Screen.height - r_
window.height);
```

Basically, we set the minimum limit of our window in the x-position to 0 and the maximum to the screen width subtracted by the window width; we also set the minimum limit of y-position to 0 and the maximum to the screen height subtracted by the window height.

We will see this result when we click **play the game** and try to drag this window off the screen. Lastly, we created a tab that can be clicked to change to a different page.

Classified Intel

In this step, we were using a GUI class to create our window, box, and button, but we can also use a GUILayout class to create the same thing as we did with GUI class. The only difference between these two classes is that GUI will need to take a Rect object to specify the size and position of the UI. On the other hand; GUILayout doesn't need to take the Rect object. It will automatically adjust the size related to the source it has. Let's say, we want to create a box that contains a text or image, GUILayout will automatically adjust the height and width to nicely fit your text or image. For the position, GUILayout will automatically set the first position to the top-left corner of the screen, which is (0, 0), and it will continue to the right or down depending on the GUILayout object that we already have on the screen. However, the downside is that we will not be able to create a fixed position or size for the GUILayout. So, both classes are very powerful to use. We can use them in different situations.

You can see more details of the GUI class at this URL:

`http://unity3d.com/support/documentation/ScriptReference/GUI.html`.

You can also see the details of the GUILayout class at this URL:

`http://unity3d.com/support/documentation/ScriptReference/GUILayout.html`.

The GUI.DragWindow() function allows us to create a draggable window by specifying the drag area on our window. You can visit the following URL to see the details:

`http://unity3d.com/support/documentation/ScriptReference/GUI.DragWindow.html`.

We will see this function take one Rect parameter, which is the area that allows the user to drag the window around. However, we didn't assign Rect parameters to our GUI.DragWindow() function, which means that we can drag the whole window area.

Creating a status tab

In this step, we will create a status page for our menu, which will show all attributes of this character, including hit points, magic points, level, experience, experience needed for the next level, attack, defense, agility, intelligence, and luck. We will also show the current equipment and skill of this character.

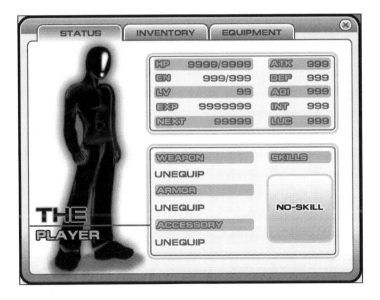

Engage Thrusters

We will start with assigning the status parameters for our character and displaying them on our menu:

1. Let's go back to `MonoDevelop` and add more code to our `Menu.js`. Include these variables before the `Start` function:

```
public var fullHP : int = 9999; //The current full HP
public var fullMP : int = 999; //The current full MP
public var currentHP : int = 9999; //The current HP
public var currentMP : int = 999; //The current MP
public var currentLV : int = 99; //The current LV
public var currentEXP : int = 9999999; //The current EXP
public var currentNEXT : int = 99999; //The current NEXT
public var currentATK : int = 999; //The current ATK
public var currentDEF : int = 999; //The current DEF
public var currentAGI : int = 999; //The current AGI
public var currentINT : int = 999; //The current INT
public var currentLUC : int = 999; //The current LUC

public var a_weapons : Item[]; //weapons array that the character
currently has
public var a_armors : Item[]; //armors array that the character
currently has
public var a_accessories : Item[]; //accessories array that the
character currently has
```

```
public var a_items : Item[]; //items array that the character
currently has
public var a_skills : Texture[]; //skills array that the character
currently has

private var currentWeapon : Item; //current weapon that character
uses
private var currentArmor : Item; //current armor that character
uses
private var currentAccessory : Item; //current accessory that
character uses
private var currentItem : Item; //current item that character uses
private var currentSkill : Texture; //current skill that character
uses

private var s_unequip : String = "UNEQUIP";
private var s_none : String = "NONE";

//Status Tab
private var maxHP : int = 9999; //Maximum limit of HP
private var maxMP : int = 999; //Maximum limit of MP
private var maxLV : int = 99; //Maximum limit of LV
private var maxEXP : int = 9999999; //Maximum limit of EXP
private var maxNEXT : int = 99999; //Maximum limit of NEXT
private var maxATK : int = 999; //Maximum limit of ATK
private var maxDEF : int = 999; //Maximum limit of DEF
private var maxAGI : int = 999; //Maximum limit of AGI
private var maxINT : int = 999; //Maximum limit of INT
private var maxLUC : int = 999; //Maximum limit of LUC

//Rect position for the GUI
private var r_statTexture1 : Rect = new Rect (252, 77, 331, 125);
private var r_statTexture2 : Rect = new Rect (252, 244, 331, 142);
private var r_hpLabel : Rect = new Rect (313, 75, 120, 25);
private var r_mpLabel : Rect = new Rect (313, 100, 120, 25);
private var r_lvLabel : Rect = new Rect (313, 124, 120, 25);
private var r_expLabel : Rect = new Rect (313, 150, 120, 25);
private var r_nextLabel : Rect = new Rect (313, 177, 120, 25);
private var r_atkLabel : Rect = new Rect (529, 75, 50, 25);
private var r_defLabel : Rect = new Rect (529, 100, 50, 25);
private var r_agiLabel : Rect = new Rect (529, 124, 50, 25);
private var r_intLabel : Rect = new Rect (529, 150, 50, 25);
private var r_lucLabel : Rect = new Rect (529, 177, 50, 25);
private var r_statBox : Rect = new Rect (237, 67, 360, 147);
private var r_weaponBox : Rect = new Rect (237, 230, 360, 207);
```

```
private var r_weaponLabel : Rect = new Rect (252, 264, 180, 40);
private var r_armorLabel : Rect = new Rect (252, 324, 180, 40);
private var r_accessLabel : Rect = new Rect (252, 386, 180, 40);
private var r_skillTexture : Rect = new Rect (464, 288, 119, 117);
private var r_skillBox : Rect = new Rect (460, 284, 127, 125);
//GUIContent
private var gui_weaponCon : GUIContent;
private var gui_armorCon : GUIContent;
private var gui_accessCon : GUIContent;
private var gui_skillCon : GUIContent;
```

Now we've got all the variables for our status page.

2. Next, we need the `Item` class to contain the information for our items. Let's add this to the preceding code:

```
//Items class to contain our information
class Item{
  public var icon : Texture;
  public var name : String;
  public var amount : int;

  private var itemName : String;

  //This function is just to put the space between name of the
item and amount of the item
  public function setUpItemName () : void {
    var in_length : int = (this.name.Length + this.amount.
ToString().Length);
    if (in_length < 25) {
      while (this.name.Length < 17 ) {
        this.name += " ";
      }
    }
    if(this.amount < 10) {
      itemName = (this.name + " " + this.amount.ToString());
    } else {
      itemName = (this.name + this.amount.ToString());
    }
  }

  public function get itemNA () : String {
    return itemName;
  }
}
```

Basically, the `Item` class will contain the information that we need to show for every item.

3. Next, we go to the `Start()` function and add the highlighted code:

```
public function Start () : void {
    b_openMenu = false; //Set our menu disabled at the first run

    gui_weaponCon = GUIContent(s_unequip);
    gui_armorCon = GUIContent(s_unequip);
    gui_accessCon = GUIContent(s_unequip);
    gui_skillCon = GUIContent("");
```

4. We just finished all the setup that we need for our status page in the menu window. Next, we go to `DoMyWindow (windowID : int)` and uncomment the highlighted line as follows:

```
switch (in_toolbar) {
    case 0 : //Status
        //Create a status page
        StatusWindow();
        break;
```

5. Next, we need to create a `StatusWindow()` function, as follows:

```
private function StatusWindow() : void {
    GUI.Box (r_statBox, "");
    GUI.Box (r_weaponBox, "");
    GUI.DrawTexture(r_statTexture1, t_statusBox1);
    GUI.DrawTexture(r_statTexture2, t_statusBox2);
    GUI.DrawTexture(r_skillBox, t_skillBox);

    CheckMax();

    GUI.Label(r_hpLabel, currentHP.ToString() + "/" + fullHP.
ToString(), "Text Amount");
    GUI.Label(r_mpLabel, currentMP.ToString() + "/" + fullMP.
ToString(), "Text Amount");
    GUI.Label(r_lvLabel, currentLV.ToString(), "Text Amount");
    GUI.Label(r_expLabel, currentEXP.ToString(), "Text Amount");
    GUI.Label(r_nextLabel, currentNEXT.ToString(), "Text Amount");

    GUI.Label(r_atkLabel, currentATK.ToString(), "Text Amount");
    GUI.Label(r_defLabel, currentDEF.ToString(), "Text Amount");
    GUI.Label(r_agiLabel, currentAGI.ToString(), "Text Amount");
    GUI.Label(r_intLabel, currentINT.ToString(), "Text Amount");
    GUI.Label(r_lucLabel, currentLUC.ToString(), "Text Amount");
```

```
   GUI.Label(r_weaponLabel, gui_weaponCon, "Text Item");
   GUI.Label(r_armorLabel, gui_armorCon, "Text Item");
   GUI.Label(r_accessLabel, gui_accessCon, "Text Item");
   GUI.Label(r_skillTexture, gui_skillCon, "Text Item");
}
```

6. Before we finish this step, we need to add another function, `checkmax()`, to the preceding code. This function will make sure that the maximum number of attributes is not over the limit. Let's add the code to create this function:

```
private function CheckMax () : void {
   fullHP = Mathf.Clamp(fullHP, 0.0, maxHP);
   fullMP = Mathf.Clamp(fullMP, 0.0, maxMP);
   currentHP = Mathf.Clamp(currentHP, 0.0, fullHP);
   currentMP = Mathf.Clamp(currentMP, 0.0, fullMP);
   currentLV = Mathf.Clamp(currentLV, 0.0, maxLV);
   currentEXP = Mathf.Clamp(currentEXP, 0.0, maxEXP);
   currentNEXT = Mathf.Clamp(currentNEXT, 0.0, maxNEXT);
   currentATK = Mathf.Clamp(currentATK, 0.0, maxATK);
   currentDEF = Mathf.Clamp(currentDEF, 0.0, maxDEF);
   currentAGI = Mathf.Clamp(currentAGI, 0.0, maxAGI);
   currentINT = Mathf.Clamp(currentINT, 0.0, maxINT);
   currentLUC = Mathf.Clamp(currentLUC, 0.0, maxLUC);
}
```

7. Now, we go back to Unity, click **play**, and press the *M* key to bring up our menu window. We will see all the attributes for our character, as shown in the following screenshot:

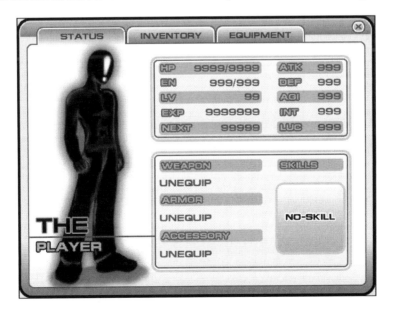

Objective Complete - Mini Debriefing

We just added an `Item` class to contain our item's information, which will be shown on the equipment box, and will use this in the next step. Then, we created a `GUIContent` to contain the image, name, and information of our items in the `Start()` function, and set it to an **UNEQUIP** stage. Next, we added and created the `StatusWindow()` function to show the status page when the player sees our menu at first click on the status tab button. We also created a `CheckMax()` function to make sure that the number of the character attributes is not over the limit.

Classified Intel

In this section, we used `GUIContent` to contain the information of our items and pass to `GUI.Label()` function. Basically, if we take a look at each `GUI` class function, we will see that it can take many variables such as `Rect`, `string`, `Texture`, `GUIContent`, and `GUIStyle`. We already know what `Rect`, `string`, and `Texture` are. `GUIStyle` is the name of the style from our `MenuSkin` object that we created, but what is `GUIContent`? It is basically a class that contains the necessary variables to apply to our `GUI`. For example, if we want our button to have an icon, name, and information when the user rolls over it, we can add this code: `GUI.Button(Rect(0,0,100,20), GUIContent("My Button Name", icon, "This is the button info")`. The first parameter is the `string` that will be shown inside the button, and next is the graphic `Texture` that will also be shown inside this button. The last `string` is the information that will be stored in this button, which we call **tooltip**. We can show this **tooltip** when the user rolls over this button by calling `GUI.tooltip`. It will automatically show the current button **tooltip** that the user rolls over. We will use it in the next section.

For more details about `GUIContent` and `GUI.tooltip`, we can check out this website:

`http://unity3d.com/support/documentation/ScriptReference/GUIContent.GUIContent.html`.

Creating an inventory tab

So, we are in the second page of our menu window, which is the inventory page. In this section, we will create an item scroll that the player can use to scroll up and down to select the item and see its name, amount, and information of the item.

Engage Thrusters

We will start with adding the parameters, which we will use to store the data in our inventory page:

1. Open `Menu.js`, and add the following code to it; first the parameters:

```
//Item Tab
private var r_itemsBox : Rect = new Rect (237, 67, 360, 247);
private var r_tipBox : Rect = new Rect (237, 330, 360, 107);
private var r_itemsButton : Rect = new Rect (257, 87, 340, 227);
private var r_tipButton : Rect = new Rect (257, 350, 340, 87);
private var r_verScroll : Rect = new Rect (600, 87, 20, 227);
private var f_scrollPos : float = 1.0;
private var scrollPosition : Vector2 = Vector2.zero;
private var scrollPosition2 : Vector2 = Vector2.zero;
private var in_toolItems : int = 0;
```

2. Then, go to the `Start()` function and add the following code at the end:

```
if (a_items.Length > 0) {
    a_items[0].setUpItemName();
    currentItem = a_items[0];
}
```

3. Next, go to `DoMyWindow (windowID : int)` and uncomment the highlighted line as follows:

```
case 1 : //Items
    //Create an item page
    ItemWindow();
    break;
```

4. Then, we need to create an `ItemWindow()` function to show this inventory page. Type this following function in `Menu.js`:

```
private function ItemWindow() : void {
    var in_items : int = 8;
    //Create Item Information box
    GUI.Box (r_itemsBox, "");
    GUI.Box (r_tipBox, "");
    scrollPosition = GUI.BeginScrollView (new Rect (257, 87, 320,
200), scrollPosition, new Rect (0, 0, 280, 40*in_items));
    // We just add a single label to go inside the scroll view.
Note how the
    // scrollbars will work correctly with wordwrap.
    var itemsContent : GUIContent[] = new GUIContent[in_items];
```

```
        //We create a GUIContent array of key item here (if you have
more than 1 items, you can also use your item array instead of the
current item)
        for (var i: int = 0; i < in_items; i++) {
            if (a_items.Length > 0) {
                if (i == 0) {
                    itemsContent[i] = GUIContent(currentItem.itemNA,
currentItem.icon, "Lorem ipsum dolor sit amet, consectetur
adipisicing elit, sed do eiusmod tempor incididunt ut labore
et dolore magna aliqua. Ut enim ad minim veniam, quis nostrud
exercitation ullamco laboris nisi ut aliquip ex ea commodo
consequat.");
                } else {
                    itemsContent[i] = GUIContent(currentItem.itemNA,
currentItem.icon, "This is key " + i);
                }
            } else {
                itemsContent[i] = GUIContent("NONE", "");
            }
        }

    //We create the grid button here.
    in_toolItems = GUI.SelectionGrid (Rect (0, 0, 280, 40*in_
items), in_toolItems, itemsContent, 1, GUI.skin.GetStyle("Selected
Item"));
        GUI.EndScrollView (); //End Scroll Area

    //Checking if there is an item information
    var s_info : String = itemsContent[in_toolItems].tooltip;
    if (s_info == "") {
      s_info = "Show items information here";
    }
    var style : GUIStyle = GUI.skin.GetStyle("Label");
    if (GUI.tooltip != "") {
      //Get height from this style
      var f_height : float = style.CalcHeight(GUIContent(GUI.
tooltip), 330.0);
        scrollPosition2 = GUI.BeginScrollView (new Rect (257, 343,
320, 75), scrollPosition2, new Rect (0, 0, 280, f_height));
        GUI.Label(new Rect (0, 0, 280, f_height), GUI.tooltip);
    } else {
      //Get height from this style
      f_height = style.CalcHeight(GUIContent(s_info), 330.0);
        scrollPosition2 = GUI.BeginScrollView (new Rect (257, 343,
320, 75), scrollPosition2, new Rect (0, 0, 280, f_height));
        GUI.Label(new Rect (0, 0, 280, f_height), s_info);
    } GUI.EndScrollView ();
}
```

In this function, first we set the maximum of our items in this container, and next we create a GUI.Box for the background of the item scroll area. Then, we create the scroll by using GUI.BeginScrollView. Next, we create a GUIContent array to contain our items, create GUI.SelectionGrid, and apply our GUIContent array to show them. Then, we get the item information from the GUIContent.tooltip, calculate the height of that information, and put it in the **Label**, which is also a scroll view.

5. Now, go back to Unity and click on the **Menu** object in the **Hierarchy** view to bring up its **inspector**. Then, click on the **A_items** option to bring up the drop-down and assign the parameters as follows:

    ❑ **Size: 1**

    ❑ **Element 0**

        ▸ **Icon**: key.png (located in Chapter2/images folder)

        ▸ **Name: Key**

    ❑ **Amount: 1**

    Now, click **play**, and press the *M* key to bring up our menu window. Click on the **INVENTORY** tab and we will see our item page. Isn't that cool?

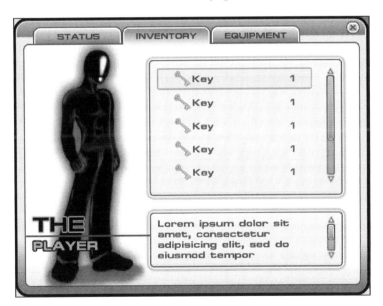

Objective Complete - Mini Debriefing

We just created our inventory page that we'll be able to view by clicking the **INVENTORY** tab. In the `Start()` function, we set up our `item` object if there is more than one item assigned in `a_items`. Next, we added `ItemWindow()` line in the `DoMyWindow()` function, and created `ItemWindow()` function to control our item page. In this function, we created a scroll view by using `GUI.BeginScrollView()` and `GUI.EndScrollView()`, and created a scrollable area that contains all the items. We also used `GUI.SelectionGrid` to create our items list from which the player can select any item. Then, we get the current tooltip from `GUIContent` and check to see whether there is any information or not. Next we check `GUI.tooltip` for any stored string; if nothing is stored here we assign the current `tooltip` from our selected items to `GUI.tooltip`, which will show the result that if we roll over each item the current information will change to the rollover item. On the other hand, if we rollover from our items list, the result of the information will show the selected item information. Next, we get the **Label** style height from the current `GUI.tooltip`. Then, we created another scroll view to show this `tooltip` information in the box area.

Classified Intel

In this step, we were using `GUI.SelectionGrid` to create the list of the items. By using `GUI.SelectionGrid`, we were able to create a list of buttons that have a fixed height and space in one line of code, which was very convenient. We can see more details on how to use `GUI.SelectionGrid` at this URL:

http://unity3d.com/support/documentation/ScriptReference/GUI.SelectionGrid.html.

We also used the `GUI.tooltip` parameter to be able to show our items' information when the player rolls over each item and show the selected item information if the player rolls out. So, how does `GUI.tooltip` work? Basically, `GUI.tooltip` will return the string from each button that contains a `tooltip` string when the player rolls over it. However, if the player rolls out or that button doesn't have any `tooltip` store, this parameter will automatically return a blank string, similar to the following code that we used:

```
if (GUI.tooltip != "") {
  //Get height from this style
  var f_height : float = style.CalcHeight(GUIContent(GUI.tooltip),
330.0);
  scrollPosition2 = GUI.BeginScrollView (new Rect (257, 343, 320,
75), scrollPosition2, new Rect (0, 0, 280, f_height));
  GUI.Label(new Rect (0, 0, 280, f_height), GUI.tooltip);
} else {
  //Get height from this style
  f_height = style.CalcHeight(GUIContent(s_info), 330.0);
```

```
    scrollPosition2 = GUI.BeginScrollView (new Rect (257, 343, 320,
 75), scrollPosition2, new Rect (0, 0, 280, f_height));
    GUI.Label(new Rect (0, 0, 280, f_height), s_info);
  }
```

We basically tell `GUI.tooltip` that we will assign rollover tooltip information to the label when the player rolls over. And if the player rolls out, we show the selected item information, for which the default is the first item as we can see in the following screenshot:

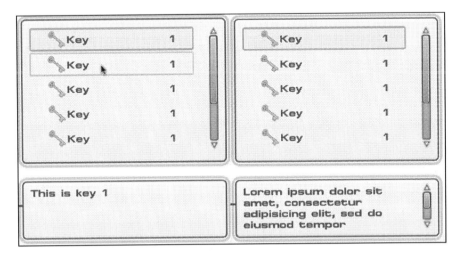

From the preceding screenshot, the left image shows that when we roll over the second key, the information box shows the tooltip of the second key. The right image shows that when we rollout from the second key, the information box shows the tooltip of the selected key, which is the first key.

 You can see more details about `GUI.tooltip` at this URL:

`http://unity3d.com/support/documentation/ScriptReference/GUI-tooltip.html`.

Creating an equipment tab

This is the last step of our menu. We will create a tab with which the player can change the weapon, armor, accessory, and skill of the character, which will also update the status tab, as we can see in the following screenshot:

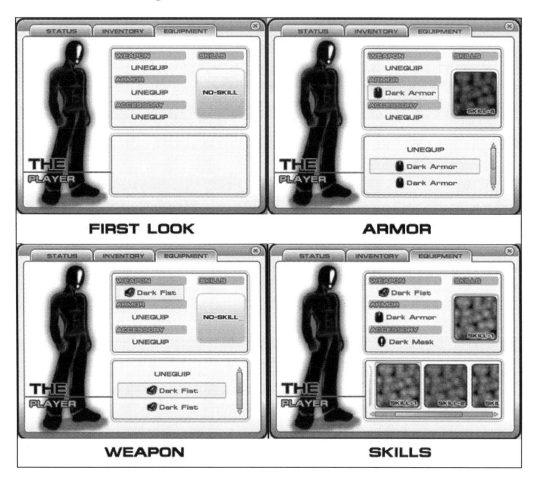

Engage Thrusters

We will start this section by adding the parameters:

1. Go back to `MonoDevelop`, open `Menu.js`, and add the following code to it:

```
//Equip tab
private var r_equipBox : Rect = new Rect (237, 67, 360, 207);
private var r_equipWeaponBox : Rect = new Rect (237, 280, 360, 157);
```

```
private var r_statTextureEquip : Rect = new Rect (252, 81, 331,
142);
private var r_skillBoxEquip : Rect = new Rect (460, 121, 127,
125);

//The position of each equip button from 0 - weapon, 1 - armor, 2
- accessory, 3 - skill
private var r_equipRect : Rect[] = [new Rect (252, 101, 180, 40),
new Rect (252, 161, 180, 40), new Rect (252, 221, 180, 40), new
Rect (464, 125, 119, 117)];
private var r_equipWindow : Rect = new Rect (500, 0, 70, 100);
private var scrollPosition3 : Vector2 = Vector2.zero;
private var scrollPosition4 : Vector2 = Vector2.zero;
private var scrollPosition5 : Vector2 = Vector2.zero;
private var scrollPosition6 : Vector2 = Vector2.zero;
private var a_equipBoolean : boolean[] = new boolean[4];
private var in_toolWeapons : int = 0;
private var in_toolArmors : int = 0;
private var in_toolAccess : int = 0;
private var in_toolskill : int = 0;
```

2. Then, go to the `Start()` function and add the following code at the end:

```
//Setup boolean equip
    for (var i : int = 0 ; i < a_equipBoolean.length; i++) {
      a_equipBoolean[i] = false;
    }
```

3. We go to `DoMyWindow (windowID : int)` and uncomment the highlighted line as follows:

```
    case 2 : //Equip
        //Create an equipment tab
    EquipWindow();
        break;
```

4. Next, we are going to create an `EquipWindow()` function, which will control our equipment tab:

```
private function EquipWindow() : void {
  GUI.Box (r_equipBox, "");
  GUI.Box (r_equipWeaponBox, "");
  GUI.DrawTexture(r_statTextureEquip, t_statusBox2);
  GUI.DrawTexture(r_skillBoxEquip, t_skillBox);

  SetupEquipBox();
}
```

5. In the next function, we will see four function calls, which are `SetupEquipBox()`, `ShowWeapon()`, `ShowArmor()`, `ShowAccess()`, and `ShowSkill()`. The first function is to set each equipment label as clickable or not. The other functions are enabled when the player clicks on each equipment label at the top box, and inside each function will contain the script that allows the player to change and select new equipment for weapon, armor, accessory, or skill. So, let's type the following code:

```
//Setting the ability to enabled or disable the button
private function SetupEquipBox () : void {
   var equipContent : GUIContent[] = [gui_weaponCon, gui_armorCon,
gui_accessCon, gui_skillCon];
   for (var i : int = 0; i < a_equipBoolean.length; i++) {
     if (a_equipBoolean[i] == true) {
       //Set up disabled Button
        GUI.Label(r_equipRect[i], equipContent[i], "Disabled
Click");
            //Show each equipment window
            switch (i) {
            case 0:
              ShowWeapon();
              break;
            case 1:
              ShowArmor();
              break;
            case 2:
              ShowAccess();
              break;
            case 3:
              ShowSkill();
              break;
          }
       } else {
          //Set up enabled Button
          if (GUI.Button(r_equipRect[i], equipContent[i], "Selected
Item")) {
            a_equipBoolean[i] = true;
            //Set others to false
            for (var j : int = 0; j < a_equipBoolean.length; j++) {
              if (i != j) {
                a_equipBoolean[j] = false;
              }
            }
          }
       }
     }
}
```

6. Next, we will start the first function with the ShowWeapon() function, which will display the weapon selection box; type the following code:

```
private function ShowWeapon () : void {
    var in_items : int = 6;
    var itemsContent : GUIContent[] = new GUIContent[in_items];
    //We create a GUIContent array of key item here (if you have
more than 1 item, you can also use your item array instead of the
current item)
        for (var i: int = 0; i < in_items; i++) {
            if (i == 0) {
            itemsContent[i] = GUIContent(s_unequip, "");
        } else {
            itemsContent[i] = GUIContent(a_weapons[0].name, a_
weapons[0].icon);
        }
    }
    scrollPosition3 = GUI.BeginScrollView (new Rect (257, 300, 320,
120), scrollPosition3, new Rect (0, 0, 280, 40*in_items));
    //We create grid button here.
    in_toolWeapons = GUI.SelectionGrid (Rect (0, 0, 280,
40*in_items), in_toolWeapons, itemsContent, 1, GUI.skin.
GetStyle("Selected Item"));
    //End the scrollview we began above.
    GUI.EndScrollView ();

    gui_weaponCon = itemsContent[in_toolWeapons];
}
```

7. Then, we will create the ShowArmor() function, which will be used to display the armor box as follows:

```
private function ShowArmor () : void {
    var in_items : int = 6;
    var itemsContent : GUIContent[] = new GUIContent[in_items];
    //We create a GUIContent array of key item here (if you have
more than 1 item, you can also use your item array instead of the
current item)
        for (var i: int = 0; i < in_items; i++) {
            if (i == 0) {
            itemsContent[i] = GUIContent(s_unequip, "");
        } else {
            itemsContent[i] = GUIContent(a_armors[0].name, a_
armors[0].icon);
        }
    }
```

```
    scrollPosition3 = GUI.BeginScrollView (new Rect (257, 300, 320,
120), scrollPosition3, new Rect (0, 0, 280, 40*in_items));
    //We create grid button here.
    in_toolArmors = GUI.SelectionGrid (Rect (0, 0, 280,
40*in_items), in_toolArmors, itemsContent, 1, GUI.skin.
GetStyle("Selected Item"));
        // End the scrollview we began above.
        GUI.EndScrollView ();

        gui_armorCon = itemsContent[in_toolArmors];
}
```

8. Next, we will create the `ShowAccess()` function, which will be used to display the accessory box as follows:

```
private function ShowAccess () : void {
    var in_items : int = 6;
    var itemsContent : GUIContent[] = new GUIContent[in_items];
    //We create a GUIContent array of key item here (if you have
more than 1 item, you can also use your item array instead of the
current item)
        for (var i: int = 0; i < in_items; i++) {
            if (i == 0) {
            itemsContent[i] = GUIContent(s_unequip, "");
            } else {
            itemsContent[i] = GUIContent(a_accessories[0].name, a_
accessories[0].icon);
            }
        }
    scrollPosition3 = GUI.BeginScrollView (new Rect (257, 300, 320,
120), scrollPosition3, new Rect (0, 0, 280, 40*in_items));
    //We create grid button here.
    in_toolAccess = GUI.SelectionGrid (Rect (0, 0, 280,
40*in_items), in_toolAccess, itemsContent, 1, GUI.skin.
GetStyle("Selected Item"));
        // End the scrollview we began above.
        GUI.EndScrollView ();

        gui_accessCon = itemsContent[in_toolAccess];
}
```

9. In the last function, we will create the `ShowSkill()` function, which will be used to display the skills box as follows:

```
private function ShowSkill () : void {
  var in_items : int = a_skills.length + 1;
  var itemsContent : GUIContent[] = new GUIContent[in_items];
  //We create a GUIContent array of key item here (if you have
more than 1 item, you can also use your item array instead of the
current item)
    for (var i: int = 0; i < in_items; i++) {
        if (i == 0) {
        itemsContent[i] = GUIContent(t_skillBox);
        } else {
        itemsContent[i] = GUIContent(a_skills[i-1]);
        }
    }
  scrollPosition3 = GUI.BeginScrollView (new Rect (253, 286, 330,
140), scrollPosition3, new Rect (0, 0, 600, 117));
  //We create grid button here.
  in_toolskill = GUI.SelectionGrid (Rect (0, 4, 600, 117), in_
toolskill, itemsContent, in_items, GUI.skin.GetStyle("Selected
Item"));
    // End the scrollview we began above.
    GUI.EndScrollView ();
    if(in_toolskill != 0) {
      gui_skillCon = itemsContent[in_toolskill];
    } else {
      gui_skillCon = GUIContent ("");
    }
}
```

10. Now, we go back to Unity and click on the **Menu** object in the **Hierarchy** to bring up its **Inspector**. Then, we set up the following properties:

   ▸ **A_weapons**
      ❑ **Size: 1**
      ❑ **Element 0**
         ❑ **Icon:** Drag-and-drop `weapon.png` from `Chapter2/ images` here
         ❑ **Name: Dark Fist**
         ❑ **Amount: 1**

- ▸ **A_armors**
  - ❏ **Size**: 1
  - ❏ **Element 0**
    - ❏ **Icon**: Drag-and-drop `armor.png` from `Chapter2/images` here
    - ❏ **Name: Dark Suit**
    - ❏ **Amount: 1**
- ▸ **A_accessories**
  - ❏ **Size**: 1
  - ❏ **Element 0**
    - ❏ **Icon**: Drag-and-drop `accessory.png` from `Chapter2/images` here
    - ❏ **Name: Dark Mask**
    - ❏ **Amount: 1**
- ▸ **A_skills**
  - ❏ **Size: 4**
  - ❏ **Element 0**: Drag-and-drop `skill1.png` from `Chapter2/images` here
  - ❏ **Element 1**: Drag-and-drop `skill2.png` from `Chapter2/images` here
  - ❏ **Element 2**: Drag-and-drop `skill3.png` from `Chapter2/images` here
  - ❏ **Element 3**: Drag-and-drop `skill4.png` from `Chapter2/images` here

We finish the last step of the menu, click **play**, open the menu window, click on the **EQUIPMENT** tab, and roll over and click on the **UNEQUIP** label or the skill box. We will be able to change the character equipment, as we can see from the following screenshot:

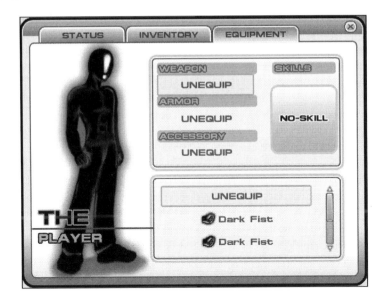

Objective Complete - Mini Debriefing

We just finished the last tab of our menu window. In this step, we created an **EQUIPMENT** button that will bring up the selection window, from which the player can choose the type of equipment or skill. It will update the current equipment status on the status tab too.

In the `ShowArmor()` function, we had the following code to display the six items in the scroll view, which is just an example to use, to set up the multiple selected items within the scroll view area when `a_armors.length = 1`:

```
var in_items : int = 6;
  var itemsContent : GUIContent[] = new GUIContent[in_items];
for (var i: int = 0; i < in_items; i++) {
    if (i == 0) {
        itemsContent[i] = GUIContent(s_unequip, "");
    } else {
        itemsContent[i] = GUIContent(a_armors[0].name, a_armors[0].
icon);
    }
  }
```

The preceding code will assign the `GUIContent` to the `itemContent[]` array and display the result, as shown in the following screenshot:

If we have set the amount of `a_armors.length` to be more than 1, we can modify the code to something like the highlighted code as follows:

```
var in_items : int = a_armors.length+1;
var itemsContent : GUIContent[] = new GUIContent[in_items];
for (var i: int = 0; i < in_items; i++) {
    if (i == 0) {
        itemsContent[i] = GUIContent(s_unequip, "");
    } else {
        itemsContent[i] = GUIContent(a_armors[i-1].name, a_armors[i-1].icon);
    }
}
```

This will set the value of the display item in the armor box related to the length of `a_armors`. We assign `in_items = a_armors.length+1` because we want to assign `unequip` as the first object. So, we add 1 to `in_items` for the `for` loop to `unequip` and the `a_armors[]`. We also subtract 1 from i in the `a_armors[i-1].name` and `a_armors[i-1].icon`. This will make sure that we aren't going out of the length, while we are looping through it.

Classified Intel

In this step, we have created a vertical and horizontal scroll view by using `GUI.BeginScrollView()` to begin the scroll view at how this function works. Basically, we can use this function, which is very convenient to use, when we want to create a scrollable area that contains any type of `GUI` object, because this function will automatically create a scrollable area from the two `Rect` parameters that we set up.

For example, in order to create a vertical scroll area at position x: 0, y: 0, width: 100 pixels, and height: 40 pixels, which contains three buttons with each button having 40 pixels height, we can have code like this:

```
var scrollPostion : Vector2 = Vector2.zero;
function OnGUI() {
    scrollPostion = GUI.BeginScrollView(Rect(0,0,100,40), scrollPostion,
Rect(0,0,80,120));
    GUI.Button(Rect(0,0,80,40),"Button 1");
    GUI.Button(Rect(0,40,80,40),"Button 2");
    GUI.Button(Rect(0,80,80,40),"Button 3");
    GUI.EndScrollView();
}
```

From the preceding code, we can see that the GUI.BeginScrollView() function returns Vector2, which is a vertical and horizontal of this scroll view. It also takes two Rect objects, the first Rect is the area that the player will see or we can call a mask area. The second Rect is the area of our content, which is based on the content that we included between GUI.BeginScrollView() and GUI.EndScrollView() functions, which are the three lines of GUI.Button. We can also see more details of this function from the following URL.

http://unity3d.com/support/documentation/ScriptReference/GUI.
BeginScrollView.html.

The following figure shows how the GUI.BeginScrollView() works in visual:

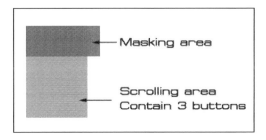

Game over-Wrapping it up

In this chapter, we just created a nice menu, which has the feature for an RPG game menu. This menu can move around the screen, and we can change the equipment of the character, too. We used a GUI class, GUI Skin, and OnGUI function to create this menu. In the GUI class, we used GUI.window to create our main menu, GUI.box to create the background box area, GUI.DrawTexture to show our character graphics, GUI.Button to create a button, GUI.ToolBar to create a tab button, GUI.SelectionGrid to create a list of clickable items, GUI.BeginScrollView, and GUI.EndScrollView to create a scrolling area, and last we also used GUI.Label to create a text label. We also used GUIContent to contain the information of our button or label. Let's take a look at what we learned from this chapter:

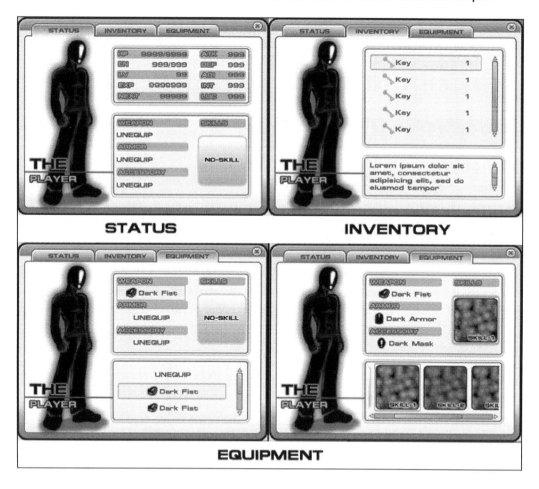

We can also go back to the **STATUS** tab to see the result when we equip all the equipments, as seen in the following screenshot:

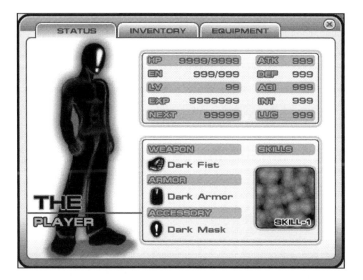

Are you ready to go gung ho?
A Hotshot challenge

Now, we have a nice menu, but we still have room to improve this menu to work better. So, why don't you try something to make this menu much more interesting?

- ▶ Add an option tab with which the player will be able to adjust music and sound volume
- ▶ Create more items or any equipment to make the menu much more interesting
- ▶ Add the ability to update the character graphics when we change the equipment or skill of the character
- ▶ Pause the game when we bring up our menu
- ▶ You can also create your own custom UI graphic and use it instead of the one in this chapter

Project 3

Model and Shade your Hero/Heroine

In the last two chapters, we have learned how to create a UI by using the `OnGUI` function, and a 2D platform game that used the 2D sprite texture to create our 2D character, and also got to know a bit of the 3D world in the first chapter. So, in this chapter, we will be using a full 3D character. We will take a close look at how to import the next generation 3D character modeling, and how to apply the material to the model. We will also get an understanding of the shader programming in Unity, and create a custom shader by writing and adapting shader programming. We can then use the Cg/HLSL shader language to write vertex and fragment programming.

> "Cg (C for Graphics) is a high-level shader language developed by NVIDIA in close collaboration with Microsoft for programming vertex and pixel shader. It is similar to HLSL (High Level Shader Language or High Level Shading Language), which is a proprietary shading language developed by Microsoft for use with the Microsoft Direct3D API." References taken from:
>
> http://en.wikipedia.org/wiki/Cg_%28programming_language%29.
>
> http://en.wikipedia.org/wiki/High_Level_Shader_Language.

The shader programming language is very complex and difficult, especially when we have to deal with lighting. It can be a nightmare, but Unity 3.x has come up with a new style of writing the shader program that is shorter and simpler. We still need to know the basics of Cg/HLSL programming, but we won't go too deep into how to create a shader from scratch or how Cg/HLSL works. We will use the new surface shader and create our own custom shader.

Mission briefing

We will create a basic custom shader and apply this shader to the character model that we already have. That's it. We might say "Hey! Why is it so short?". Well, it's short to say but it takes a long time to explain the whole concept of writing a shader.

1. First, we will open the character model in 3Ds Max (this is an optional step).

 We can get the trial version for free from this website:
`http://usa.autodesk.com/adsk/servlet/`
`download/item?siteID=123112&id=16324410.`

2. Then, we will set up its scale and rotation, and export it as an FBX file format to work with Unity. Then, we will import the character model to Unity and start applying a build material in Unity.

3. Next, we will start creating a shader, which includes diffuse texture, bump map (normal map) texture, ambient color, specular color and glossiness, rim light (or back light) color and power, and ramp texture, as shown in the following screenshot:

Diffuse   Bump   Ambient   Specular   Rim Light   Toon Ramp

4. Then, we will apply all of them together to create our custom toon shade style, as shown in the following screenshot:

Our Toon Shade

What does it do?

In this project, we will start with opening the character model in 3D Studio Max, set up the unit scale and rotation, export it as an FBX file, and then put it in our Unity project. This will give us a basic understanding of how to export the FBX file format from 3D Studio Max.

Next, we will create our first shading language by using the surface shaders, which are included in Unity 3.0.

"Surface shaders in Unity is the code generation approach that makes it much easier to write lit shaders than using low level vertex/pixel shader programs, which is much more complicated. However, there is no easy way to write the shader programming, we still have to write the code in Cg/HLSL."

Reference: `http://unity3d.com/support/documentation/Components/SL-SurfaceShaders.html`.

We will start creating by adding the diffuse texture and bump (normal) texture and using the built-in lighting models, which are `Lambert` (diffuse lighting) and `BlinnPhong` (specular lighting) that are located in the `Lighting.cginc` file inside the Unity application. This way, we can see the structure and algorithm of the shader programming, and it will be helpful when we adapt it to our custom shader.

`Lambert`, or diffuse reflection, will cause all closed polygons to reflect light equally in all directions when rendered. This algorithm is named after *Johann Heinrich Lambert* who invented it.

`Blinn-Phong`, or Blinn-Phong reflection, is the shading model that is the modification of the *Phong* reflection model developed by *Jim Blinn*.

`Phong` reflection model is the shading model that includes a model for the reflection of light from surfaces. It also has a compatible method of estimating pixel colors using interpolation surface normals across rasterized(or bitmap) polygons developed by *Bui Tuong Phong*.

Reference:

`http://en.wikipedia.org/wiki/Lambertian_reflectance.`

`http://en.wikipedia.org/wiki/Phong_shading.`

`http://en.wikipedia.org/wiki/Blinn%E2%80%93Phong_shading_model.`

Next, we will add the ambient color and specular color, and create the custom lighting model. In this step, we will learn how to create a custom lighting model in a surface shader.

Finally, we will add the rim light (back light) and the ramp texture to create the toon shader style, and see a result similar to the previous figure.

Why Is It Awesome?

When we complete this chapter, we will know how to set up the export unit scale and rotation from 3D Studio Max to Unity, which will be the same scale from MAYA or other 3D software. We will also be able to understand the basics of how to create our custom shader and the custom lighting model by using the surface shader in Unity, which we will be able to adapt to a more advanced shader in the future.

Your Hotshot Objectives

Since we are not shader programmers, and we just want to understand how the shader programming in Unity works, we will go through four steps from exporting our character from 3D Studio Max to creating a custom shader in Unity, as follows:

1. Exporting FBX from 3D Studio Max.

2. Shader programming—Diffuse and bump (normal) map.

3. Shader programming—Ambient and specular light.

4. Shader programming—Rim light and toon ramp.

Mission Checklist

First, we need a 3D character model with all the textures included. So, browse to `http://www.packtpub.com/support?nid=8267` and download the `Chapter3.zip` package; unzip it and we will see the `3DSMax` folder and `Chapter3.unitypackage` file. The `3DSMax` folder will contain the 3D Studio Max file that we will only use in the first step and the `Chapter3.unitypackage` file will contain all the assets (FBX file exported from 3D Studio Max, textures, and scene) that we will use for this chapter.

 If you already know how to export an FBX file from 3D Studio Max, use a Mac or other 3D software, or if you don't have 3D Studio Max installed, we can skip the *Exporting FBX from 3D Studio Max* step and go to the *Diffuse and bump (normal) map* step, right away. (The FBX file that was exported from 3D Studio Max is already included in the `Chapter3.unitypackage` file.)

Exporting from 3D Studio Max

As we know, Unity can read .FBX, .dae, .3DS, .dxf, and .obj files, which can be exported from other 3D software (3D Studio Max, MAYA, and so on.). However, if we are running our 3D software in the same OS as Unity, we can basically save our 3D files to the Unity project. Unity will convert a lot of 3D file formats such as (.ma or .mb) MAYA, (.c4d) Cinema4D, (.blend) Blender, (.lxo) Modo, (.jas) Cheetah3D, (.max) 3D Studio Max file to .FBX file format excepting (.lwo) Lightwave file format (need to export to .FBX manually). You can find the information on how to export a 3D file at the following URL:

http://unity3d.com/support/documentation/Manual/HOWTO-importObject.
html.

In most cases, this works perfectly if we are working on the same machine or the same operating system. But wait! Let's say we create a 3D model in 3D Studio Max on our PC and we want to use it on another machine, or even the same machine, but on a different operating system, such as a Mac. Here is what we are going to do in this section: we will set up the unit scale in 3D Studio Max and rotation. Then, we will export it as an FBX file format.

 Although this step will teach us how to export our 3D file to .FBX, it is recommended to save the 3D file directly to the Unity project, which will be the right flow of work when we have to go back and forth between Unity and our 3D software.

Prepare for Lift Off

In this step, we will use 3D Studio Max 2010 and the FBX version 2011.3.1 for exporting the FBX format. Let's browse to the following website:

http://usa.autodesk.com/adsk/servlet/pc/
item?siteID=123112&id=16126683.

Then, we click on FBX 2011.3.1 Plug-in for 3ds Max 2010 (exe - 16019Kb) to make sure that we have the same FBX version 2011.3.1 that is suitable for 3D Studio Max 2009 – 2011. However, if you have the older version of 3D Studio Max, the FBX exporter might not look the same as shown here. You can check the FBX exporter plugin from the following Autodesk website:

http://usa.autodesk.com/adsk/servlet/pc/
item?siteID=123112&id=10775920.

Then, we install the plugin file to our 3D Studio Max. Next, we will make sure that we have our 3D Studio Max file for this chapter. Let's check the 3DSMax folder to make sure that we have the Heroine.max file.

Engage Thrusters

Now, we are ready! Let's start by following these steps:

1. Open up 3D Studio Max and open the character file `Heroine.max`. We will see our character without any texture, as shown in the following screenshot:

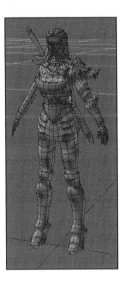

2. Then, go to (**Customize | Units Setup**). You will see the **Units Setup** window pop up. Under the **Display Unit Scale**, choose **Metric** and then **Meters**, and you will see something similar to the following screenshot:

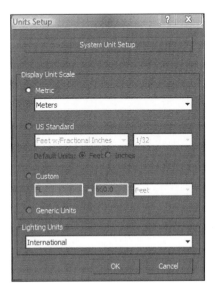

3. Click on **System Unit Setup** to bring up the **System Unit Setup** window. Under the **System Unit Scale**, we choose **Meters** for the **Unit**, and leave the rest as it is. And now we have done the unit scale setup; click **OK** on both the windows to close them.

4. Since 3D Studio Max uses the Z-axis to represent the vertical direction (which is very different from other 3D software such as Unity, which uses the Y-axis to do this), we need to rotate the pivot point of our model. So, we need to adjust our pivot before we export it to use in Unity; go to the **Hierarchy** toolbar by clicking on the **Hierarchy** icon on the right-hand side, as shown in the following screenshot:

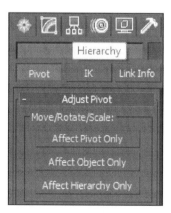

5. You will see the **Hierarchy** window. Click on the **Pivot** button and then on the **Affect Pivot Only** button, as shown in the preceding screenshot, to bring up the pivot of our character.

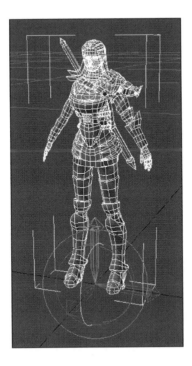

6. Now, we can see the pivot of our character which is made up of the colored coordinate axes at the bottom. Press the *E* key to bring up the rotation gizmo and rotate it by having the Z-axis point out from the character and Y-axis point up (rotate 90 degrees on the X-axis in other words), as you can see in the following screenshot:

7. Finally, we have to export our file to the FBX format. Let's go to **Export**, choose **Autodesk(*.FBX)**, name it `Heroine`, and put it in the `3DSMax` folder. Now we will see the FBX exporter pop up; go through each step as follows:

   ▸ **Include**

      ❑ **Animation**: Uncheck the **Animation** toggle box. (If we have the animation included in the character we will check this box.)

      ❑ **Cameras**: Uncheck the **Cameras** toggle box. (We don't need a camera.)

      ❑   **Lights**: Uncheck the **Lights** toggle box. (We don't need a light.)

   ▸ **Advanced Options**

      ❑   **Units**

          ❑ **Automatic**: Uncheck the toggle box.

          ❑ **Scene units converted to**: **Meters** (make sure that you have the **Scale Factor** as **1.0**).

   ▸ **Axis Conversion**

      ❑   **Up Axis**: **Y-up**

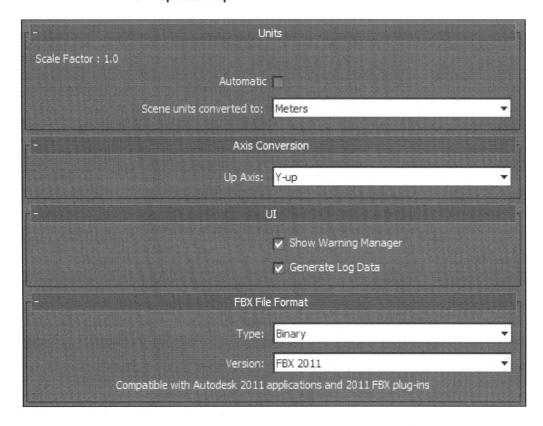

Then, click on the **OK** button and you have finished the first step.

Objective Complete - Mini Debriefing

Basically, what we have done here is set up the unit scale, transformed the rotation of our character, and exported it to a FBX format that will fit with Unity's world scale and space. We set up the unit scale in 3D Studio Max to have 1 unit equal to 1 meter and convert to meters. In some cases, you might want to set 1.0 unit equal to 1 inch or anything else; just make sure that when you export to the FBX format under **Units**, you choose the same unit that you set in 3D Studio Max and make sure that the **Scale Factor** equals 1.0. We also rotate the pivot of the character 90 degrees on the X-axis to create the Y-up axis that is suitable to use in Unity.

Classified Intel

You might have a question—why do we need to do something like this to export the FBX and import it to Unity? Well, this method of setup will make sure that we won't get any wrong scale and rotation when we put our model in Unity. Since the FBX exporter from 3D Studio Max will convert the unit scale and the rotation for our character, sometimes we might get the FBX file the transformation already attached to it. For example, if we set the unit scale in 3D Studio Max to have 1 unit equal to 1 inch and export FBX to meters, it will work fine in Unity; however, the start of the XYZ scale of our character might be **0.0254** (as one inch equals 0.0254 meters) instead of 1, as you can see in the following screenshot:

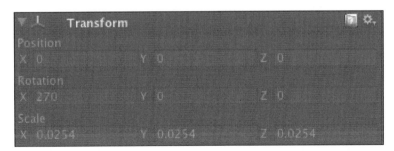

This is because the FBX exporter will convert the unit in 3D Studio Max file to the unit that we set up for export in the FBX exporter. So, we need to make sure that **Scale Factor** in the FBX exporter window is equal to 1.0. Also, if we didn't rotate the pivot of the character 90 degrees on the X-axis, export it to FBX, and put it in Unity, it would still work, but you would see the default rotation of the character in the X-axis as 270 degrees instead of all being 0.

Why do we need the default number to be 1 (for scale) or 0 (for rotation)? The answer is that when we write the script to control our model, we will have to deal with lots of numbers. If we don't have the default setting for the model as 1 for scale or 0 for rotation, it can be really difficult to write the script to control our model.

Shader programming—Diffuse and bump (normal) map

From the last step, we have a FBX model ready to use in Unity. In this step, we will import `Chapter3.unitypackage` (which is already included in the FBX model that we export from the 3D Studio Max), and begin creating a shader programming, which will include all properties that we can edit from the **Material Inspector**. We will start with assigning the diffuse and bump (normal) map. Then, we will use the Lambert lighting model, which comes with Unity, to see our result.

Prepare for Lift Off

Now, we can start the shader programming by implementing the following steps:

1. Let's create a new project named `Shader` similar to that in the last chapter and click on the **Create Project** button, as shown in the following screenshot:

2. Import the assets package by going to (**Assets | Import Package | Custom Package...**), choose the `Chapter3.unitypackage`, which we downloaded earlier, and then click on the **Import** button in the pop-up window, as shown in the following screenshot:

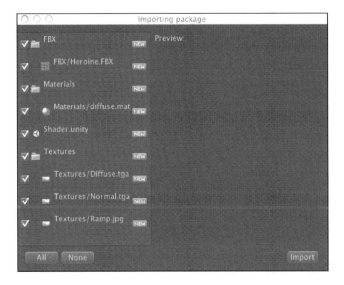

3. Wait until it's done, and you will see the **FBX**, **Materials**, and **Textures** folders, as we can see in the following screenshot:

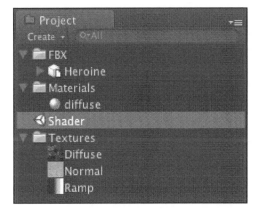

4. Next, double-click on the **Shader** scene, as shown in the preceding screenshot, to open the scene that we will work on in this chapter. When you double-click on the **Shader** scene, Unity will bring up the pop-up and ask whether we want to save the current scene or not, similar to what we saw in the last chapter. Just click on the **Don't save** button to open up the **Shader** scene.

5. Then, go to the `FBX` folder, and click on `Heroine.FBX` in this folder to bring up its **Inspector** view. In the **Inspector** view, make sure that the **(FBXImporter) | Scale Factor** properties equals **1**, and then click on the **Apply** button, as shown in the following screenshot:

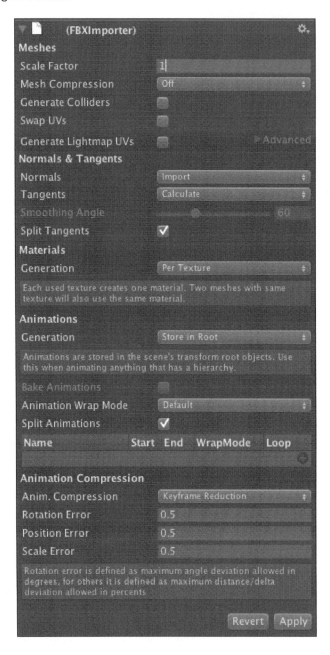

6. Then, go to the `Textures` folder, and click on `Normal.tga` to bring up its **Inspector** view. In the **Inspector** view, change the **(Texture Importer)** | **Texture Type** to **Normal Map**, then uncheck **Generate from greyscale**, and click on the **Apply** button, as shown in the following screenshot:

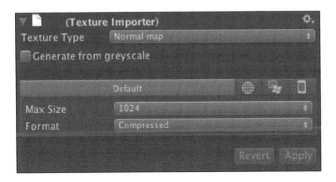

 Why do we set it up this way? First, we want our model scale factor default equal to 1. Then, we set the **Texture Type** for the `Normal.tga` to **Normal map** type, which we will use for the bump map.

Engage Thrusters

Here, we will put the 3D model into our scene and start writing our custom shader programming:

1. First, we drag the `Heroine.FBX` model in the `FBX` folder from the **Project** view to the **Hierarchy** view.

2. Next, we will click on the `Heroine.FBX` model in the **Hierarchy** view to bring up its **Inspector** view. Then, we will go to the **Inspector** view and set rotation **Y** to **180**, as shown in the following screenshot:

If we go to the material component, we will see **Diffuse** applied to the **Shader** in this material, which has two properties: **Main Color** and **Base (RGB)**. **Main Color** takes the color that we can edit and it will apply the color to our model. **Base (RGB)** takes the texture, which is used for our model. Both properties can be edited and adjusted in the Unity editor to get the best look for our model, as shown in the following screenshot:

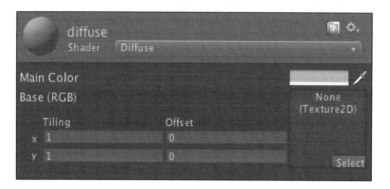

3. Now, we will start coding by going to **Assets | Create | Shader**, and naming it `MyShader`. Then, we right-click on it and choose **Sync MonoDevelop Project** to open our **MonoDevelop**.

 Warning: The **Sync MonoDevelop Project** step might not work if we didn't set the MonoDevelop as our default editor. (This was discussed in the first chapter.)

4. In MonoDevelop, you will see the default setup of the shader script, as shown in the following screenshot:

```
MyShader.shader ×
1   Shader "New Shader" {
2       Properties {
3           _MainTex ("Base (RGB)", 2D) = "white" {}
4       }
5       SubShader {
6           Tags { "RenderType"="Opaque" }
7           LOD 200
8
9           CGPROGRAM
10          #pragma surface surf Lambert
11
12          sampler2D _MainTex;
13
14          struct Input {
15              float2 uv_MainTex;
16          };
17
18          void surf (Input IN, inout SurfaceOutput o) {
19              half4 c = tex2D (_MainTex, IN.uv_MainTex);
20              o.Albedo = c.rgb;
21              o.Alpha = c.a;
22          }
23          ENDCG
24      }
25      FallBack "Diffuse"
26  }
27
```

 If you create the shader inside the MonoDevelop, the default setup of the shader script will be different from the preceding screenshot and similar to the following screenshot.

```
MonoDevelop.shader ×
1   Shader "NewShader" {
2       Properties {
3           _Color ("Main Color", Color) = (1,1,1,1)
4           _MainTex ("Base (RGB)", 2D) = "white" {}
5           _BumpMap ("Bump (RGB) Illumin (A)", 2D) = "bump" {}
6       }
7       SubShader {
8           UsePass "Self-Illumin/VertexLit/BASE"
9           UsePass "Bumped Diffuse/PPL"
10      }
11      FallBack "Diffuse"
12  }
13
```
Default Shader File Create in MonoDevelop

5. Next, go to the first line in `MyShader.shader` and modify the existing code as follows:

```
Shader "My Shader/Toon Rim Light" {
```

In this line, we change the position and name our shader, which will appear in the drop down **Shader** when we select the **Shader** properties in the object's **Inspector** view.

6. Then, go back to Unity and click on the `Heroine.FBX` model in the **Hierarchy** view to bring up its **Inspector**.

7. In the **Shader** properties in the material component, we will click on the small arrow on the right side to bring up the drop-down, then select the **My Shader | Toon Rim Right**, as shown in the following screenshot:

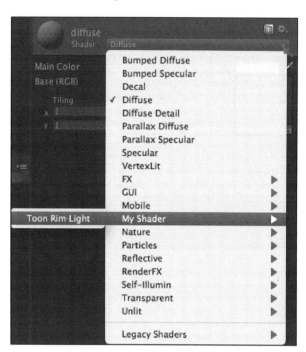

8. Then, we go back to MonoDevelop again, and go to the next line of the `MyShader.shader` and start modifying the `Properties` section, as follows:

```
Properties {
  _MainTex ("Texture", 2D) = "white" {}
_BumpMap ("Bumpmap", 2D) = "bump" {}
}
```

Then, we go to `SubShader` section to modify and add the following code:

```
SubShader {
    Tags { "RenderType"="Opaque" }
LOD 300

    CGPROGRAM
    #pragma surface surf Lambert
```

```
    sampler2D _MainTex;
sampler2D _BumpMap;

    struct Input {
       float2 uv_MainTex;
    float2 uv_BumpMap;
    };

    void surf (Input IN, inout SurfaceOutput o) {
       half4 c = tex2D (_MainTex, IN.uv_MainTex);
       o.Albedo = c.rgb;
       o.Alpha = c.a;
    o.Normal = UnpackNormal (tex2D (_BumpMap, IN.uv_BumpMap));
    }

    ENDCG
}
```

9. Finally, we go back to Unity and apply the texture to our model.

Let's click on the `Heroine.FBX` model in the **Hierarchy** view to bring up its **Inspector** view. In the **Inspector** view, we will go to the material component and set the following:

*   **Texture**: Drag-and-drop the `Diffuse.tga` in the `Textures` folder from the **Project** view to this thumbnail
*   **Bumpmap**: Drag-and-drop the `Normal.tga` in the `Textures` folder from the **Project** view to this thumbnail

You will see the **Inspector** view, as shown in the following screenshot:

Now, click **Play** and behold the result:

Objective Complete - Mini Debriefing

Let's take a look at what we did here.

First, we added the new property (_BumpMap), which will be used to get the **surface normals** from our character.

Properties can be created by using the following syntax:

```
name ("display name", property type) = default value
```

▸ name is the name of property inside the shader script

▸ display name is the name that will be shown in the material inspector

▸ property type is the type of the property that we can use in our shader programming, which can be Range, Color, 2D, Rect, Cube, Float, or Vector

▸ default value is the default value of our property

Every time you add new properties in the `Properties` section, you will need to create the same parameter inside the `CGPROGRAM` in the `SubShader` section, as shown in the following code:

```
Properties {  _BumpMap ("Bumpmap", 2D) = "bump" {}  }
SubShader {

        .........
        CGPROGRAM
        #pragma surface surf Lambert
        sampler2D _BumpMap;

        ....... . .
        ENDCG

}
```

We can see more details at the following website and see what each parameter does:

```
http://unity3d.com/support/documentation/Components/
SL-Properties.html
```

Then, we set `LOD` (Level of Detail) for our shader to 300. The Level of Detail is the setup that will limit our shader to use the maximum of detail to the number that we set. We used 300 because we have included the bump map to our shader, which is the same number of the Unity built-in setup for the diffuse bump. You can take a look at the following link to get more information on the Shader Level of Detail:

```
http://unity3d.com/support/documentation/Components/SL-ShaderLOD.html
```

We added the `sampler2D _BumpMap;` line, which is the same property that gets passed from the `Properties` section (`_BumpMap ("Bumpmap", 2D) = "bump" {}`).

`sampler2` is basically the type of parameter that is used in the Cg/HLSL shader programming language, which is a two-dimensional texture. We can get more information about the Cg parameter from the following website:

```
http://http.developer.nvidia.com/CgTutorial/cg_
tutorial_chapter03.html
```

Next, we added `float2 uv_BumpMap` in `struct Input {}`, which will be used to calculate the color information from our `_BumpMap`. The `uv_BumpMap` parameter is the texture coordinate, which is the `vector2`.

In the `surf()` function, we have the following:

```
half4 c = tex2D (_MainTex, IN.uv_MainTex);
   o.Albedo = c.rgb;
   o.Alpha = c.a;
   o.Normal = UnpackNormal (tex2D (_BumpMap, IN.uv_BumpMap));
```

> `surf(Input IN, inout SurfaceOutput o)` function is basically the function that will get the input information from `struct Input {}`. Then, we will assign the new parameter to `SurfaceOutput o`. This parameter will get passed and used next in the vertex and pixel processor.
>
> We can get more details on the `Input struct` and the default parameter of `SurfaceOutput struct` here:
>
> `http://unity3d.com/support/documentation/Components/`
> `SL-SurfaceShaders.html`.

The `tex2D` function will return the color value (Red, Green, Blue, Alpha) or (R,G,B,A) from the sample state (`_MainTex`) and the texture coordinate (`IN.uv_MainTex`), which we will then assign to the `o.Albedo` and `o.Alpha`. The `o.Albedo` parameter will store the color information (RGB) and the `o.Alpha` parameter will store the alpha information.

> *"Albedo or reflection coefficient, is the diffuse reflectivity or reflecting power of a surface. It is defined as the ratio of reflected radiation from the surface to incident radiation upon it."*
>
> Reference from `http://en.wikipedia.org/wiki/Albedo`

The next line is to get the `normal` information, which is the vector that contains the position (x, y, and z). Then, we used the `tex2D` function to get the color value (R,G,B,A) from the sample state (`_BumpMap`) and the texture coordinate (`IN.uv_BumpMap`). Then, we used the `UnpackNormal` function to get the `Normal` as the result of the `tex2D` function.

Classified Intel

Talking about shader programming, there are a lot of things to get to know and understand, for example, how the shader works. We will take a look at the basic structure of the shader programming in Unity.

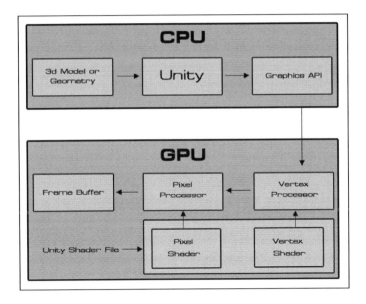

 The preceding diagram is from **Amir Ebrahimi** and **Aras Pranckevčius**, who presented the Shader Programming course at Unite 2008, and represents how the shader works in Unity. We can get more information from the following website. (Warning: this presentation might be difficult to understand, since it showed how to create the shader without using any *surface shader* and it used the old version of Unity.)

```
http://unity3d.com/support/resources/unite-
presentations/shader-programming-course
```

Let's get back to the diagram—you will see that the shader file that we are writing is working on the vertex and pixel (fragment) level. Then, it will show the result to the frame buffer, but what are vertex and pixel shaders? These are the different types of processors in the GPU. First, the vertex processor gets the vertex data, which is the position and color of each vertex in the 3D model; then, draw a triangle from these vertices and pass the data to the pixel processor. The pixel processor will get that value and translate it to the per pixel screen. It is similar to taking a vector art from Illustrator or Flash and translating it to a pixel art in Photoshop. Then, it interpolates color data to each pixel, as shown in the following diagram:

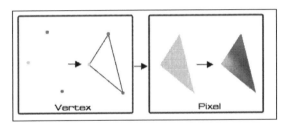

From the explanation, we know that we need to deal with the vertex and pixel shader programming when we want to write a shader program. For example, if we want to create a shader, we will need to get the vertex data from our geometry, calculate the data, and pass it out to the pixel level. At the pixel level, we will calculate the color of the geometry, light, and shadow, and then we will get the result.

However, this can be very complex when we have to handle lighting manually. That's why we are using the surface shaders, so we don't have to deal with various types of lightning, rendering, and so on.

If you check out the ShaderLab link in Unity, you will see that there are a lot of things to do, but don't be afraid because we don't need to understand everything that's there to create our custom shader. In the next step, we will create the custom lighting models in surface shaders.

Shader programming–Ambient and specular light

In this step, we will add the ambient and specular light to our script as well as create our custom lighting models.

The custom lighting model is basically the function that will be used to calculate our surface shader, which is the output of (surf () function) interaction with the lights.

surf () function is the function that will take any UVs or data we need as input, and fill in the output structure SurfaceOutput (the predefined structure, such as Albedo, Normal, Emission, Specular, Gloss, and Alpha).

Engage Thrusters

1. Go to MonoDevelop, open MyShader.shader file, and go to the Properties section and add the highlighted script as follows:

```
Properties {
    _MainTex ("Texture", 2D) = "white" {}
    _BumpMap ("Bumpmap", 2D) = "bump" {}
  _AmbientColor ("Ambient Color", Color) = (0.1, 0.1, 0.1, 1.0)
  _SpecularColor ("Specular Color", Color) = (0.12, 0.31, 0.47, 1.0)
  _Glossiness ("Gloss", Range(1.0,512.0)) = 80.0
  }
```

2. Next, go to the `SubShader` section, modify, and add the following highlighted code:

```
SubShader {
    Tags { "RenderType"="Opaque" }
    LOD 400

    CGPROGRAM
    // Custom lighting function that uses a texture ramp based on
angle between light direction and normal

    #pragma surface surf RampSpecular

        sampler2D _MainTex;
        sampler2D _BumpMap;

    fixed4 _AmbientColor;
    fixed4 _SpecularColor;
    half _Glossiness;

        struct Input {
            float2 uv_MainTex;
            float2 uv_BumpMap;
        };
```

3. We set `LOD` to `400`, and set `#pragma surface surf` to `RampSpecular` instead of `Lambert`, and get the other three properties for **Ambient** and **Specular** light. Now, we will need the custom lighting models function. Let's add the following highlighted code under the `surf()` function:

```
    void surf (Input IN, inout SurfaceOutput o) {
    fixed4 c = tex2D (_MainTex, IN.uv_MainTex);
        o.Albedo = c.rgb;
        o.Alpha = c.a;
        o.Normal = UnpackNormal (tex2D (_BumpMap, IN.uv_BumpMap));
    }

    inline fixed4 LightingRampSpecular (SurfaceOutput s, fixed3
lightDir, fixed3 viewDir, fixed atten) {
        //Ambient Light
        fixed3 ambient = s.Albedo * _AmbientColor.rgb;

        //Diffuse
        fixed NdotL = saturate(dot (s.Normal, lightDir)); //Get the
direction of the light source related to the normal of character
        fixed3 diffuse = s.Albedo * _LightColor0.rgb * NdotL;
```

```
        //Specular - Gloss
    fixed3 h = normalize (lightDir + viewDir); // Get the Normalize
of the lighting direction and view direction
            float nh = saturate(dot (s.Normal, h)); //Make sure that
the return number isn't lower than 0 or greater than 1
            float specPower = pow (nh, _Glossiness);

            fixed3 specular = _LightColor0.rgb * specPower * _
SpecularColor.rgb;

        //Result
        fixed4 c;
        c.rgb = (ambient + diffuse + specular) * (atten * 2);
        c.a = s.Alpha + (_LightColor0.a * _SpecularColor.a * specPower
* atten);

        return c;
    }


    ENDCG
    }
```

We have finished this step. We can now go back to Unity, and click **Play** to see our result with the specular reflection, as shown in the following screenshot:

Objective Complete - Mini Debriefing

In this step, we first added the new properties `_AmbientColor`, e, and `_Glossiness`, which will be used to calculate in our custom lighting models function to get the specular reflection.

Next, we increased the `LOD` to `400` because we wanted to increase the **Level of Detail** for our custom lighting model that will calculate the specular lighting. Then we changed `#pragma surface surf` from `Lambert` to `RampSpecular`, which means that we changed our lighting calculated from the `Lambert` built-in to `RampSpecular` (our custom lighting function, `LightingRampSpecular`).

In the `surf()` function, we have changed the first line from `half4 c = tex2D (_MainTex, IN.uv_MainTex);` to `fixed4 c = tex2D (_MainTex, IN.uv_MainTex);` to increase the performance of our shader. Also, since the return value from the `tex2D()` function is the color value (R,G,B,A), which has a range from 0 to 1, it will be expensive to use `half` or `float`.

What are `half` and `fixed` parameters for? When we are writing a shader in **Cg/HLSL**, there are three types of the parameter that we can use, which are `fixed`, `half`, and `float`. These parameters determine the precision of computations. The parameter `fixed` is low precision (11 bits, the range of -2.0 to +2.0 and 1/256th precision), `half` is medium precision (16 bits, the range of -60000 to +60000 and 3.3 decimal digits of precision), and `float` is high precision (32 bits, similar to the float in regular programming language).

Reference from:

`http://unity3d.com/support/documentation/Components/`
`SL-ShaderPerformance.html`

However, it follows a trend wherein the more precision we have, the more calculation we need. If we use all `float` for our shader, it will cause the game to slow down. So, if we want to improve the performance of our game, we should use the lowest precision as possible.

Then, we created our custom lighting function, which is `inline half4 LightingRampSpecular (SurfaceOutput s, half3 lightDir, half3 viewDir, half atten)`. This function passes four parameters, `SurfaceOutput`, `light Direction`, `view direction`, and `light attenuation` that we will use to calculate the output for our shader.

Why is the name of this function not RampSpecular? First, we call this function by using #pragma surface surf RampSpecular, but to have this function working properly, we need to add Lighting in front of the name of our custom lighting function, so that Unity will know that this function is a custom lighting function. This is the way that the surface shaders are set up in Unity. You can find out more details from the following website:

http://unity3d.com/support/documentation/Components/
SL-SurfaceShaderLighting.html

In this function, we first get the ambient color value by getting s.Albedo, which is the parameter from the surf() function o.Albedo, and then multiply the s.Albedo by _AmbientColor.rgb, where _AmbientColor is the color information from the **Properties** section at the beginning of our code.

The fixed, half, and float parameters in **Cg/HLSL** can contain one, two, three, or four values of floating number such as 1.0, (1.0, 1.0), (1.0, 1.0, 1.0), or (1.0, 1.0, 1.0, 1.0) by calling it fixed, fixed2, fixed3, fixed4, half, half2, half3, half4, float, float2, float3, float4. We can also access the value in these parameters by using (x, y, z, w) or (r, g, b, a). For example, if you have fixed4 color = (1.0, 0.5, 0.3, 0.8); and you want to create another parameter, which will contain only three values (1.0, 0.5, 0.3) from the fixed4 color, you can do it like this: fixed3 newColor = color.rgb;. However, if we want the newColor value equal to (0.5, 1.0, 0.3), you can do it like this: fixed3 newColor = color.grb;.

Then, we calculate the diffuse color by getting the dot product of the surface normal of the object (s.Normal) that we pass out from the surf() function (o.Normal), and the light direction (fixed NdotL = dot (s.Normal, lightDir);). Then, we use that value to multiply with the object diffuse texture (s.Albedo) and light color (_LightColor0.rgb), which is similar to the Lambert model.

Next, we calculate the specular color by first getting the normalize vector of light direction and view direction (fixed3 h = normalize (lightDir + viewDir);). In float nh = saturate(dot (s.Normal, h));, we calculate the dot product of the surface normal and normalize vector, and make sure that the return number isn't greater than 1 or lower than 0 by using saturate(). Then, we use nh to calculate the specular power by powering it with the _Glossiness properties (float specPower = pow (nh, _Glossiness);), and we get the specular color from multiplying the light color, specular power, and the specular color properties (_LightColor0.rgb * specPower * _SpecularColor.rgb;), which is similar to the Blinn-Phong model.

In the last step, we add ambient, diffuse, and specular together, and multiply the lighting attenuation value doubled, to get the smooth specular effect (`c.rgb = (ambient + diffuse + specular) * (atten * 2);`).

A major part of the code is in the Cg/HLSL language, so you might not be familiar with it. However, you can still get an idea of how it works by trying to see more examples and taking a look at the Cg/HLSL language:

```
http://http.developer.nvidia.com/CgTutorial/cg_
tutorial_appendix_e.html
```

We can also see an example of the custom lighting model from the following Unity website:

```
http://unity3d.com/support/documentation/Components/
SL-SurfaceShaderExamples.html
```

Classified Intel

How exactly do the surface shaders work?

First, we get the parameters from the `Input struct`, and these parameters will get passed to the `SurfaceOutput struct` inside the `surf` function. Then, the return of the `SurfaceOutput struct` will go to the lighting model function to calculate both the vertex and pixel (fragment) shader. Lastly, the result from the lighting model function will be passed to the frame buffer, as shown in the following diagram:

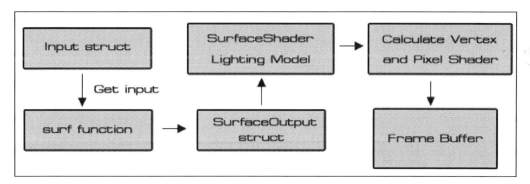

Shader programming—Rim light and toon ramp

In this last step, we will add the last three properties, `_RimColor`, `_RimPower`, and `_Ramp` to get the toon shader result. The `_RimColor` and `_RimPower` properties basically control the back lighting effect of our character. The `_Ramp` properties will be the ramp textures that are used to calculate the lighting effect based on the angle between **light direction** and **surface normal** of the object.

Engage Thrusters

This is the last section, after which you will be able to see the result of your custom shader.

1. Go to MonoDevelop, open the `MyShader.shader` file, and go to the `Properties` section and add the highlighted script as follows:

```
Properties {
    _MainTex ("Texture", 2D) = "white" {}
    _BumpMap ("Bumpmap", 2D) = "bump" {}
    _AmbientColor ("Ambient Color", Color) = (0.1, 0.1, 0.1, 1.0)
    _SpecularColor ("Specular Color", Color) = (0.12, 0.31, 0.47,
1.0)
    _Glossiness ("Gloss", Range(1.0,512.0)) = 80.0
 _RimColor ("Rim Color", Color) = (0.12, 0.31, 0.47, 1.0)
   _RimPower ("Rim Power", Range(0.5,8.0)) = 3.0
   _Ramp ("Shading Ramp", 2D) = "gray" {}
    }
```

2. Go to the `SubShader` section, modify, and add the highlighted code as follows:

```
SubShader {
    Tags { "RenderType"="Opaque" }
    LOD 400

    CGPROGRAM
        // Custom lighting function that uses a texture ramp based on
    angle between light direction and normal
        // We use exclude_path:prepass because this lighting model won't
    work on the deferred lighting
    // Since we don't have the angle between the light direction and
    normal to calculate in the prepass

    #pragma surface surf RampSpecular exclude_path:prepass

        sampler2D _MainTex;
```

```
    sampler2D _BumpMap;
  sampler2D _Ramp;

    fixed4 _AmbientColor;
    fixed4 _SpecularColor;
    half _Glossiness;

  fixed4 _RimColor;
  half _RimPower;

    struct Input {
      float2 uv_MainTex;
      float2 uv_BumpMap;
    half3 viewDir;
    };
```

3. Add the following highlighted code inside the `surf()` function as follows:

```
void surf (Input IN, inout SurfaceOutput o) {
    fixed4 c = tex2D (_MainTex, IN.uv_MainTex);
    o.Albedo = c.rgb;
    o.Alpha = c.a;
    o.Normal = UnpackNormal (tex2D (_BumpMap, IN.uv_BumpMap));

    fixed rim = 1.0 - saturate(dot (normalize(IN.viewDir),
o.Normal));
    o.Emission = (_RimColor.rgb * pow (rim, _RimPower));
    }
```

4. Finally, go to the custom lighting models function. Let's modify and add this highlighted code as follows:

```
inline fixed4 LightingRampSpecular (SurfaceOutput s, fixed3
lightDir, fixed3 viewDir, fixed atten) {
    //Ambient Light
    fixed 3 ambient = s.Albedo * _AmbientColor.rgb;

  //Ramp - Diffuse color
    fixed NdotL = saturate(dot (s.Normal, lightDir));
  fixed diff = NdotL * 0.5 + 0.5;
  fixed3 ramp = tex2D (_Ramp, float2(diff, diff)).rgb;
  fixed3 diffuse = s.Albedo * _LightColor0.rgb * ramp;

    //Specular - Gloss
    fixed3 h = normalize (lightDir + viewDir); // Get the
Normalize of the lighting direction and view direction
```

```
        float nh = saturate(dot (s.Normal, h)); //Make sure that
the return number isn't lower than 0 and greater than 1
        float specPower = pow (nh, _Glossiness);

        fixed3 specular = _LightColor0.rgb * specPower * _
SpecularColor.rgb;

        //Result
        fixed4 c;
        c.rgb = (ambient + diffuse + specular) * (atten * 2);
        c.a = s.Alpha + (_LightColor0.a * _SpecularColor.a *
specPower   * atten);

        return c;
    }
```

Finally, we go back to Unity and apply the ramp texture to our model. Let's click on the Heroine.FBX model in the **Hierarchy** view to bring up its **Inspector** view. In the **Inspector** view, we will go to the material component in the new property **Shading Ramp** and set the following:

- ▶ **Shading Ramp**: Drag-and-drop the Ramp.jpg in the Textures folder from the **Project** view to this thumbnail

After finishing, we will see the **Inspector** view, as shown in the following screenshot:

Now, we can click **Play** to see the result, as shown in the following screenshot:

We can also move or rotate our camera to see our character with the shader in a different angle.

Next, we will go to our custom lighting function, `LightingRampSpecular()`. In this function, we will add the following highlighted code:

Next, we calculate the diffuse color by using the `Half Lambert` or `Warp Lambert` method to get the lighting warp around our model, and then we get the ramp texture from the property, and multiply it with the light color and our main color texture.

Objective Complete - Mini Debriefing

In this section, first we added three properties (`_RimColor, _RimPower, _Ramp`) in the **Properties** section, which will be used to calculate the rim light as well as the toon ramp shader style.

Then, we put `exclude_path:prepass` after `#pragma surface surf RampSpecular`. This means that we set our shader to compile without the deferred rendering. Why would we want to do this? Because our toon ramp shader needs the angle data between the **light direction** and **surface normals** to calculate the lighting that can't be calculated in the deferred rendering, so we exclude it.

In Unity, we can choose three types of **Rendering Paths**: **Vertex Lit**, **Forward**, and **Deferred Lighting**. **Vertex Lit** is basically the lowest lighting quality and doesn't support any real-time shadows. **Forward** is shader-based, which is the default setting in Unity and only supports real-time shadow from one directional light. **Deferred Lighting** is the rendering path with the most lighting and shadow quality, which is only for the Unity Pro with no support on mobile devices. We can get more information about the **Rendering Path** from the following website:

```
http://unity3d.com/support/documentation/Manual/
RenderingPaths.html
```

Next, we add `half3 viewDir;` in `struct Input {}`, which will allow us to get the user view direction vector. This parameter will be used to calculate the specular reflection on our model.

Inside the `surf()` function, we calculated the rim power or the brightness of our backlight, which is `fixed rim = 1.0 - saturate(dot (normalize(IN.viewDir), o.Normal));` by using the saturation of the dot product of the view direction normalize and surface normals. In the next line (`o.Emission = (_RimColor.rgb * pow (rim, _RimPower));`), we multiply the rim light color with the power of the rim power that we got. Then, we assigned the result to `o.Emission` to show the rim light effect on our object.

Then, in the `LightingRampSpecular()` function, we changed the calculation of the lighting by using the Half-Lambert model, which will make our object brighter with the light that will warp around the object by dividing it by half and plus half (`fixed diff = NdotL * 0.5 + 0.5;`).

Half-Lambert lighting is a technique first developed in the original Half-Life. It is designed to prevent the rear of an object losing its shape and looking too flat. Half Lambert is a completely non-physical technique and gives a purely perceived visual enhancement and is an example of a forgiving lighting model.

Reference from `http://developer.valvesoftware.com/wiki/ Half_Lambert`.

Next, we use `diff` to calculate the ramp texture, `_Ramp`, to get the color result by using the `tex2D()` function (`fixed3 ramp = tex2D (_Ramp, float2(diff, diff)).rgb;`). Then we multiply this value with the diffuse color and light color (`fixed3 rampDiffuse = s.Albedo * _LightColor0.rgb * ramp;`), and we will get a result which is different from the previous section, as shown in the following screenshot:

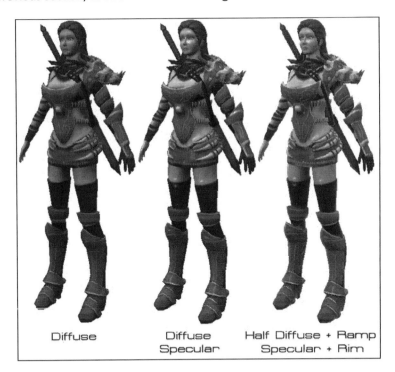

Game over-Wrapping it up

In this chapter, we have learned how to export the model from 3D Studio Max, and how to set the proper scale and rotation to use in Unity. We also learned the basic concept of shader programming and created by using surface shader, and created the custom lighting model for the shader. Some of you might find shader programming to be very complex with a lot of things to learn; well, yes, that's true. There is no easy way to write code using shader programming. However, if you want to know more about shader programming, you should definitely learn Cg/HLSL language, which will help you to understand more about the structure and the syntax of the shader language. Now, let's see our result in the following screenshot:

 We can also get more detail on shader programming in Unity from the following websites:

(Unity Shader Reference):

```
http://unity3d.com/support/documentation/Components/
SL-Reference.html
```

(Unity ShaderLab forum):

```
http://forum.unity3d.com/forums/16-ShaderLab
```

Are you ready to go gung ho? A Hotshot challenge

Now, we learned the basic concepts of how to write a custom shader by using surface shader in Unity 3. Why don't we try out something to get more familiar with it by playing with the properties to get a different type of rendering style?

- ▶ Adjust a value in the material editor in our shader to create a different lighting color and effect
- ▶ Create the new ramp texture and apply it to the shader to see the new result of just changing the ramp texture
- ▶ Try taking out some properties and using new properties such as cube and so on
- ▶ Try changing some parameters in the custom lighting function by adding a different method to calculate the lighting direction
- ▶ Adjust some equations by changing plus to multiple or have more properties to get the different types of rendering techniques
- ▶ You can also create your own custom lighting models

Project 4

Add Character Control and Animation to our Hero/Heroine

Here we are in part two of Hero/Heroine. In this chapter, we will make our character come to life by using the animation script to control our character to walk, jump, and run with smooth transition from one animation to another.

We will learn how to set up the animation clip for our imported 3D model, understanding the concept of a built-in third-person controller, and creating a custom third-person controller and camera, which is similar to the built-in third-person controller script. This way we will obtain a good understanding of the built-in script and can adapt it to use for the specific extra controller or animation later on.

Mission briefing

We will create a basic custom third-person controller and third-person camera script to control our character's animation. This will allow us to control our character similar to the *Hack and Slash* style game, such as the Devil May Cry series, Gods of Wars, Tomb Raider, and so on.

What does it do?

In this chapter, we will start with setting up the animation clip from the imported FBX model with animation (walk, run, jump, and fall), which is created from other 3D software.

Next, we will add the Physics **Character Controller** component instead of the Physics **Rigidbody**. This **Character Controller** will give us the ability to access collision detection as the well as Move() function, which is very easy to use.

> We will use the Move() function to move our character while playing the animation. This function can be accessed from the CharacterController class when we add the **Character Controller** component to our game object. The Move() function will return the CollisionFlags, which will tell us which part of our character hits other collider objects.

Then, we will apply the built-in third-person character controller script to our character, and take a look at the script to get the basic idea for creating the custom character control script and camera.

After that we will get rid of the built-in script and start creating the custom script to control our character's walk, run, and jump by using the Move() function in the Character Controller class. In this step, we will also create the transition between each animation clip by using the Animation class in Unity, which allows us to adjust the speed of animation clip, type of playing, and fading time. Next, we will create the camera script to follow our character. We will then attach the script to our character and make it move on the level.

Why Is It Awesome?

After we complete this chapter, we will know how to set up the animation clip from FBX file, which we already exported from another 3D software. We will also be able to create a custom controller script to control our character in the 3D world and blend the animation from idle to walk, walk to run and jump, and so on. We will also learn how to create the third-person camera to follow our character.

This chapter will give you an understanding of how to create the third-person character control script and you will be able to use it for other controllers.

Your Hotshot Objectives

Even though Unity is already provided with built-in third-person controller script, we will create our third-person controller to get a good understanding of how to use the built-in character controller. Here is what we will learn:

- ▶ Setting up character animation and level
- ▶ Creating character controller and built-in script
- ▶ Creating a custom character control script

- ▶ Creating cross fade animation
- ▶ Creating a third-person camera to follow our character

Mission Checklist

As we have already learned how to export the FBX file format from 3D Studio Max in the previous chapter, we will download the new chapter package, which will include the new FBX character with all the animation cycles, textures, and necessary assets for this chapter. Download the `Chapter4` package from this book's website, unzip it, and then you will see · `Chapter4.unitypackage`, which will contain all the assets for this chapter.

> There is also a built-in animation system in Unity (that we will not cover in this chapter), which we can use to animate a simple object such as a moving platform or the animation of an opening door. You can get more details from the following Unity website:
>
> `http://unity3d.com/support/documentation/Manual/Animation.html`.

Setting up character animation and level

From the last chapter, we have imported the 3D character model from 3D Studio Max and created the shader for it, but the model doesn't have any animation set up in it, yet. So, in this chapter we will learn more about how to set up the animation clip from the FBX model that is already exported from 3D software (in this book, we have used 3D Studio Max), and use it in Unity.

In Unity, we can import the FBX format file with the rigging animation and set it up for multiple clips to use, as we want. The concept is that we have one file that includes all small clips from walking, running, or jumping. Then, we divide it to each type of animation by telling Unity the range of frames for this animation. For example, if we create a walking cycle animation from frames 1 to 30, we can just tell Unity that we want to use the range of frames from 1 to 30 for the walking animation. This concept is very flexible to adjust and change the animation clip on the fly.

Prepare for Lift Off

In this section, we will begin with setting up the new FBX file, which is the same model and shader from the last chapter, but this FBX file will include all the necessary animations that we need for this section:

1. Create a new project with the name `CharacterAnimation`, and this time we will include the built-in `Character Controller` package by checking on the **Character Controller.unityPackage** in the **Project Wizard**, as shown in the following screenshot:

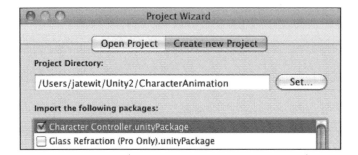

2. Next, import the assets package by going to **Assets | Import Package | Custom Package....** Choose `Chapter4.unityPackage`, which we just downloaded, and then click on the **Import** button in the pop-up window, as shown in the following screenshot:

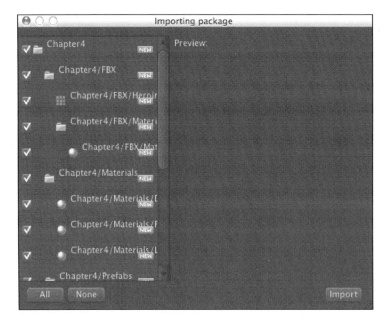

3. Wait until it's done, and you will see the **Chapter4** and **Standard Assets** folders in the **Window** view, as shown in the following screenshot:

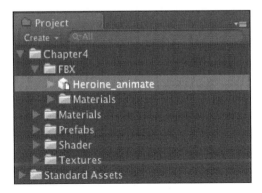

Engage Thrusters

Now we are ready to start this section:

1. Let's go to the FBX folder; click on Heroine_animate to bring up the **Inspector** view. Then, scroll down a bit until you see the **Animations** section in the **FBXImporter**. In the **Animations** section, you will see a small window below the word **Split Animations**:

Here, we will see five parameters, which are **Name**, **Start**, **End**, **WrapMode**, and **Loop**. The **Name** parameter is the name of the animation that we want to assign. The **Start** parameter is the start frame of the clip. The **End** parameter is the end frame of the clip. The **WarpMode** parameter is the type of animation that we want, such as loop, default, once, and so on. And the last one, **Loop**, is the true or false parameter; if it is checked, Unity will automatically increase an extra frame at the end of animation to match with the first frame.

There are two ways to import the animations to use in Unity. The first method is the one that we mentioned previously. We import a single model that contains all animations and split the animation by setting the duration of the frame. In the second method, we don't have to set up the animation frame from start to end. Unity will automatically export the animation clip for you. However, this method will need to import the multiple model files, each file having a different animation clip such as idle, walk, run, and so on. Also, we need to follow the naming convention for Unity to be able to import the animation clip properly. For example, we have imported the base FBX model name `Heroine_animate` without any animation clip. Then we will import another FBX model that contains only idle animation; we should name it `Heroine_animate@idle`, as we can see in the following screenshot:

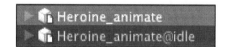

For more details, see the following website:
`http://unity3d.com/support/documentation/Manual/Character-Animation.html.`

2. Next, we will create each animation clip by clicking on the plus sign on the right-hand side. After you click on the plus sign, you will see the clip added to this window. This is the animation clip that we can use in our game. For this chapter, we need five clips, so after clicking on the plus sign five times, we set it as follows:

- **Name: idle** **Start: 7** **End: 210** **WrapMode: Loop** **Loop: uncheck**
- **Name: walk** **Start: 230** **End: 280** **WrapMode: Loop** **Loop: uncheck**
- **Name: run** **Start: 290** **End: 320** **WrapMode: Loop** **Loop: uncheck**
- **Name: jump** **Start: 325** **End: 339** **WrapMode: Default** **Loop: uncheck**
- **Name: fall** **Start: 340** **End: 360** **WrapMode: Default** **Loop: uncheck**

3. Then, click on the **Apply** button at the end of the **Inspector** view. Now, we have finished adding our animation clip.

4. Next, we want to add the level to our scene. Go to the **Project** view under the `Prefabs` folder and drag the **Level** Prefabs to the **Hierarchy** view, as we can see in the following screenshot:

5. Then, we need to add light to our scene. Go to **GameObject | Create Other | Directional Light**. In its **Inspector** view, set the **Rotation** in the **X-axis** to **30**. (If you have the Unity Pro version, you can set it up to use the **Hard Shadows** or **Soft Shadows** to get a nice shadow on the ground.)

6. Before we finish this step, we will add our character to the scene. Go to the `FBX` folder in the **Project** view and drag `Heroine_animate` to the **Hierarchy** view.

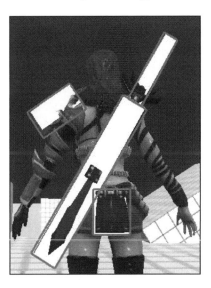

In the preceding screenshot, we can see the red frame, which shows the white boxes on the character that represent extra bones to control the extra objects on our character. In this case, the extra objects are the sword, sword sheath, dragonhead on the shoulder, and the back plate.

The extra bone meshes are usually exported from other 3D software, depending on the artist or animator who sets it up. Sometimes, we can use these meshes for collision detection for the attack action, if we have a fighting animation attached on the character.

We don't need to show the mesh here, so we can remove or hide it, but we will remove it because we don't have to use the **Mesh Renderer** component in this case.

7. Let's do this by clicking on the Heroine_animate in the **Hierarchy** view.

8. Then, we will use the search box in the **Hierarchy** view to search and put bone in this box, as we can see in the following screenshot:

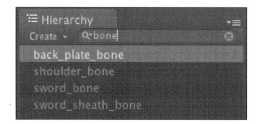

9. Let's click on the first bone back_plate_bone to bring up its inspector and go to the **Inspector** view, then right click on the **Mesh Renderer** component, and click **Remove Component** to remove it as we can see in the following screenshot:

This will bring up the **Losing Prefab** popup; we just click **Continue** button to break it.

10. Then, we go to the next bone `shoulder_bones`, `sword_bone`, and `sword_sheath_bone` and perform tasks similar to what we performed for the `back_plate_bone`, and we will see all the white boxes disappear as seen in the following screenshot:

Objective Complete - Mini Debriefing

Basically, what we have done here is set up the animation clip for idle, walk, run, jump, and fall. Then, we also created the level and directional light for our scene. Next, we added our character, which included the animation clips that we have set up. Lastly, we removed the **Mesh Renderer** of the extra bones, because we don't want to show it in our scene.

> If you click on the `Body` object (the child of `Heroine_animate`) in the **Hierarchy** view to bring up its **Inspector** view, you will see the **Skinned Mesh Renderer** in the **Inspector** view. The **Skinned Mesh Renderer** is automatically added to the imported object when the imported object is skinned. The **Skinned Mesh Renderer** will take care of drawing the mesh attached to the animation. The advantage of using **Skinned Mesh** is that we can enable or disable the bone by using scripting, which is very good for the ragdoll physics. We can take a look at the details from the following website:
>
> `http://unity3d.com/support/documentation/Components/class-SkinnedMeshRenderer.html`.

Classified Intel

In the last chapter, we exported the 3D model from 3D Studio Max, but we did so without the animation or rigging. So, we'd like to talk a bit about how to export the animation from 3D Studio Max with animation and all the rigs with it.

As we know, 3D Studio Max uses the Z-axis as the upward direction, but Unity uses the Y-axis for the same purpose. In *Chapter 3*, *The Hero/Heroine Part I – Models and Shaders*, when we exported the 3D model, we set the **X** rotation of the character pivot to **-90 degrees**. However, if we try to set up the character as the last, we will have the problem with the biped setup. To problem the problem this time, we don't have to set up the rotation in the **X**-axis of the pivot as in *Chapter 3*, *The Hero/Heroine Part I – Models and Shaders*. So, this means that we will leave the rotation of the pivot as default, as shown in the following screenshot:

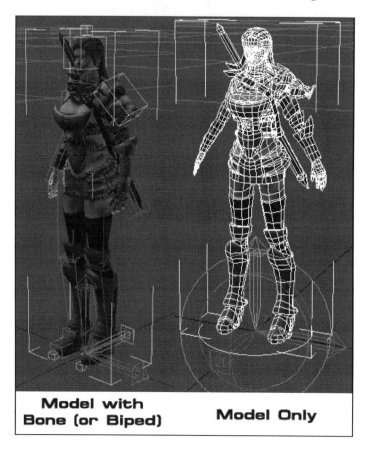

This is because our character has two objects attached to it—the model and the bone. Then, when we import it to Unity, the **FBXImporter** in Unity will basically create the container and add both objects and its children, which will solve the problem of wrong rotation and set the default rotation of the model to **X: 0, Y: 0, Z: 0**, as we can see in the following screenshot:

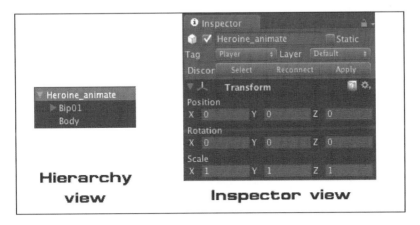

Some of you might be curious—how do we know when to rotate the pivot or not rotate the pivot in 3D Studio Max? Well, it's very simple; just remember that any 3D model that is static and not complicated or has only one mesh object included, will rotate the pivot. On the other hand, if we have a character model with rigging or maybe a simple mesh for detecting the collision, we can just leave it as it is.

We can also fix the rotation of the imported model in Unity by creating the empty object as a parent of the imported model. For more information on how to fix the rotation of the imported model in Unity, we can go to the following website:

http://unity3d.com/support/documentation/Manual/
HOWTO-FixZAxisIsUp.html.

Next, we will take a look at how to set up the FBX exporter to export the 3D model with animation included. We can follow the next screenshot, which shows the extra parameter that we need to set when exporting the FBX file from 3D Studio Max:

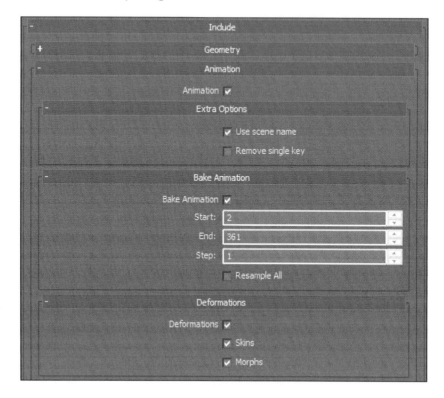

Then, we will take a look at the animation clip in the **FBXImporter**. We can see the action of each animation clip in Unity by clicking on **Heroine_animate** in the **Heirarchy** view; then go to **Window | Animation**, and we can bring up the **Animation** window. Here, we can click the **play** button to play each animation clip, and we can see the result on the editor. We can also change the animation clip by clicking on the name of the animation clip beside the character name below the play button, as we can see in the following screenshot:

Then, we can click to choose the animation that we want to see, as shown in the following screenshot:

Creating the character controller and built-in script

In the last section, we have a ready FBX with an animation clip, and a scene to use. In this step, we will add a character controller script to our character. This script will allow us to be able to access all the character control classes, which we can use to move the character, detect the collision, limit the slope we can walk up, and how big of stairs (step offset) we can climb. Then, we will add a third-person character controller and third-person camera script to our character and set up the parameter to be able to control our character.

Prepare for Lift Off

Make sure to include the unity built-in **Character Controllers** package included in our project. (We have already done this at the beginning of this chapter)

 If you didn't do it earlier, you can go to **Assets | Import Package | Character Controller** to import this package.

Engage Thrusters

First, we will add the character controller script to our character by clicking on `Heroine_animate`, and then we go to **Component | Physics | Character Controller**. Now, go to the **Inspector** view, under **Character Controller**, and change the parameters as follows:

- ▶ **Height**: 1.7
- ▶ **Radius**: 0.2
- ▶ **Slope Limit**: 45
- ▶ **Step Offset**: 0.3
- ▶ **Skin Width**: 0.08
- ▶ **Min Move Distance**: 0
- ▶ **Center**: X: 0, Y: 0.89, Z: 0

Right here, we set up the character controller script to fit with our character. We can see more details about each parameter from the following link:

`http://unity3d.com/support/documentation/Components/class-CharacterController.html`.

We can find all the animation clips of our character from the **Project** view in the **Chapter4 | FBX | Heroine_animate**, as shown in the following screenshot:

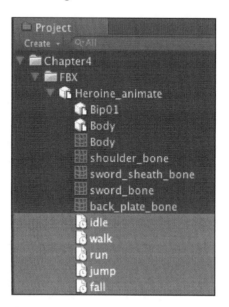

Next, we will attach the `Third-person Controller` script to the character by going to **Component | Scripts | Third-person Controller** and set the following:

- ▸ **Idle Animation**: idle
- ▸ **Walk Animation**: walk
- ▸ **Run Animation**: run
- ▸ **Jump Pose Animation**: jump
- ▸ **Walk Max Animation Speed**: 1.5
- ▸ **Trot Max Animation Speed**: 1.5
- ▸ **Run Max Animation Speed**: 1.5
- ▸ **Jump Animation Speed**: 4
- ▸ **Land Animation Speed**: 0.1
- ▸ **Walk Speed**: 2
- ▸ **Trot Speed**: 2
- ▸ **Run Speed**: 8
- ▸ **In Air Control Acceleration**: 5
- ▸ **Jump Height**: 2
- ▸ **Gravity**: 20
- ▸ **Speed Smoothing**: 10
- ▸ **Rotate Speed**: 300
- ▸ **Trot After Seconds**: 3
- ▸ **Can Jump**: check the box

Lastly, we will add the `Third-person Camera` script to make the camera follow our character smoothly; go to **Component | Scripts | Third-person Camera** and then go to the **Inspector** view and set the following:

- ▸ **Camera Transform**: Drag the **Main Camera** in the **Hierarchy** view here
- ▸ **Distance**: 3
- ▸ **Height**: 1
- ▸ **Angular Smooth Lag**: 0.1
- ▸ **Angular Max Speed**: 175
- ▸ **Height Smooth Lag**: 0.3
- ▸ **Snap Smooth Lag**: 0.2
- ▸ **Snap Max Speed**: 720

- ▸ **Clamp Head Position Screen Space: 0.6**
- ▸ **Lock Camera Timeout: 0.2**

Before we finish this step, we need to create a new prefab for this game object. So, we go to **Assets | Create | Prefab**, name it `Heroine_BuiltIn`, and drag `Heroine_animate` in the **Hierarchy View** to the `Heroine_BuiltIn` prefab.

Finally, we click on **Play** and control the character by pressing *W, A, S, D,* or up, down, left, right arrow keys to move the character, Space key for jumping, and holding the *Shift* with pressing the move key to run. If we didn't press any key, the character will be playing the idle animation.

Objective Complete - Mini Debriefing

We just added the character controller and the built-in third-person character controller script to our character and set up the parameters that are suitable for our character.

Classified Intel

In this step, we added the built-in third-person character controller, which is a good starting point to set up the third-person character. We can set up and adjust the parameter the way we want, such as the height or distance of the camera, speed of the animation clip, and so on, as we can see in the following screenshot:

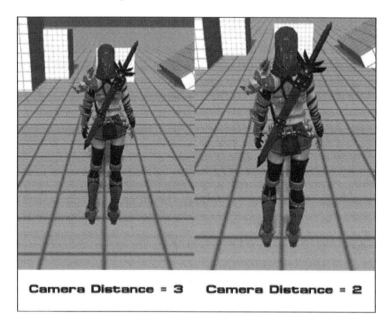

Camera Distance = 3   Camera Distance = 2

However, the built-in third-person character controller has its own limitations. For example, if we walk down from the box or try to fall down from the big box, we will see that our character still uses the walk animation. This is because the built-in third-person controller doesn't support the fall animation. We will solve this problem in the next step by creating our custom `CharacterControl` script and `CharacterCamera` and adapt some of the code from the built-in script to get a result similar to the following screenshot:

Creating a custom character control script

From the last section, we know how to set up the character controller using the built-in third-person character controller, which works very well. If we look at the built-in character controller closely, we will see that it takes only four animation clips, but we want to add one more clip, which is the fall animation (for the model that we had, it's the backward of the jump animation clip). However, if we have more than four animation clips, we will need to build our own script because there is no support for including a falling animation in the built-in script. So, we will create our character control script which is similar to, but much simpler than, the built-in third-person controller script.

Prepare for Lift Off

Before we start coding, we need to get rid of the built-in `Third-person Controller` and `Third-person Camera` scripts. So, let's go to `Heroine_animate` in the **Hierarchy View**, under the **Inspector** view, right-click the **Third-person Camera** script, and then click **Remove Component**. We will see the pop-up window that says we'll lose the prefab if we remove it. We can just click on the **OK** button to remove it because we already created our prefab. Then, we go to **Third-person Controller**, right-click and select **Remove Component** to remove it. Now, we are ready to create our character control script.

Engage Thrusters

Now we will create the script to control our character:

1. Go to **Assets | Create | JavaScript** and name it `CharacterControl`, and then right-click on this script and click **Sync MonoDevelop Project** (or double-click it if you have already set **MonoDevelop** as your main editor, if not it will open the default script editor either **Unitron** or **UniScite**) to open **MonoDevelop**, and we are ready to code.

2. We start by adding these parameters as follows:

```
// Require a character controller to be attached to the same game
object
@script RequireComponent (CharacterController)

//All Animation Clip Params
public var idleAnimation : AnimationClip;
public var walkAnimation : AnimationClip;
public var runAnimation : AnimationClip;
public var jumpPoseAnimation : AnimationClip;
public var fallPoseAnimation : AnimationClip;

//Animation Clip Speed
public var jumpAnimationSpeed : float = 4;
public var fallAnimationSpeed : float = 0.1;
public var runAnimationSpeed : float = 1.5;
public var walkAnimationSpeed : float = 1.5;
public var idleAnimationSpeed : float = 0.5;

public var speed : float = 2; //Walk speed
public var runSpeed : float = 5.0;
public var jumpSpeed : float = 8.0;
public var gravity : float = 20.0;

private var controller : CharacterController;
```

```
//Move Params
private var f_verticalSpeed : float = 0.0;
private var f_moveSpeed : float = 0.0;
private var v3_moveDirection : Vector3 = Vector3.zero;

//Boolean
private var b_isRun : boolean;
private var b_isBackward : boolean;
private var b_isJumping : boolean;

//Rotate Params
private var q_currentRotation : Quaternion; //current rotation of
the character
private var q_rot : Quaternion; //Rotate to left or right
direction
private var f_rotateSpeed : float = 1.0; //Smooth speed of
rotation

//Direction Params
private var v3_forward : Vector3; //Forward Direction of the
character
private var v3_right : Vector3; //Right Direction of the character

private var c_collisionFlags : CollisionFlags; //Collision Flag
return from Moving the character

//Create in air time
private var f_inAirTime : float = 0.0;
private var f_inAirStartTime : float = 0.0;
private var f_minAirTime : float = 0.15; // 0.15 sec.
```

Here, we have all the necessary parameters to use in our script. In the first line, we want to make sure that we have the character controller script attached when we use this script. Then, we have the animation clip parameters to contain all the animation that we want to play when we control our character. Next, we have the animation speed to control how fast we want our animation clip to play when it uses. We also have the speed for the walk, run, jump and gravity parameters. We need the gravity property because we will use the Move() function in the CharacterController class, which doesn't have the gravity parameter included.

3. Next, we will start creating the first function `Awake()` using the following code:

```
//Using Awake to set up parameters before Initialize
public function Awake() : void {
  controller = GetComponent(CharacterController);
  b_isRun = false;
  b_isBackward = false;
  b_isJumping = false;
  f_moveSpeed = speed;
  c_collisionFlags = CollisionFlags.CollidedBelow;
}
```

4. In this function, we set up the necessary parameters before we initialize it. Then, we create the `Start()` function and initialize it as follows:

```
public function Start() : void {
  f_inAirStartTime = Time.time;
}
```

We use the `Start()` function to set up `f_inAirStartTime` because we need to get the time when we first start the scene.

5. Next, we will add the scripts to check the stage of our character, such as jumping, moving backward, on the ground, and in the air. Let's type this as follows:

```
//Checking if the character hit the ground (collide Below)
public function IsGrounded () : boolean {
   return (c_collisionFlags & CollisionFlags.CollidedBelow);
}
//Getting if the character is jumping or not
public function IsJumping() : boolean {
  return b_isJumping;
}
//Checking if the character is in the air more than the minimum
time
//This function is to make sure that we are falling not walking
down slope
public function IsAir() : boolean {
  return (f_inAirTime > f_minAirTime);
}
//Geting if the character is moving backward
public function IsMoveBackward() : boolean {
  return b_isBackward;
}
```

6. Now we will set up the `Update()` function to make the character move; add the following code:

```
public function Update() : void {
  //Get Main Camera Transform
  var cameraTransform = Camera.main.transform;

  //Get forward direction of the character
  v3_forward = cameraTransform.TransformDirection(Vector3.
forward);
    v3_forward.y = 0; //Make sure that vertical direction equals zero
    // Right vector relative to the character
    // Always orthogonal to the forward direction vector
    v3_right = new Vector3(v3_forward.z, 0, -v3_forward.x); // -90
degree to the left from the forward direction
```

In the preceding section, we get the transform from the main camera, the forward direction, and right direction from this transform, because the controls are relative to the camera orientation not the character orientation.

7. We need to get the **Input** button from the user by using the `Input.GetAxis` `"Horizontal"` and `"Vertical"`:

```
  //Get Horizontal move - rotation
  var f_hor : float = Input.GetAxis("Horizontal");
  //Get Vertical move - move forward or backward
  var f_ver : float = Input.GetAxis("Vertical");
```

8. We check whether the character is moving backward or forward by checking if the result of `f_ver` is lower than `0`, as shown in the following script:

```
  //If we are moving backward
  if (f_ver < 0) {
    b_isBackward = true;
  } else {
    b_isBackward = false;
  }
```

9. We get the target direction by multiplying the horizontal value with the camera transform right direction and add the value of vertical multiply with forward direction of the camera, as shown in the following script:

```
  //Get target direction
  var v3_targetDirection : Vector3 = (f_hor * v3_right) + (f_ver *
v3_forward);
```

10. We calculate the move direction here by using `Vector3.Slerp()`, and normalize it, because we only need the direction where our character moves from the user input, as shown in the following script:

```
//If the target direction is not zero - that means there is no
button pressing
if (v3_targetDirection != Vector3.zero) {
    //Rotate toward the target direction
    v3_moveDirection = Vector3.Slerp(v3_moveDirection, v3_
targetDirection, f_rotateSpeed * Time.deltaTime);
    v3_moveDirection = v3_moveDirection.normalized; //Get only
direction by normalizing our target vector
} else {
    v3_moveDirection = Vector3.zero;
}
```

> `Vector3.Slerp()` is the function that we can use to interpolate between two vectors spherically by amount of time, and the return vector's magnitude will be the difference between the magnitudes of the first vector and the second vector. This function is usually used when we want to get the smooth rotation from one vector to another vector in a fixed amount of time. You can see more details at the following Unity website:
>
> `http://unity3d.com/support/documentation/`
> `ScriptReference/Vector3.Slerp.html.`

11. We get the moving speed of our character by checking if our character is walking or running. In this section, we also check whether the character is grounded or not. We will make sure that we cannot press the **Run** or **Jump** buttons while the character is in the air:

```
//Checking if character is on the ground
if (!b_isJumping) {
    //Holding Shift to run
    if (Input.GetKey (KeyCode.LeftShift) || Input.GetKey (KeyCode.
RightShift)) {
        b_isRun = true;
        f_moveSpeed = runSpeed;
    } else {
        b_isRun = false;
        f_moveSpeed = speed;
    }
        //Press Space to Jump
        if (Input.GetButton ("Jump")) {
            f_verticalSpeed = jumpSpeed;
            b_isJumping = true;
        }
}
```

12. We apply the gravity and calculate in-air timing of our character. We need to apply the gravity here because the `Move()` function in the character controller script doesn't have any gravity applied to it. We will use the in-air time to track the time when the character is in the air. This will make sure that our character can walk down on the slope without any bugs:

```
// Apply gravity
if (IsGrounded()) {
    f_verticalSpeed = 0.0; //if our character is grounded
    b_isJumping = false; //Checking if our character is in the air
or not
    f_inAirTime = 0.0;
    f_inAirStartTime = Time.time;
} else {
    f_verticalSpeed -= gravity * Time.deltaTime; //if our
character in the air
    //Count Time
    f_inAirTime = Time.time - f_inAirStartTime;
}
```

13. We calculate the movement of our character and use the `Move()` function to move our character:

```
// Calculate actual motion
var v3_movement : Vector3 = (v3_moveDirection * f_moveSpeed) +
Vector3 (0, f_verticalSpeed, 0); // Apply the vertical speed if
character fall down
v3_movement *= Time.deltaTime;

// Move the controller
c_collisionFlags = controller.Move(v3_movement);
```

14. Finally, we apply rotation to our character when the user controls our character left or right:

```
//Update rotation of the character
if (v3_moveDirection != Vector3.zero) {
    transform.rotation = Quaternion.LookRotation(v3_
moveDirection);
}
}
```

Next, we will assign this script to our character by going back to Unity and dragging the `CharacterControl` script to the `Heroine_animate` in the **Hierarchy** view; we will be able to control our character, but there will be no animation applied to our character yet. We will apply animation to our character/character animation in the next section.

Objective Complete - Mini Debriefing

In this section, we have created a custom character control script to create the character movement by using the `Move()` function in `CharacterController` class. This function needs only the direction and it returns the collision flags, which are very convenient to use. We also apply the **Gravity** and **Jump** buttons to make our character fall down when there is no collider.

Classified Intel

In the first chapter, we created a 2D platform game which used a plane object to show a sprite animation. We also attached `Rigidbody` to the character to be able to use a gravity and access to the `Rigidbody` class to get a nice Physics movement.

However, in this chapter we didn't use `Rigidbody`, but we used `CharacterController` to control our character. We can add `Rigidbody` to our character if we want to create a `ragdoll` object, but we aren't doing it in this chapter. We will take care of the `ragdoll` object in *Chapter 7, Creating a Destructible and Interactive Virtual World*.

The `CharacterController` script has a lot of advantages. In this case, we will talk about the `Move()` function. This function takes one parameter, `Vector3`, which will be the motion of our movement per frame. So, we basically need to get the direction from the input, multiply the speed and `Time.deltaTime`, and pass it to this function.

The `Move()` function also returns the `CollisionFlags`, which we can check for each part of our character collide to another object. This is very useful when we want to check if the top of the character hit the ceiling, or the side of our character hit the wall, and so on. We can read more details of the `Move()` function and `CollisionFlags` from the following link:

```
http://unity3d.com/support/documentation/ScriptReference/
CharacterController.Move.html
```

```
http://unity3d.com/support/documentation/ScriptReference/
CollisionFlags.html
```

Creating CrossFade animation

In this section, we will apply and create the animation clip to our character and make it suitable for each action such as idle, walk, run, jump, and fall animation.

Engage Thrusters

We will start with creating the `Awake()` function:

1. Go to the `Awake()` function to set up `warpMode` of the animation, and type the following highlighted script:

```
//Using Awake to set up parameters before Initialize
public function Awake() : void {
    controller = GetComponent(CharacterController);
    b_isRun = false;
    b_isBackward = false;
    b_isJumping = false;
    f_moveSpeed = speed;
    c_collisionFlags = CollisionFlags.CollidedBelow;

    //Set warpMode for each animation clip
    animation[jumpPoseAnimation.name].wrapMode = WrapMode.ClampForever;
    animation[fallPoseAnimation.name].wrapMode = WrapMode.ClampForever;
    animation[idleAnimation.name].wrapMode = WrapMode.Loop;
    animation[runAnimation.name].wrapMode = WrapMode.Loop;
    animation[walkAnimation.name].wrapMode = WrapMode.Loop;
}
```

2. Go back to the `Update()` function in the `CharacterControl.js` file between `c_collisionFlags = controller.Move(v3_movement);` and `if (v3_moveDirection != Vector3.zero)` near the bottom line of this function; add the following highlighted script:

```
// Move the controller
    c_collisionFlags = controller.Move(v3_movement);

//Play animation
if (b_isJumping) {
 if (controller.velocity.y > 0 ) {
    animation[jumpPoseAnimation.name].speed = jumpAnimationSpeed;
    animation.CrossFade(jumpPoseAnimation.name, 0.1);
 } else {
    animation[fallPoseAnimation.name].speed = fallAnimationSpeed;
    animation.CrossFade(fallPoseAnimation.name, 0.1);
 }
} else {
 if (IsAir()) { // Fall down
    animation[fallPoseAnimation.name].speed = fallAnimationSpeed;
    animation.CrossFade(fallPoseAnimation.name, 0.1);
 } else { //Not fall down
```

```
        //If the character has no velocity or very close to 0 show idle
animation
        if(controller.velocity.sqrMagnitude < 0.1) {
            animation[idleAnimation.name].speed = idleAnimationSpeed;
            animation.CrossFade(idleAnimation.name, 0.1);
        } else { //Checking if the character walks or runs
          if (b_isRun) {
              animation[runAnimation.name].speed = runAnimationSpeed;
              animation.CrossFade(runAnimation.name, 0.1);
          } else {
              animation[walkAnimation.name].speed = walkAnimationSpeed;
              animation.CrossFade(walkAnimation.name, 0.1);
          }
        }
      }
    }
  }


        //Update rotation of the character
      if (v3_moveDirection != Vector3.zero) {
          transform.rotation = Quaternion.LookRotation(v3_
moveDirection);
        }
    }
```

We just added the script to check what the animation clip should play when the character is in each action. In the first section, we are checking if we are jumping. If we are, we play also, **Jump and not jump**. If we are falling down, we play the **Fall and not fall**. Then, if we are moving by walking, we play **Walk Animation**. If we are running, we play **Run Animation**. If we are not doing anything, we play **Idle Animation**.

3. Finally, we go back to Unity and add the animation clip to our character by clicking on the `Heroine_animate` object in the **Hierarchy View** to bring up its **Inspector** view, under the **Character Control** component in the **Inspector** view, and set the following:

    □   **Idle Animation: idle**

    □   **Walk Animation: walk**

    □   **Run Animation: run**

    □   **Jump Animation: jump**

    □   **Fall Animation: fall**

We will see the result of the **Inspector** view, as shown in the following screenshot:

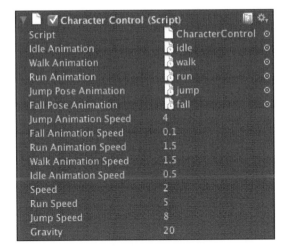

 We can find all the animation clips by going to the **Project** view in **Chapter4 | FBX | Heroine_animate**, as shown in the following screenshot.

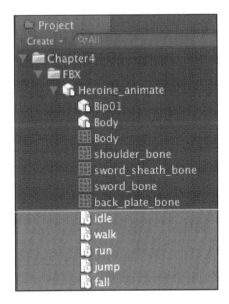

Objective Complete - Mini Debriefing

We just added a new script to check what the animation clip should play when the character is in each action. We also set the speed of each animation by using `animation[name].speed`, set the `warpMode` by using `animation[name].warpMode`, and we used the `animation.CrossFade(name, time)` to blend one animation clip to another.

Classified Intel

In this step, we set the speed of our animation by using `animation[name].speed`, where `animation[name]` is the animation clip that we have already set up in the first step.

The `speed` parameter is basically the speed with which the animation clip is played. For example, if we set our animation from 3D Software to play this animation in one second, and we set the speed of this animation equal to `1`, then the animation clip will play at the same speed as the source animation. On the other hand, if we set up the speed to `2`, this animation clip will play twice as fast as our source animation. Also, if we set the number lower than `1`, the animation will play that many times slower than the source.

The `animation.CrossFade()` function will cross fade from the current animation clip to another animation, and we pass its name to this function. We can also control how much time we want to cross fade for by setting the number of times. More details on this function are available at: `http://unity3d.com/support/documentation/ScriptReference/Animation.CrossFade.html`.

Creating a third-person camera to follow our character

From the last section, we got the controllable character with the animation, but the camera isn't actually following the character at all. So, in this section we will create the third-person camera to follow our character.

Prepare for Lift Off

Create a new JavaScript in **Unity** by going to **Assets | Create | JavaScript**, and name it **CharacterCamera**. Then right-click on this script and click **Sync MonoDevelop Project** (or double-click it if we already set **MonoDevelop** as our main editor; if not it will open the default script editor, either **Unitron** or **UniScite**) to open **MonoDevelop**. Now we are ready to code.

Engage Thrusters

Now, we will begin coding the `CharacterCamera` script:

1. Type the parameters script as follows:

```
//Make sure that we have CharacterControl included in this
gameobject
@script RequireComponent(CharacterControl)

//Angular smooth
public var smoothTime : float = 0.1;
public var maxSpeed : float = 150.0;

public var heightSmoothTime : float = 0.1;

public var distance : float = 2.5;
public var height : float = 0.75;

private var f_heightVelocity : float = 0.0;
private var f_angleVelocity : float = 0.0;

private var v3_velocity : Vector3;
//Transform
private var target : Transform;
private var cameraTransform : Transform;

private var f_maxRotation : float;
//Character Control
private var c_characterControl : CharacterControl;

//Target
private var f_targetHeight : float = Mathf.Infinity;
private var v3_centerOffset = Vector3.zero;
```

Using the preceding code, we created all the parameters to use in this script.

2. Next, we will set up the parameters by using the `Awake()` function:

```
public function Awake () : void {
   //Get Our Main Camera from the scene
   cameraTransform = Camera.main.transform;
   target = transform;
   c_characterControl = GetComponent(CharacterControl);

   //Get target center offset
   var characterController : CharacterController = target.collider;
```

```
    v3_centerOffset = characterController.bounds.center - target.
position;
}
```

In this function, we get the camera transform and the `CharacterController` script to get the center position of the target, which is the character we are pointing at.

3. Then, we will create a function to get the angle distance between the current angle and target; let's add the following code:

```
//Get the angle distance between two angle
//This function took from the built-in Third-person Camera Script
public function AngleDistance (a : float, b : float) : float {
    //Loop the value a and b not higher than 360 and not lower than
0
    a = Mathf.Repeat(a, 360);
    b = Mathf.Repeat(b, 360);

    return Mathf.Abs(b - a);
}
```

4. Next, we will create the `LateUpdate()` function to update the camera position and rotation after all the objects have their `Update` functions called. So, let's add the following code.

> The `LateUpdate()` function is the function that will be called after the `Update()` function has been called. This function will make sure that all the calculation in the `Update()` function is finished before we start the `LateUpdate()` function. We can see more details of this function at the following Unity website:
>
> `http://unity3d.com/support/documentation/ ScriptReference/MonoBehaviour.LateUpdate.html.`

```
//We use LateUpdate here because we need to wait for the user
input before we update our camera.
public function LateUpdate () : void {
    var v3_targetCenter : Vector3 = target.position + v3_
centerOffset;

    //Calculate the current & target rotation angles
    var f_originalTargetAngle : float = target.eulerAngles.y;
    var f_currentAngle : float = cameraTransform.eulerAngles.y;
    var f_targetAngle : float = f_originalTargetAngle;
```

```
    // Lock the camera when moving backwards!
    // * It is really confusing to do 180 degree spins when turning
around. So We fixed the camera rotation
    if (AngleDistance (f_currentAngle, f_targetAngle) > 160 && c_
characterControl.IsMoveBackward ()) {
        f_targetAngle += 180;
    }
    //Apply rotation to the camera
    f_currentAngle = Mathf.SmoothDampAngle(f_currentAngle, f_
targetAngle, f_angleVelocity, smoothTime, maxSpeed);

    //Update camera height position
    f_targetHeight = v3_targetCenter.y + height;

    // Damp the height
    var f_currentHeight : float = cameraTransform.position.y;
    f_currentHeight = Mathf.SmoothDamp (f_currentHeight, f_
targetHeight, f_heightVelocity, heightSmoothTime);

    // Convert the angle into a rotation, by which we then
reposition the camera
    var q_currentRotation : Quaternion = Quaternion.Euler (0, f_
currentAngle, 0);

    // Set the position of the camera on the x-z plane to:
    // distance meters behind the target
    cameraTransform.position = v3_targetCenter;
    cameraTransform.position += q_currentRotation * Vector3.back *
distance;

    // Set the height of the camera
    cameraTransform.position.y = f_currentHeight;

    // Always look at the target
    SetUpRotation(v3_targetCenter);
}
```

5. Finally, we will create the `SetupRotation()` function to update the rotation of our camera. Type the following code:

```
private function SetUpRotation (v3_centerPos : Vector3) {
    var v3_cameraPos = cameraTransform.position; //Camera position
    var v3_offsetToCenter : Vector3 = v3_centerPos - v3_cameraPos;
//Get the camera center offset

    //Generate base rotation only around y-axis
```

```
   var q_yRotation : Quaternion = Quaternion.
LookRotation(Vector3(v3_offsetToCenter.x, v3_offsetToCenter.y +
height, v3_offsetToCenter.z));
   //Apply the rotation to the camera
   var v3_relativeOffset = Vector3.forward * distance + Vector3.
down * height;
   cameraTransform.rotation = q_yRotation * Quaternion.
LookRotation(v3_relativeOffset);
   }
```

So, we are done with this chapter. We can go to Unity and click **Play** to see our result. We will see that now the camera is following our character.

Objective Complete - Mini Debriefing

We just created a third-person camera to follow our character. This script also allows us to set the distance from our character and the height of our camera position by using some code from the third-person camera built-in script and adapting it to our character.

Classified Intel

Why do we need the `LateUpdate()` function instead of the `Update()` function for this script? Well, we used it to guarantee that the player position is already updated when we are doing the camera calculations. If we are doing the calculation in the `Update()` function, the camera position might be calculated before the player position is updated. This will result in jitter.

We can also explain it this way: We wait for the input from the user and then get the direction where the character will go in the `Update()` function. Then, we use the position of the character as the target position that our camera will follow, and calculate the camera position in the `LateUpdate()` function. This way, we will be able to track each movement of our character and the camera will follow the direction smoothly without any jitter, as we can see in the following diagram:

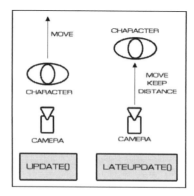

Game over-Wrapping it up

In this chapter, we have learned how to set up the animation from a 3D model and we also learned a bit about how to export the model with animation from 3D Studio Max to use in Unity. Then, we used the `CharacterController` script to our character and added the built-in `Third-person Controller` and `Third-person Camera` to apply it to our character and make it move.

Next, we created our `CharacterControl` script to control our character and add the fall animation that we want to use for our character. We also learned how to use the `Move()` function in the `CharacterController` script, and how to speed up or slow down the animation clip by setting the speed of the clip. We also learned how to use `Animation.crossFade()` to cross fade the current animation to another, giving animation clip. Lastly, we created our `CharacterCamera` to follow our character by using the `LateUpdate()` function to track the position of the character.

We will see a result similar to the following screenshot:

Are you ready to go gung ho? A Hotshot challenge

Now we know how to create a custom character control script, camera, and animation from our custom script. Even though our custom script works great with this character, it still has a lot of things that we can improve to make our script much more flexible. Let's do something to make our script better, and much more flexible. Give the following ideas a try:

- Add your own character with a different animation, even if the character has more than five animation clips
- Use a different method to make the camera not follow the character when our character jumps (or basically just rotate the camera)
- Change some parameters such as distance or height in the `CharacterCamera` script to see how the game will look
- Create more action for the character such as slide or crawl and create a script to show using `crossFade` to fade from one action to another
- Add the backward walk or run by setting the negative speed for those animation clips and using the `b_isBackward` property to check it

Project 5

Build a Rocket Launcher!

In this chapter, we will learn how to create a rocket launcher. Here, we will first use the FPS camera and controller from the Unity built-in FPS package, but we will tweak our camera view to see from the character's shoulder as in Resident Evil 4 or 5. We will also take the character model and animation from the FPS tutorial package from Unity, which we can download from the following website:

`http://unity3d.com/support/resources/tutorials/fpstutorial.html`.

Then, we will adapt the built-in FPS controller script to be able to play the animation of the character, and make the controller similar to the Resident Evil style controller. Next, we will create a rocket prefab and the rocket launcher script to fire our rocket, which will also include the use of the built-in fire explosion particle and custom smoke particle effect from the launcher when we fire.

Mission briefing

We will create a character that carries a rocket launcher and is able to shoot it as well as creating the camera view looking back from the character shoulder (third-person camera view). Then, we will add the character controller script to control our character, and the player will have to hold the **Aim** button to be able to shoot the rocket, similar to the Resident Evil 4 or 5 styles.

What does it do?

We will start with applying the built-in `CharacterMotor`, `FPSInputController`, and `MouseLook` scripts from the built-in FPS character controller. Then, we will add the character model and start creating a new script by adapting part of the code in the `FPSInputController` script. Then, we will be able to control the animation for our character to shoot, walk, run, and remain idle.

Next, we will create a rocket prefab and the rocket launcher script to fire our rocket. We will use and adapt the built-in explosion and fire trial particle in Unity, and attach them to our rocket prefab. We will also create a new smoke particle, which will appear from the barrel of the rocket launcher when the player clicks **Shoot**.

Then, we will create the scope target for aiming. We will also create the launcher and smoke `GameObject`, which are the start position of the rocket and the smoke particle.

Finally, we will add the rocket `GUITexture` object and script to track the number of bullets we have left, after each shot. We will also add the **Reload** button to refill our bullet when the character is out of the bullet.

Why Is It Awesome?

When we complete this chapter, we will be able to create the third-person shooter style camera view and controller, which is very popular in many games today. We will also be able to create a rocket launcher weapon and particle by using the prefab technique. Finally, we will be able to create an outline text with the `GUITexture` object for tracking the number of bullets left.

Your Hotshot Objectives

In the last chapter, we already talked about how to create a third-person controller script to control our character. In this chapter, we will use a similar concept and combine it with the built-in first-person controller prefab style to create our third-person shooter script to fire a rocket from the rocket launcher. Here is what we will do:

- ▸ Setting up the character with the first-person controller prefab
- ▸ Creating the `New3PSController` and `MouseLook_JS` scripts
- ▸ Create a rocket launcher and a scope target
- ▸ Create the rockets and particles
- ▸ Create the rocket bullet UI

Mission Checklist

First, we need the `chapter 5` project package, which will include the character model with a gun from the Unity FPS tutorial website, and all the necessary assets for this chapter.

So, let's browse to `http://www.packtpub.com/support?nid=8267` and download `Chapter5.zip` package. Unzip it and we will see `Chapter5.unitypackage`, and we are ready.

Setting up the character with the first-person controller prefab

In the first section of this chapter, we will make all the necessary settings before we create our character on the scene. We will set up the imported assets and make sure that all the assets are imported in the proper way and are ready to use by using the `Import Package` in the **Project** view inside Unity. Then, we will set the light, level, camera, and put our character in the scene with the first-person controller prefab.

We will import the `Chapter5.unitypackage` package to Unity, which contains the `Chapter5` folder. Inside this folder, we will see five subfolders, which are `Fonts`, `Level`, `Robot Artwork`, `Rocket`, and `UI`. The `Fonts` folder will contain the `Font` file, which will be used by the GUI. The `Level` folder will contain the simple level prefab, its textures, and materials that we used in _Chapter 3, The Hero/Heroine Part I – Models and Shaders_, and _Chapter 4, The Hero/Heroine Part II – Animation and Controls_ . **Robot Artwork** is the folder that includes the character `FBX` model, materials, and textures, which can be taken from the Unity FPS tutorial. The `Rocket` folder contains the rocket and rocket launcher `FBX` models, materials, and textures, which can be taken from the Unity FPS tutorial. Finally, the `UI` folder includes all the images, which we will use to create the `GUI`.

Prepare for Lift Off

In this section, we will begin by importing the `chapter 5` Unity package, checking all the assets, setting up the level, and adding the character to the scene with the FPS controller script.

First, let's create a new project and name it **RocketLauncher**, and this time we will include the built-in `Character Controller` package and `Particles` package by checking the **Character Controller.unityPackage** and **Particles.unityPackage** checkboxes in the **Project Wizard**. Then, we will click on the **Create Project** button, as shown in the following screenshot:

Next, import the `assets` package by going to **Assets | Import Package | Custom Package...**. Choose `Chapter5.unityPackage`, which we just downloaded, and then click on the **Import** button in the pop-up window link, as shown in the following screenshot:

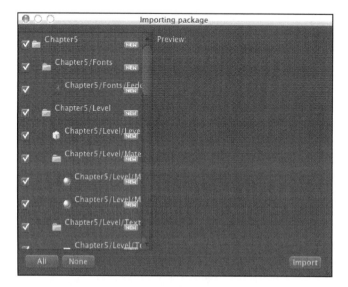

Wait until it's done, and you will see the `Chapter5` folder in the **Window** view. Make sure that we have all five folders, which are **Fonts**, **Level**, **Robot Artwork**, **Rocket**, and **UI**, inside this folder. Now, let's create something.

Engage Thrusters

In this section, we will set up the scene, camera view, and place our character in the scene:

1. First, let's begin with creating the directional light by going to **GameObject | Create Other | Directional Light**, and go to its **Inspector** view to set the rotation **X** to **30** and the position (**X: 0, Y: 0, Z: 0**).

2. Then, add the level to our scene by clicking on the **Chapter5** folder in the **Project** view. In the **Level** folder, you will see the **Level Prefab**; drag it to the **Hierarchy** view and you will see the level in our scene.

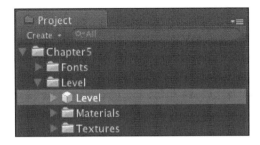

3. Next, remove the **Main Camera** from the **Hierarchy** view because we will use the camera from the built-in **First Person Controller** prefab. So, right-click on the **Main Camera** on the **Hierarchy** view and choose **Delete** to remove it.

4. Then, add the built-in **First Person Controller** prefab to the **Hierarchy** view by going to the **Standard Assets** folder. Under the **Character Controllers** folder, you will see the **First Person Controller** prefab; drag it to the **Hierarchy** view.

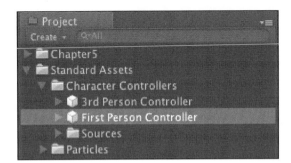

5. In the **Hierarchy** view, click on the arrow in the front of the **First Person Controller** object to see its hierarchy, similar to the one shown in the following screenshot:

6. Then, we go back to the **Project** view. In the **Chapter5** folder inside **Robot Artwork**, drag the `robot.fbx` object (as shown in the following screenshot) on top of the `Main Camera` inside the `First Person Controller` object in the **Hierarchy**.

7. This will cause the editor to show the window that tells us this action will break the prefab, so we just click on the **Continue** button to break it. It means that this game object will not be linked to the original prefab.

8. Next, remove the `Graphics` object above the `Main Camera`. Right-click on it and choose **Delete**. Now we will see something similar to the following screenshot:

 We have put the `robot` object as a child of the camera because we want our character to rotate with the camera. This will make our character always appear in front of the camera view, which is similar to the third-person view. This setup is different from the original FPS prefab because in the first person view, we will not see the character in the camera view, so there is no point in calculating the rotation of the character.

9. Now, click on the **First Person Controller** object in the **Hierarchy** view to bring up the **Inspector** view, and set up the **Transform | Position** of **X: 0, Y: 1.16, Z: 0**. Then, go to the **Character Controller**, and set all values as follows:

    ▸   **Character Controller (Script)**

    ▸   **Height: 2.25**

    ▸   **Center**

        ❑   **X: -0.8, Y: 0.75, Z: 1.4**

10. Move down one step by clicking on **Main Camera** in the **Hierarchy** view and go to its **Inspector** view to set the value of **Transform** and **Mouse Look** as follows:

    ▸   **Transform**

    ▸   **Position**

        ❑   X: 0, Y: 1.6, Z: 0

    ▸   **Mouse Look (Script)**

    ▸   **Sensitivity Y: 5**

    ▸   **Minimum Y: -15**

We will leave all the other parameters as default and use the default values.

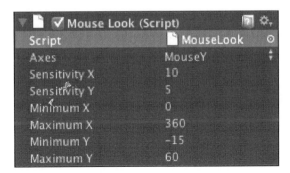

Then, we will go down one more step to set the **Transform** of the robot by clicking on it to bring up its **inspector** view, and set the following:

▸   **Transform**

    ❑   **Position**

        ❑   **X: -0.8, Y: -0.8, Z: 1.4**

    ❑   **Rotation**

        ❑   **X: 0, Y: 10, Z: 0**

Now, we are done with this step. In the next step, we will adjust and add some code to control the animation and movement of our character the `FPSInputController` script.

Objective Complete - Mini Debriefing

Basically, what we have done here is preparing the scene ready for the next step. In this step, we added the directional light, level prefab, and the built-in `First Person Controller` prefab to the scene. We also adjusted the built-in `First Person Controller` prefab by removing the `Graphics` object from the prefab object and adding the `robot` prefab as a child of the `Main Camera` of the `First Person Controller` prefab object for the new graphics, which we will see from the `Main Camera`, as shown in the following screenshot:

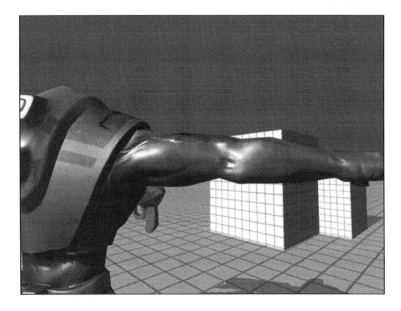

However, we will see the character's arm block half of the screen, which is because we don't have the script to control the animation, yet. We will do that in the next step.

Classified Intel

At the beginning of this chapter, we imported the `Chapter5.unityPackage` file, but what about exporting?

A good way to share assets between projects is by exporting them as `unitypackage`. A `unitypackage` also saves the import settings of the assets. To make it easier to include all needed assets, the export dialog automatically checks for dependencies. To export assets as `unitypackage`, just select the items, right-click, and choose **Export Package**.

For example, if we copy the `png` file from another project to the `Unity Assets` folder or import in the **Project** view, the default **Texture Importer | Texture Type** in Unity will always set to **Texture**. On the other hand, if we export this file by using `unityPackage`, we will be able to set the **Texture Type** to **GUI** or **Normal map**. Then, when we import this `unityPackage` to other projects, we will get the same settings we can see in the following screenshot:

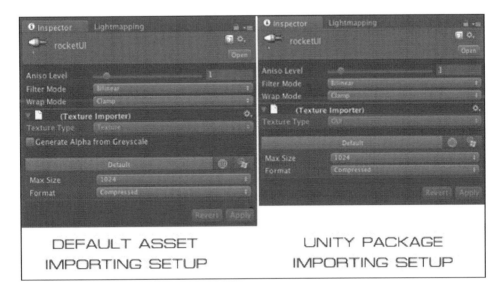

We can easily create the `unityPackage` file by just right-clicking on the file or folder in the **Project** view that we want to export and choosing **Export Package...** to bring up the **Exporting package** window as we can see in the following screenshot (we have selected the **Chapter 5** folder for the example):

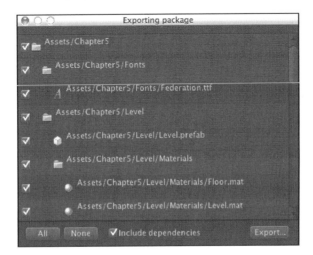

In this window, we can choose what we want to export by enabling the checkbox. Then, we can click on the **Export Package...** button and choose the path that we want to export.

> When the file is chosen in the **Project** window and we choose **Export Package...**, Unity will collect all the dependencies for that file and show them in the **Exporting package** window. So, selecting a scene file and exporting that will automatically export all the assets used in that scene. If an asset is only loaded from code and is not used directly in the scene or referenced from a public member variable, Unity will not know that it needs to be included. More information on the topic can be found at:
>
> `http://unity3d.com/support/documentation/Manual/HOWTO-exportpackage.html.`

Creating the New3PSController and MouseLook_JS scripts

In the last section, we imported the `Chapter5` Unity package and created our scene, which included all the basic setup. In this step, we will create a `New3PSController` script by using the old built-in `FPSInputController` script, and add some script to control the animation or the character to run, walk, aim, or shoot. We will also create the `MouseLook_JS` script, which is the JavaScript version of the `MouseLook` built-in script that is written in C#. The `MouseLook_JS` script is used to control the rotation of the camera in our scene.

Prepare for Lift Off

We are first going to create the `New3PSController` script.

We will start by creating a new `MouseLook_JS` by going to **Assets | Create | Javascript** and name it `MouseLook_JS`, then double-click to open it in **MonoDevelop** and replace the script as follows:

```
@script AddComponentMenu("Camera-Control/Mouse Look JS")

enum RotationAxes { MouseXAndY, MouseX, MouseY }
public var axes : RotationAxes = RotationAxes.MouseXAndY;
public var sensitivityX : float = 15;
public var sensitivityY : float = 15;

public var minimumX : float = -360;
public var maximumX : float = 360;
```

```
public var minimumY : float = -60;
public var maximumY : float = 60;

private var rotationY : float = 0;

public function Start () : void {
  // Make the rigid body not change rotation
  if (rigidbody)
    rigidbody.freezeRotation = true;
}

public function Update () : void {
  if (axes == RotationAxes.MouseXAndY)
  {
    var rotationX : float = transform.localEulerAngles.y + Input.
GetAxis("Mouse X") * sensitivityX;

    rotationY += Input.GetAxis("Mouse Y") * sensitivityY;
    rotationY = Mathf.Clamp (rotationY, minimumY, maximumY);

    transform.localEulerAngles = new Vector3(-rotationY, rotationX,
0);
  }
  else if (axes == RotationAxes.MouseX)
  {
    transform.Rotate(0, Input.GetAxis("Mouse X") * sensitivityX, 0);
  }
  else
  {
    rotationY += Input.GetAxis("Mouse Y") * sensitivityY;
    rotationY = Mathf.Clamp (rotationY, minimumY, maximumY);

    transform.localEulerAngles = new Vector3(-rotationY, transform.
localEulerAngles.y, 0);
  }
}
```

 This script is the JavaScript version of the MouseLook built-in script. This way we can edit and adapt the script without bothering anything in the built-in script. Even though, in Unity we can use both C# and JavaScript languages in the same project (we will talk about this in more detail in *Chapter 8, Let the World See your Carnage! Saving, Loading, and Posting your High Score*), it's better to pick one language for the entire project because it will be very difficult to access the parameters between different languages.

Then, we will go back to Unity and create a new script named `New3PSController` by going to **Assets | Create | Javascript**. Then, we will right-click it and choose **Sync MonoDevelop Project** (if you set **MonoDevelop** as the main editor) or just double-click it to open the script. It will open the new script in **MonoDevelop** (or your default editor **Unitron/UniScite**).

In **MonoDevelop**, at the top left in the **Solution** view, you will see the name of our project; click on the arrow in front of it. In the **Assets** folder, go to **Assets | Standard Assets | Character Controllers | Sources | Scripts**. Double-click the **FPSInputController** file to open it.

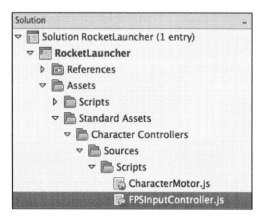

Next, we go to the `FPSInputController` file, copy the code in it to the `New3PSController` file that we just created. Then, we close the `FPSInputController` file, and go to the `New3PSController` file at the end of this script. We will see the following line of code:

```
@script AddComponentMenu ("Character/FPS Input Controller")
```

Change the preceding line of the script to the following one:

```
@script AddComponentMenu ("Character/New 3PS Controller")
```

We are changing the name of this script because we don't want to replace the built-in script with the new one. This script will be added to the **Component** menu, which we will see in the Unity Editor **Component | Character | New 3PS Controller**.

Engage Thrusters

Now we are ready to create our script. We will start by creating the new parameters that will be used to control our character:

1. Go to `New3PSController.js`, and set up the new parameters. Go to the first line of this script and type the following highlighted code:

```
//Character movement speed
public var runSpeed : int = 6;
public var walkSpeed : int = 2;
private var int_moveSpeed : int;
//Animation Params
public var _animation : Animation;
public var idleAnimation : AnimationClip;
public var walkAnimation : AnimationClip;
public var runAnimation : AnimationClip;
public var shotAnimation : AnimationClip;
public var walkAnimationSpeed : float = 1.5;
public var idleAnimationSpeed : float = 1.0;
public var runAnimationSpeed : float = 2.0;
public var shotAnimationSpeed : float = 0.5;
//Camera Rotation Limit
public var minRotateY : float = -15;
public var maxRotateY : float = 60;

//Mouse Look
private var mouseLook : MouseLook_JS;

//Character Motor
private var motor : CharacterMotor;
```

Here, we just set up the necessary parameters for controlling the animation of our character, as we did in the last chapter, and set the Y-axis camera limit rotation.

2. Next, we will add some code in the `Awake()` function. Go to the function and add the following highlighted code:

```
// Use this for initialization
public function Awake () : void {
  motor = GetComponent(CharacterMotor);
  //Hide cursor
  Screen.showCursor = false;
  //Setup the character move speed to walk speed
  int_moveSpeed = walkSpeed;

  //Get MouseLook component
```

```
    mouseLook = Camera.main.GetComponent(MouseLook_JS);

    //Setup Animation
    _animation[walkAnimation.name].speed = walkAnimationSpeed;
    _animation[walkAnimation.name].wrapMode = WrapMode.Loop;
    _animation[runAnimation.name].speed = runAnimationSpeed;
    _animation[runAnimation.name].wrapMode = WrapMode.Loop;
    _animation[idleAnimation.name].speed = idleAnimationSpeed;
    _animation[idleAnimation.name].wrapMode = WrapMode.Loop;
}
```

Here, we just add the code to hide the mouse cursor, set the character movement speed value equal to the walk speed, get the mouse look component, and set up the animation speed and warp mode.

3. Go to the `Update()` function and add the highlighted code after the `if (directionVector != Vector3.zero) {}` statement:

```
// Update is called once per frame
public function Update () : void {
    // Get the input vector from keyboard or analog stick
    var directionVector = new Vector3(Input.GetAxis("Horizontal"),
0, Input.GetAxis("Vertical"));

    if (directionVector != Vector3.zero) {
        ..............
    }

    if (Input.GetKey(KeyCode.E)) {
        //Set the maximum and minimum limit rotation on Y-axis for the
main camera
        mouseLook.minimumY = minRotateY;
        mouseLook.maximumY = maxRotateY;
            //No Movement Direction
        motor.inputMoveDirection = Vector3.zero;
    } else {
        //No Y-axis Rotation
        mouseLook.minimumY = 0;
        mouseLook.maximumY = 0;
            //Change the movement speed of the character
        if (Input.GetKey(KeyCode.LeftShift) || Input.GetKey(KeyCode.
RightShift)){
            int_moveSpeed = runSpeed;
        } else {
            int_moveSpeed = walkSpeed;
        }
```

```
    motor.movement.maxForwardSpeed = int_moveSpeed;
    motor.movement.maxSidewaysSpeed = int_moveSpeed;
    motor.movement.maxBackwardsSpeed = int_moveSpeed;
    ////////////////////////////////////////////////////
    //Checking if the character is moving or not
    if (directionVector != Vector3.zero) {
      if (int_moveSpeed == walkSpeed) {
        _animation.CrossFade(walkAnimation.name);
      } else {
        _animation.CrossFade(runAnimation.name);
      }
    } else {
      _animation.CrossFade(idleAnimation.name);
    }
    // Apply the direction to the CharacterMotor
    motor.inputMoveDirection = transform.rotation *
directionVector;
    motor.inputJump = Input.GetButton("Jump");
  }
}
```

In the preceding function, we have used `Input.GetKey(KeyCode.E)` for aiming and `Input.GetKey(KeyCode.LeftShift) || Input.GetKey(KeyCode.RightShift)` for running, which will get the input as the *E* key and right arrow/left arrow keys on the keyboard. However, this isn't flexible if we want to change the input or if we want to put this game on another platform that doesn't have a keyboard. We can solve this by setting the custom **Input** button via the **Input Manager** and using `Input.GetButton()` instead of `Input.GetKey()`, which is much more dynamic for adjusting the input controller for different platforms. We can go to the **Input Manager** (**Edit | Project Settings | Input**), which we have already mentioned in the first chapter.

4. Go back to Unity, click on the **First Person Controller** object in the **Hierarchy** view, go to its **Inspector** view, and right-click the **FPSInput Controller (Script)** and choose **Remove Component** to remove it. Then, we will go to the **Project** view and drag the `New3PSController` script that we just created to the **First Person Controller** object in the **Hierarchy** view.

5. Go to the **Inspector** view of **First Person Controller** object in the **New3PSController** component and set the following:

   - **Animation: robot** (`robot` game object in the **Hierarchy** view)
   - **Idle Animation: idle** (`Chapter5/Robot Artwork/robot@idle/idle`)
   - **Walk Animation: walk** (`Chapter5/Robot Artwork/robot@walk/walk`)
   - **Run Animation: run** (`Chapter5/Robot Artwork/robot@run/run`)

- ☐ **Shoot Animation**: **shoot** (`Chapter5/Robot Artwork/robot@idle/shoot`)

The **Idle**, **Walk**, **Run**, and **Shoot Animation** will be located in the **Project** view inside `robot@idle`, `robot@walk`, `robot@run`, and `robot@shoot` objects, as shown in the following screenshot:

6. Before we finish the section, we will add our `MouseLook_JS` script to the **First Person Controller** instead of the old `MouseLook`. So, click on the **First Person Controller** object in the **Hierarchy** view, go to its **Inspector** view. In the **Mouse Look (Script)** component, we will click on the circle icon at the right of **Script** and choose **MouseLook_JS**, as shown in the following screenshot:

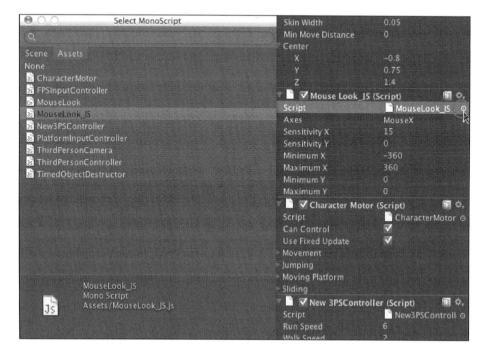

7. Then, go down one step and click on the **Main Camera** object in the **Hierarchy** view; go to its **Inspector** view. In the **Mouse Look (Script)** component, click on the circle icon at the right of **Script** and choose **MouseLook_JS** as we did earlier.

Now, click **Play** to see the result. You will be able to control your character's moves; run by holding the *Shift* key and jump by pressing the space bar. However, pressing the *E* key will stop our character's movements because we didn't set up the aiming and shoot animation in our script yet. We will do this in the next section.

Objective Complete - Mini Debriefing

We just created our `New3PSController.js` script by using the old built-in `FPSInputController.js` script as the base script. We also added the new code section to control the animation of the character while it is moving, running, or idle. Then, we limited the movement and rotation of the camera by applying the character movement direction to **Character Motor** and the **Main Camera**.

Then, in the `Update()` function, we added the new section of the code to control the animation of our character. At first, we check whether or not the user has pressed *E*:

▶ If the user presses it, we want the character to stop moving and play the shooting animation to prepare the character to be able to fire. We also set the maximum and minimum of the camera rotation on the Y-axis, which limits the camera to rotate up and down only. Then, we set the `motor.inputMoveDirection` to `Vector3.zero` because we don't want our character to move while he/she is executing the shooting action.

▶ On the other hand, if the user doesn't press *E*, we check for the user input. If the user presses the right arrow or left arrow, we change the speed to run speed; if not we set it to walk speed. Then, we applied the movement speed to `motor.movement.maxForwardSpeed`, `motor.movement.maxSidewaysSpeed`, and `motor.movement.maxBackwardsSpeed`.

Next, we checked the character movement direction to play the run animation, walk animation, or idle animation (we can also have the jump animation in here, but in this example we don't have the jump animation, so we just leave it).

At last, we applied the movement direction and jump to the character motor for the user to be able to control the movement of this character, and we are done with this step. In the next step, we will add the shoot animation and function, fire script, rocket launcher, and scope target to our character.

Classified Intel

In this step, we have access to the `Character Motor` and can change `MouseLook` script to `MouseLook_JS` script. If we take a look at the `Character Motor` script, we will see that it has a lot of parameters to adjust. In our case, we only pass the `inputMoveDirection`, `inputJump`, `movement.maxForwardSpeed`, `movement.maxSidewaysSpeed`, and `movement.maxBackwardsSpeed` parameters. We don't need to go to every parameter in the `Character Motor`, but there is something that we will need to know to be able to use it with our script. The `Character Motor` will help us to calculate the smooth movement speed including moving forward, backward, and sideways. It will calculate the gravity when the character is jumping and falling as well as check for the moving platform.

Next, we will take a look at the `MouseLook` script. If we open up this script, we will see that it is written in C#, but we need not worry as Unity allows us to access the parameters even though we are using JavaScript. As we know, we can use C# (and also Boo) scripting language to write the script in Unity similar to JavaScript. So, let's open the `MouseLook` and look inside—it's very similar to what we did for `MouseLook_JS` in JavaScript. However, there are numerous differences between writing JavaScript and C#, but we will talk about the basics of syntax.

Both of the preceding scripts do the same thing, but use different syntaxes. For example, if we want to create a `float` variable in JavaScript, we can use the following line of code:

```
public var myNumber : float = 0;
```

To create a function we can use the following line of code:

```
public function Myfuncion () : void { //dosomething }
```

On the other hand, if we are using C#, we can write the following line of code:

```
public float myNumber = 0F;
```

 We put the `F` here to tell the complier that it is a float value.

And for the function, we will use the following line of code:

```
public void Myfuncion () { //dosomething }
```

There is also some difference in syntax between both the languages. For more information, we can go to the following websites:

```
http://unity3d.com/support/documentation/ScriptReference/index.
Writing_Scripts_in_Csharp.html
```

```
http://answers.unity3d.com/questions/12911/what-are-the-syntax-
differences-in-c-and-javascrip.html.
```

We can also see the syntax for each language in the Unity scripting document, as shown in the following screenshot:

```
// Performs a mouse look.                                    JavaScript ▼
                                                            JavaScript
var horizontalSpeed : float = 2.0;                                C#
var verticalSpeed : float = 2.0;                                 Boo
function Update () {
    // Get the mouse delta. This is not in the range -1...1
    var h : float = horizontalSpeed * Input.GetAxis ("Mouse X");
    var v : float = verticalSpeed * Input.GetAxis ("Mouse Y");
    transform.Rotate (v, h, 0);
}
```

You can also buy the JavaScript to C# converter package or C# to Javascript converter package there.

Creating the rocket launcher and scope target

From the last section, we have the setup for the **Aiming** button to stop our character's movement as well as control the animation of our character by using crossFade(). In this section, we will add the aiming animation, shot animation, scope target UI, rocket launcher script, and rocket launcher object.

Engage Thrusters

We will start with creating a rocket launcher and adding the New3PSController script to it. Then, our character will be able to shoot the rocket:

1. Go to Unity editor, **GameObject | Create Empty**, and name the object RocketLauncher, and then we drag this object inside the **Main Camera** object in the **Hierarchy** view as shown in the following screenshot:

2. Then, go to the **Inspector** view of the `RocketLauncher` to set up the **Transform | Position, X: 0, Y: 0, Z: 2**. Next, we create the **GUITexture** for the scope target by going to **GameObject | Create Other | GUI Texture** and naming it `ScopeUI`. Go to its **Inspector** and set the following:

    ▸ **GUITexture**

        ❑ **Texture**: `scopeTarget.png` (`Chapter5/UI folder/ scopeTarget`)

        ❑ **Pixel Inset**

            ❑ **X: -16, Y: -16, Width: 32, Height: 32**

3. Create a new `RocketLauncher` script by going to **Assets | Create | Javascript** and name it `RocketLauncher`, double-click on it to open **MonoDevelop**. Then, go to the script and replace the code as follows:

```
public var speed : float = 10;
public var ammoCount : int = 20;

private var lastShot : float = 0.0;

public function Fire(_reloadTime : float) : void {
   if (Time.time > (_reloadTime + lastShot) && ammoCount > 0) {

      //Get the last shot time
      lastShot = Time.time;
      //Decrease the bullet
      ammoCount--;
   }
}

public function Reload () : void {
   ammoCount = 20;
}
```

    ❑ Here, we create the `Fire` and `Reload()` functions to trigger when the user presses *R* to reload the bullet or presses *E* to aim, which will be called from `New3PSController`.

4. Go back to Unity and go to the **Project** view and drag your `RocketLauncher` script to the `RocketLauncher` object in the **Hierarchy** view.

5. Go to the `New3PSController` script to add the highlighted code between the `maxRotateY` and `mouseLook` parameters (before the `Awake()` function), as shown next:

```
//Camera Rotation Limit
public var minRotateY : float = -15;
public var maxRotateY : float = 60;

//Scope UI
public var scopeUI : GUITexture;
//Rocket Launcher
public var rocketLauncher : RocketLauncher;
//Shot Params
private var b_isPrepare : boolean = false;
private var b_isShot : boolean = false;

//Mouse Look
private var mouseLook : MouseLook_JS;
//Character Motor
private var motor : CharacterMotor;
```

6. Then, go to the `Update()` function and add the code before and inside `if (Input.GetKey(KeyCode.E)) {` (after `if (directionVector != Vector3.zero) {` statement) as highlighted:

```
if (directionVector != Vector3.zero) {


}

//Reload the rocket bullet

if (Input.GetKey(KeyCode.R)) {
    BroadcastMessage("Reload");
}

if (Input.GetKey(KeyCode.E)) {
    //Show the Scope UI
    scopeUI.enabled = true;
    //Set the maximum and minimum limit rotation on Y-axis for the
main camera
    //Set the maximum and minimum limit rotation on Y-axis for the
main camera
    mouseLook.minimumY = minRotateY;
    mouseLook.maximumY = maxRotateY;

    //Checking if the character is playing the shot animation
```

```
            if (!b_isPrepare) {
              b_isShot = false;
              //Play the shot preparing animation function
              WaitForPrepare();
            } else {
              //If the player click fire play the shot animation again
              if ((Input.GetButton("Fire1")) && (!b_isShot)) {
                b_isShot = true;
                //Play the shot animation function
                WaitForShot();
              }
            }
            //No Movement Direction
            motor.inputMoveDirection = Vector3.zero;
          }
```

7. Go to the `else` section and add the highlighted code at the first line before `if (Camera.main.GetComponent(MouseLook))` `{`, as follows:

```
else {
      //Hide the Scope UI
      scopeUI.enabled = false;
      //Set the prepare animation to false
      b_isPrepare = false;

      //No Y-axis Rotation
    mouseLook.minimumY = 0;
    mouseLook.maximumY = 0;

      //Change the movement speed of the character
        if (Input.GetKey(KeyCode.LeftShift) || Input.GetKey(KeyCode.
RightShift)) {
```

8. We are now done with the adding part for the `Update()` function. We will need to add other two functions for the `WaitForPrepare()` and `WaitForShot()` functions. So, let's go to the `Update()` function before `@script RequireComponent (CharacterMotor)` line and add the following two functions:

```
private function WaitForShot () : IEnumerator {
  _animation[shotAnimation.name].speed = shotAnimationSpeed;
  _animation[shotAnimation.name].wrapMode = WrapMode.ClampForever;
  _animation.PlayQueued(shotAnimation.name, QueueMode.PlayNow);
  BroadcastMessage("Fire", shotAnimation.length); //Call Fire
function in attached scripts of this GameObject or any of its
children
```

```
    yield WaitForSeconds (shotAnimation.length);
    b_isShot = false;
}

private function WaitForPrepare () : IEnumerator {
    _animation[shotAnimation.name].speed = shotAnimationSpeed * 2;
    _animation[shotAnimation.name].wrapMode = WrapMode.ClampForever;
    _animation.CrossFade(shotAnimation.name, 0.6);

    yield WaitForSeconds(shotAnimation.length);
    b_isPrepare = true;
}
```

The preceding two functions are basically to play the aiming and shooting animation. Now, we are done with adding the `New3PSController` script.

9. Then, go back to Unity and click on the **First Person Controller** object in the **Hierarchy** view, and go to its **Inspector** view; at the **New 3PSController (Script)** drag both objects that we just created, as follows:

   ❑ **Scope UI: ScopeUI** (Drag **ScopeUI** object here)

   ❑ **Rocket Launcher: RocketLauncher** (Drag **RocketLauncher** object here)

We are done with this section. Click **Play** to see the result. Now, if you hold the *E* key, the scope target will appear and our character will start playing aiming animation. If we left-click on the mouse while holding the *E* key, the character will start playing the shot animation. However, there is no rocket coming out right now. We will create the rocket and the particle object in the next section.

Objective Complete - Mini Debriefing

In this step, we just added some code to our `New3PSController.js` for controlling the aiming and shot animation as well as created the rocket launcher object and script that will trigger when the user presses fire or aim. We also created the `GUITexture` object to show the scope target graphic, which will show when the player presses *E* to aim and hide when the player doesn't press *E*.

In the `Fire()` function, we added the rocket launcher object. We checked for the time that our rocket will be fired after the shot animation ended by checking for the reloaded time plus the last time that the character was shot. We also decreased the amount of bullet when the character clicks shot. In the next section, we will add the rocket prefab and the particle object in the `Fire()` function.

Classified Intel

If we take a look at `New3PSController.js`, we will see that we used the `BroadcastMessage("Reload");` and `BroadcastMessage("Fire", shotAnimation.length);`. Both of these functions basically call all the functions named `Reload` or `Fire`, in this game object or any of its children. This is a great way to make our script and object more organized.

> Performance wise, `BroadcastMessage()` is slower than a function call because it iterates through all possible target objects, finds matches of the desired function, and executes them. Therefore, it won't cause a huge increase in performance if we don't have a large number of function calls.

We can have different scripts attached to the children of this object and trigger at the same time. For example, `BroadcastMessage("Fire", shotAnimation.length)` will call the `Fire(var f:float)` function in each component attached to the object (irrespective of whether we're calling it on the **Component** or the **GameObject**). So, when the user hits fire, we will have the rocket shot at the same time with the smoke coming out from the launcher without having to code everything in one big script. We can see more details from the following links:

`http://unity3d.com/support/documentation/ScriptReference/Component.BroadcastMessage.html.`

`http://unity3d.com/support/documentation/ScriptReference/GameObject.BroadcastMessage.html.`

Next, we will take a look at the `waitForShot()` function, we will see that we use `_animation.PlayQueued(shotAnimation.name, QueueMode.PlayNow);` instead of the `CrossFade()` function. This is because we want to play the shot animation as soon as the player presses fire. The `PlayQueued()` function will help us to fade between the same animation smoothly. We can see further details of this function from the following website:

`http://unity3d.com/support/documentation/ScriptReference/Animation.PlayQueued.html.`

Creating the rockets and particles

In this section, we will continue creating the rocket prefab, which will shoot out from the launcher. We will also create the trail smoke the follows this rocket, the smoke from the launcher barrel, and the explosion when the rocket hits something.

Engage Thrusters

We will start with creating the **SmokePosition**, which is the position of the smoke particle when the character fires the rocket.

1. Go to the Unity editor to create the smoke position by going to **GameObject | Create Empty** to create an empty game object and name it **SmokePosition**, and drag it inside the **gun** object, which is a child of the **robot** object, as shown in the following screenshot. By doing this we will break the prefab again, so we just click on **continue** to break it.

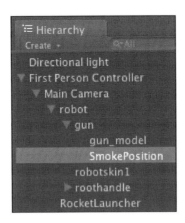

2. Then, we set **Transform** as follows:

   ❑ **Position**: **X: 1.5, Y: -0.08, Z: 0.25**

   ❑ **Rotation**: **X: 90, Y: 0, Z: 0**

   ❑ **Scale**: **X: 1, Y: 1, Z: 1**

   Now, we got the smoke position from the launcher barrel.

3. Next, create a `smoke` prefab object by going to the **Project** view, and click on the folder in this order: **Standard Assets | Particles | Smoke**, we will see `Fluffy Smoke` prefab, drag it to the **Hierarchy** view. Then, we will go to its **Inspector** view and start changing the parameters as follows:

   ❑ **Ellispsoid Particle Emitter**:

   ❑ **Min Size: 0.5**

   ❑ **Max Size: 0.75**

   ❑ **Min Energy: 0.75**

   ❑ **Max Energy: 1.5**

   ❑ **Min Emission: 8**

- ❑ **Max Emission**: 12
- ❑ **Local Velocity**: X: 0, Y: 0.75, Z: 0
- ❑ **Rnd Velocity**: X: 0, Y: 0, Z: 0
- ❑ **Ellispsoid**: X: 0.1, Y: 0, Z: 0.1
- ❑ **Particle Animator**:
- ❑ **Color Animation[0]**: R: 162, G: 162, B: 162, A: 0
- ❑ **Color Animation[1]**: R: 147, G: 147, B: 147, A: 199
- ❑ **Color Animation[2]**: R: 114, G: 114, B: 114, A: 143
- ❑ **Color Animation[3]**: R: 126, G: 126, B: 126, A: 87
- ❑ **Color Animation[4]**: R: 59, G: 59, B: 59, A: 0
- ❑ **Size Grow**: -0.1
- ❑ **Rnd Force**: X: 0, Y: 0, Z: 0

4. Create the Smoke script by going to **Assets | Create | Javascript** and name it Smoke. Then, we go to the script and type the following code:

```
public var timeOut : float = 0.5; // Destroy after 0.5 seconds.

// Use this for initialization
public function Start () : void {
   Invoke("KillObject", timeOut);
}

public function KillObject () : void {
   //Stop the emit the particle
   var emitter : ParticleEmitter = GetComponentInChildren(ParticleE
mitter);
   if (emitter != null) {
     emitter.emit = false; // Stop Emit
   }

   //In here We set the particle to auto destruct to destroy itself
after a life time (or we can setup it up in the editor)
   var particleAnimator : ParticleAnimator = GetComponentInChildren
(ParticleAnimator);
   if (particleAnimator != null) {
     particleAnimator.autodestruct = true;
   }
}
```

This `Smoke` script will be added to the `Fluffy Smoke` object that we just created. In this function, we use the `Invoke()` function, which will tell the script to call the `KillObject()` function after the `timeout` (0.5 seconds).

5. Next, we will drag our `Smoke` script which we created to this `Fluffy Smoke` object (this will break the prefab again, so click on **continue** to break the prefab).

6. Now, create a new prefab for our new `Fluffy Smoke` object by going to **Assets | Create | Prefab** and name it `ShotSmoke`. Then, drag the `Fluffy Smoke` object in the **Hierarchy** view to the `ShotSmoke` prefab in the **Project** view. Finally, we remove the `Fluffy Smoke` object in the **Hierarchy** view by right-clicking on the `Fluffy Smoke` object in the **Hierarchy** view and choosing **Delete**; now we have the new `ShotSmoke` prefab.

7. Create the rocket prefab by dragging the **rocket (FBX)** model in the **Project** view, inside (**Chapter5/Rocket**) to the **Hierarchy** view.

8. Click on the `rocket` model and go to its **Inspector** view to remove the **Animation** by right-clicking and choosing **Remove Component**. (This will bring up the losing prefab pop-up, so we just click **Continue** to break the prefab.)

In Unity, every imported FBX model will have the **Animation** component attached to itself automatically, but for our rocket, we don't need to use the **Animation** component, so we removed it from our model.

9. We will now create the `Rocket` script, so go to **Assets | Create | Javascript** and name it `Rocket`; double-click on it to open **MonoDevelop**. Then, go to the script and replace the code as follows:

```
@script RequireComponent(ConstantForce)

public var timeOut : float = 3.0; // Destroy after 3.0 seconds.
public var explosionParticle : GameObject;


// Use this for initialization
public function Start () : void {
  Invoke("KillObject", timeOut);
}

public function OnCollisionEnter (others : Collision) : void {
  //Create the explosion on the first impact point of the rocket
and collider
  var contactPoint : ContactPoint = others.contacts[0];
```

```
   var rotation : Quaternion = Quaternion.FromToRotation(Vector3.
up, contactPoint.normal);
   GameObject.Instantiate(explosionParticle, contactPoint.point,
rotation);

   KillObject();
}

public function KillObject () : void {
   //Stop the emit the particle
   var emitter : ParticleEmitter = GetComponentInChildren(ParticleE
mitter);
   if (emitter != null) {
      emitter.emit = false; // Stop Emit
   }

   //In here We set the particle to auto destruct to destroy itself
after a life time (or we can setup it in the editor)
   var particleAnimator : ParticleAnimator = GetComponentInChildren
(ParticleAnimator);
   if (particleAnimator != null) {
      particleAnimator.autodestruct = true;
   }

   //Detach the trail renderer in our particles
   transform.DetachChildren();

   //Destroy this Object
   GameObject.Destroy(gameObject);
}
```

10. Next, add the `Rocket` script that we created by dragging the script to the `rocket` object in the **Hierarchy**.

11. Then, go to the object's **Inspector** view to add the **Box Collider** to the `rocket` object by going to **Component | Physics | Box Collider**.

 When we add the **Box Collider** to the new object, the **Box Collider** will automatically adjust its size to fit around the object. This is why we don't have to set up the size or the position of the **Box Collider**.

12. Then, we go to the **Inspector** view and set the following:

    ❑ **Transform**

    ❑ **Position: X: 0, Y: 0, Z: 0**

- ❑ **Rigidbody**
- ❑ **Use Gravity**: Uncheck (We don't need the gravity for our rocket)
- ❑ **Rocket (Script)**
- ❑ **Explosion Particle**: **explosion** (Drag the explosion built-in prefab in the **Standard Assets | Particles | Legacy Particles | explosion**)

13. Next, we will add the built-in `Smoke Trail` prefab as a child of this `rocket` object. Go to the **Project** view, and click on **Standard Assets | Particles | Smoke** and drag the `Smoke Trail` prefab to the `rocket` object in the **Hierarchy** view.

14. Then, we will click on the `Smoke Trail` object in the **Hierarchy** view and set the following in its **Inspector** view:

   - ❑ **Transform: X:0, Y: 0, Z: -0.25**
   - ❑ **Ellispsoid Particle Emitter**:
   - ❑ **Min Size: 0.25**
   - ❑ **Max Size: 0.65**
   - ❑ **Min Energy: 0.75**
   - ❑ **Max Energy: 1**
   - ❑ **Particle Animator**
   - ❑ **Size Grow: 0.5**

15. Next, we will create a new prefab for our `rocket` object. Go to **Assets | Create | Prefab** and name it `Rocket`, and then drag our `rocket` object in the **Hierarchy** view to `Rocket` prefab, which we just created in the **Project** view. Finally, we remove the `rocket` object from the **Hierarchy** view by deleting it, and now we have the new `Rocket` prefab.

16. Go back to the `RocketLauncher` script by going to the **Project** view, double-click on the `RocketLauncher` script to go to **MonoDevelop**, and add the following new script at the beginning:

```
public var smoke : GameObject;
public var smokePosition : Transform;
public var rocket : ConstantForce;
public var speed : float = 10;
public var ammoCount : int = 20;

private var lastShot : float = 0.0;
```

17. Go to the `Fire()` function and add the following highlighted code:

```
public function Fire(_reloadTime : float) : void {
   if (Time.time > (_reloadTime + lastShot) && ammoCount > 0) {
```

```
    var rocketPrefab : ConstantForce = ConstantForce.
Instantiate(rocket, transform.position, transform.rotation);
    rocketPrefab.relativeForce = new Vector3(0, 0, speed);

    var smoke : GameObject = GameObject.Instantiate(smoke,
smokePosition.position, smokePosition.rotation);

    //We ignore the collision between rocket and character
    Physics.IgnoreCollision(rocketPrefab.collider, transform.root.
collider);

    //Get the last shot time
    lastShot = Time.time;
    //Decrease the bullet
    ammoCount--;
  }
}
```

18. Go back to Unity and click on the `First Person Controller` object in the **Hierarchy** view. Then, go down two more steps inside this object until we see the `RocketLauncher` object, as shown in the following screenshot:

19. Click on the `RocketLauncher` object to bring up its **Inspector** view. Then set the following:

   ❑ **Rocket Launcher (Script)**

   ❑ **Smoke: ShotSmoke** (Drag the **ShotSmoke** prefab that we created in the **Project** view here)

   ❑ **Smoke Position: Smoke Position** (Drag the **SmokePosition** object inside the **gun** child in the **Hierarchy** here)

   ❑ **Rocket: Rocket** (drag the **Rocket** prefab that we created in the **Project** view here)

Now, we can click **Play** to see the result. We should be able to walk around by pressing the arrow, *W, A, S, D,* or *Space* key to jump, move the mouse to rotate around, press *E* to aim, press *R* to reload the rocket, and click on the left mouse button to fire the rocket. However, we won't be able to see the number of bullets right now, because we don't have any UI set up to show the number yet. So, in the next step, we will create a bullet count UI by using **GUITexture** and `OnGUI()`.

Objective Complete - Mini Debriefing

In this section, we just created the rocket and particle effect that will appear when the player presses fire. It seems like a lot to do in one section, but it was worth it.

First, in the `Rocket` script, we used `@script RequireComponent(ConstantForce)` to tell the script to require the **ConstantForce** for this rocket; this will tell Unity to basically add the **ConstantForce** automatically when we add this script to the object.

 ConstantForce is one of the **Physics** components in Unity that will add a constant force to the **RigidBody** object (the **ConstantForce** works with the **RigidBody** components, so when we add the **ConstantForce** to our object, Unity will automatically add the **RigidBody** as well), which will contain the properties that we can use to control the rocket movement. For more details please have a look at the following website:

http://unity3d.com/support/documentation/Components/
class-ConstantForce.html.

Next, we have the `timeout` and `explosion` parameters. We then have the `Invoke()` function calling the `KillObject()` function after the `timeout` (3.0 seconds). Then, we check for the collision object—if the rocket hits something, it will get to the position where the collision occurs, add the explosion object to that position, and then the rocket object will kill itself.

The `KillObject()` function basically stops the particle emitter, makes sure that the particle will destroy itself by setting the `autodestruct` parameter to `true`, detaches the particle, and destroys the game object itself.

Now, we create the script for the rocket and smoke particle. Then, we use the built-in particle package and adapt to the way we want for smoke and smoke trial. Finally, we put everything together and get the result as expected.

Classified Intel

In this section, we used the `Instantiate()` function to clone a new game object from the **prefab** object in the **Project** view. The `Instantiate()` function takes three parameters, which are the original **Object, Position (Vector3)**, and **Rotation (Quaternion)**. The **Position** and **Rotation** objects are the transform parameters at the start position of the object, which will be created in the scene. The `Instantiate()` function can take any kind of object and the result can also be returned to any kind of objects. We can also see more examples and details from the Unity document at:

```
http://unity3d.com/support/documentation/ScriptReference/Object.
Instantiate.html
```

```
http://unity3d.com/support/documentation/Manual/Instantiating%20
Prefabs.html.
```

Next, we will talk about the `Invoke()` function, which we used to call the function after the time we have set in seconds. If some of you have experience with **Actionscript**, this function is very similar to the `setTimeOut()` function. We can also use `InvokeRepeating()` to call the method similar to the `Invoke()` function, but this function will repeat calling that function every time we set in seconds. We can see more details about the `Invoke()` function from the Unity document at:

```
http://unity3d.com/support/documentation/ScriptReference/
MonoBehaviour.Invoke.html.
```

For the `InvokeRepeating()` function, refer to the following website:

```
http://unity3d.com/support/documentation/ScriptReference/
MonoBehaviour.InvokeRepeating.html.
```

Finally, let's talk about the position of the rocket that launches from the same position of the scope target UI. This is a bit tricky because we want the player to be able to aim and shoot the rocket exactly to the same position that he/she is aiming at. So, we add the `RocketLauncher` object as a child of the `Main Camera` because we want it to move or rotate with the user view, which is the `Main Camera`. Then, we add the scope target UI at the center of the screen because it is easier for the player to aim than than if we put it on one side. So, we set up the positions X and Y of `RocketLauncher` object to 0 because it is the same position to the `Main Camera` and if we get the position of the `Main Camera` to the screen position it will be the center of the screen. Then, we set up the Z position of `RocketLauncher` object to 2 because it is the same depth as our character weapon graphics. This is to make the rocket not too close to the camera. We can also see it from the following diagram:

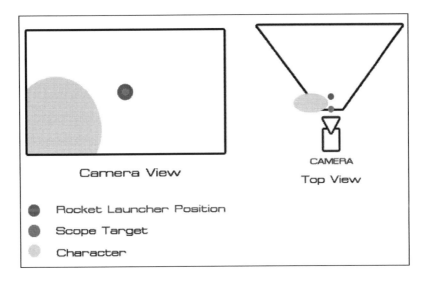

Camera View

CAMERA
Top View

● Rocket Launcher Position
● Scope Target
● Character

Creating the rocket bullet UI

Here we are at the last section of this chapter. As we know from the last step, we need a way to show the number of rockets left on the screen. In this step, we will create the rocket UI, which will show the number of rockets left and the rocket graphics. We will use both **GUITexture** and `OnGUI()` to create the UI.

Engage Thrusters

This is the last section, which will create the `RocketUI` script to display the remaining rocket bullets on the screen:

1. Go to **Assets | Create | Javascript** and name it `RocketUI`. Then, double-click on it to open **MonoDevelop** and replace the script as follows:

```
public var rocketLauncher : RocketLauncher;
public var customSkin : GUISkin;
public var width : float = 80;
public var height : float = 25;
public var pixelShift : int = 2;

public function OnGUI() : void {
  GUI.skin = customSkin;
  DrawShadowText(new Rect(Screen.width*transform.position.x,
(Screen.height*(1.0 - (transform.position.y - 0.005))), width,
height), rocketLauncher.ammoCount.ToString(), customSkin.
GetStyle("RocketText"), Color.white);
```

```
    }

    //Draw a 45 degree black shadow text by shifting 2 pixel bottom-
    right
    public function DrawShadowText (position : Rect, text : String,
    style : GUIStyle, textColor : Color) : void {
      var backupStyle : GUIStyle = style;
      //Draw a Shadow Text
      style.normal.textColor = Color.black;
      //Shift 2 pixel left and 2 pixel bottom
      position.x += pixelShift;
      position.y += pixelShift;
      GUI.Label(position, text, style);
      ///////////////////////////////////////////////
      //Draw a Text
      style.normal.textColor = textColor;
      //Shift pixel back
      position.x -= pixelShift;
      position.y -= pixelShift;
      GUI.Label(position, text, style);
      style = backupStyle; // Set style back
    }
```

2. Now, go back to Unity editor. Create the new **GUISkin** by going to **Assets | Create | GUI Skin** and name it **CustomSkin**; then click to bring up its **Inspector** view and set the following:

   ▸ **Font: Federation** (Drag the **Federation** font in `Chapter5/Fonts` folder here)

   ▸ **Custom Styles**

   ▸ **Size: 1**

   ▸ **Element 0**:

      ❑ **Name: RocketText**

      ❑ **Normal**

         ❑ **Text Color: R: 255, G: 255, B: 255, A: 255**

      ❑ **Font: Federation**

      ❑ **Font Size: 20**

      ❑ **Font Style: Bold**

   Other than the parameters mentioned earlier, we will leave everything as default.

3. Next, create the new `GUITexture` object by going to **GameObject | Create Other | GUI Texture** and name it as `RocketUI`. Next, we drag our `RocketUI` script, which we just created on this object. Then set the following:

   ❑ **Transform: Position**: **X: 0.91, Y: 0.08, Z: 0**

   ❑ **GUITexture**:

   ❑ **Texture: rocketUI** (Drag the `rocketUI.png` in the `Chapter5/UI` folder from the **Project** view here)

   ❑ **Pixel Inset: X: -64, Y: -32, Width: 128, Height:** 64

   ❑ **Rocket UI (Script)**

   ❑ **Rocket Launcher: RocketLauncher** (Drag **RocketLauncher** child of the **First Person Controller** here)

   ❑ **Custom Skin: CustomSkin** (Drag the **CustomSkin** that we just created in the **Project** view here)

We are now done with this chapter. We can click **Play** to see the result, and now if we press the *R* key to reload the bullet, we will see the number changes to 20 as we set the maximum number of bullets.

Objective Complete - Mini Debriefing

We just created the UI to show the rocket graphics UI and the number of bullets left by using **GUITexture** and `OnGUI()`. Here, we also created the text with a shadow by drawing another text layer and shifting the position bottom-right 2 pixels each, and then we drew the top layer by using the default position and color.

Classified Intel

In Unity, there is no easy way to create an outline or shadow for the dynamic text that can be easily adjustable like other software such as Flash, Photoshop, and so on. So we can create it by drawing another layer to act as the outline of the shadow, as we did for the onGUI() function in this chapter.

This is not the best way to create the outlined text or the shadow text because if we adjust the size of the pixel by shifting more than 2 pixels, we will see that the background text shifts too much and doesn't look like the outline or shadow, as we can see in the following screenshot:

In this section, we can just use this technique to create the shadow or outlined text because it is a quick way to create the outline or shadow for the dynamics text.

 To create the outlined text, we just create four text labels and shift each corner, top-left, top-right, bottom-left, bottom-right like we did for creating the shadow, and then create the last text labels on the top layer.

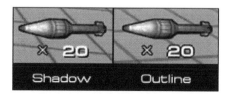

Game over-Wrapping it up

In this chapter, we have created the Resident Evil camera game style by adapting the built-in `First Person Controller`. We have also learned how to set up the FPS Character Controller, created the `New3PSController` script to control the character animation, created a rocket launcher, created the rocket prefab, and used the built-in particle to create the smoke from the launcher barrel, smoke trial from the rocket, and the explosion.

Next, we also learned how to use the `Instantiate()` function to clone the game object and display it in the scene. Then, we use `Invoke()` to call the function after the time that we assigned. Lastly, we created the UI to track the number of rockets left by using **GUITexture** and the `OnGUI()` function.

So, let's take a look at the following screenshot of what we have done so far:

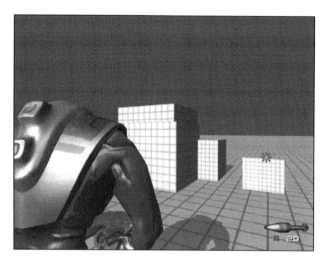

The preceding screenshot shows the camera view of the character.

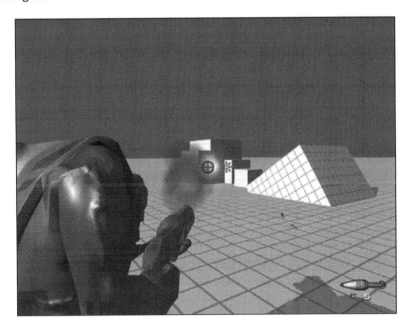

The preceding screenshot shows the character shooting.

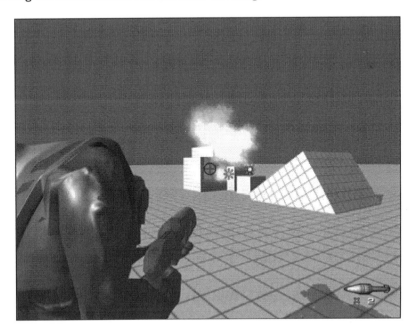

The preceding screenshot shows the rocket hitting the obstacle.

Are you ready to go gung ho? A Hotshot challenge

Now, we know how to create the First Person Controller, the rocket launcher weapon using particles, and the shadow text by using the `OnGUI()` function. Let's make this project more fun by:

- Including your own character or even your own type of weapon
- Adjusting the particle, or using a different particle effect to create the smoke effect or explosion
- Adding the ability to change the type of rocket or bullet; you can even have a different type of rocket that is slower or faster than the one in this chapter or even add gravity to it and make it as a grenade launcher
- Adding sound for each action
- Adding physics and explosions to our rocket when the rocket hits something
- Creating the dynamics outline text by using the `OnGUI()` function and the technique we used for the dynamics shadow text.

Project 6
Create Smart AI

Creating AI can be the most difficult and complex task in the development of a game because we have to calculate every possible way to make it as smart as a human brain. Most games need the AI for the enemy to be able to react to the player. The AI will run towards and attack the player, or when the player hits the wall, he or she will jump or walk avoiding the obstacles, and so on.

However, we have to be careful with the balance between making the AI smart and the performance speed to get the best moves. To get the best moves means more calculation, so it might cause a problem with performance slowing down.

We can use A* Algorithm for the pathfinder or Minimax Algorithm to calculate the best move, but these algorithms are very complex for a beginner.

A* Algorithm or **A Star Algorithm** is a computer algorithm that is widely used in path finding and graph traversal nodes. Noted for its performance and accuracy, it enjoys widespread use. Peter Hart, Nils Nilsson, and Bertram Raphael first described the algorithm in 1968. It is an extension of Edsger Dijkstra's 1959 algorithm. Reference from:

http://en.wikipedia.org/wiki/A*_search_algorithm.

Minimax Algorithm is a decision rule used in decision theory, game theory, statistics, and philosophy for minimizing the possible loss while maximizing the potential gain. Alternatively, it can be thought of as maximizing the minimum gain (maximin). Originally formulated for two-player zero-sum game theory, covering both the cases where players take alternate moves and those where they make simultaneous moves, it has also been extended to more complex games and to general decision making in the presence of uncertainty. Reference from:

http://en.wikipedia.org/wiki/Minimax.

The AI code is a lot to cover, and can be written in a whole new book, but we will learn how to create a simple and easy way to make our AI look smart by using a simple method like the random function instead of using search algorithm to get the possible move for the enemies. It might not make our AI as smart as using those algorithms, but we will get the basic idea of how to create the smart AI.

In this chapter, we will continue from *Project 5, Creating a Rocket Launcher*, reuse the code assets from the last chapter to implement the AI enemy. We will be creating an enemy by implementing the simple AI but smart enough to detect when to jump, run, walk, stop, or shoot at the player by creating the waypoint for the enemy to walk to each point, run towards the player then shoot when the player gets closer, and jump when it detects the wall.

Mission briefing

We will be creating an enemy that responds to our character. This enemy will be able to walk from one point to another and check to see if the player is in shooting range, and he can then shoot or run towards the player.

Finally, we will add the hit point bar to the player character and AI character as well as the damage cost for the character weapon, which is the rocket from the last chapter.

What does it do?

We will start by adapting the old scripts from *Project 5, Creating a Rocket Launcher*, which are New3PSController, RocketLauncher, and Rocket to be able to apply the hit damage to the player or enemy.

Then, we will create the AIController script to control the enemy by adapting the CharacterControl script from *Project 4, The Hero/Heroine Part II – Animation and Controls*. In the CharacterControl script, we will use the Physics class to check if there are any walls in front of the direction in which the enemy is moving, so that it jumps over it.

Next, we will create the Waypoint script, which will control the AI moving towards each waypoint position randomly or in an order. The Waypoint script will also use the OnDrawGizmos() function, which will allow us to see the wireframe, ray cast line, icons, and the area while we are playing in the game or editing in the editor. This is very powerful for debugging.

In the last section, we will add the hit point bar for our character and the enemy to show how much is the damage caused when we are attacked by the enemy or when we shoot at the enemy.

Why Is It Awesome?

When we complete this chapter, we will be able to create the simple AI behavior, which is smart enough to detect the player and response to the player's reaction. From this chapter, we begin to create a smart AI for any kind of game. Most of the methods or equations in this chapter are very straightforward and easy enough to create a simple AI, and can be developed to make the AI smarter.

Your Hotshot Objectives

We will use the `New3PSController` script from the last chapter for our character and the rocket launcher. For the enemy, we will adapt the `CharacterControl` script from *Project 4, The Hero/Heroine Part II – Animation and Controls*, to control the AI movement and behavior by implementing the new waypoint system to limit the movable area of our enemy. Then, we will create the hit point UI for both player and enemy, as well as the **Restart** button when either one dies. Here are the steps that we will go through in this chapter:

- ▶ Creating the waypoint and gizmos
- ▶ Creating an AI enemy
- ▶ Creating the enemy movement with `AIController` script
- ▶ Creating a hit-point UI

Mission Checklist

First, we need the project created in *Project 5, Creating a Rocket Launcher*, and assets for this chapter . We can start a new project by going to the URL `http://www.packtpub.com/support?nid=8267` and downloading the `Chapter 6` package. The package will contain all resources from *Project 5, Creating a Rocket Launcher*, and some new assets for this chapter.

Then, we run the Unity editor, create a new project, and name it as AI. Next, we import the Chapter6.unitypackage to our project as we did in the last chapter by going to **Assets | Import Package | Custom Package...**, choose Chapter6.unityPackage, which we just downloaded, and then click on the **Import** button on the pop-up window link, as shown in the following screenshot:

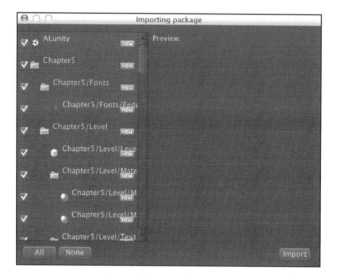

In the **Project** view, we will see the **AI** scene, **Chapter5** folder, **Chapter6** folder, **CustomSkin GUISkin**, **Prefabs** folder, **Scripts** folder, and the **Standard Assets** folder. The **Chapter5** folder will contain the entire Chapter 5 assets. The **Chapter6** folder will contain the Chapter 6 assets. The **Prefabs** folder will contain the Rocket prefabs and ShotSmoke prefab, and the **Scripts** folder will contain all the scripts we used in the last chapter.

Then, we need to double-click the **AI** scene to open the scene from the last chapter, as shown in the following screenshot:

Creating the waypoint and gizmos

In the first section, we will create the `waypoint` script to place the waypoint for our AI movement direction, which can be edited in the editor. We will also learn how to use the `OnDrawGizmos()` function, which we have used in *Project 1, Creating a Sprite and Platform Game*.

In this chapter, we will add the functions below the `OnDrawGizmos()` function to show the visual for our waypoint.

We use the `Gizmos.DrawIcon()` function to draw the icon image, see the direction line between two waypoints by using the `Gizmos.Draw Line()` function, to draw the line between two waypoints, and show the visual of the waypoint by using the `Gizmos.DrawWireSphere()` function to draw the wire sphere at the position of the waypoint.

Prepare for Lift Off

First, we need to drag-and-drop the **Gizmos** folder, which is located outside the **Chapter6** folder, as shown in the following screenshot:

Why did we move the folder outside the `Chapter6` folder?

Take a look at this: `http://unity3d.com/support/documentation/ScriptReference/Gizmos.DrawIcon.html`.

We see that the function takes two parameters: the first is the position of the object to draw the icon, and the second is the name of the icon image, which is `string`. The documentation says:

> *"The icon's path can be found in the* `Assets/Gizmos` *folder or in the* `Unity.app/Contents/Resources` *folder."*

This simply means that if we want to have our custom icon image, we basically need to put our image inside either of the folders mentioned earlier. Both the paths have advantages and disadvantages. If we want to use the image icon for every project in the same machine, we can put it inside the `Unity.app/Contents/Resources` folder, but this will be difficult when we want to move the project to another person. On the other hand, if we want to use only the icon image in this project, we can create a `Gizmos` folder in the **Project** view and put the icon image inside that folder, which we just did.

Engage Thrusters

Now we are ready to start the first section:

1. Create a new JavaScript file (we can add it to our `Scripts` folder to make it more organized) by going to **Assets | Create | Javascript**, and name it `Waypoints`.

2. Double-click to open it in **MonoDevelop** and start creating the necessary parameters for this waypoint script. Let's replace the script as follows:

```
//Name of the icon image
public var iconName : String = "wayIcon.psd";
//Radius of each way point - use for checking the collision
detection with the enemy
public var radius : float = 1.0;
//Toggle this to make the enemy move by order from the first index
to last index (Looping)
public var orderDirection : boolean = false;

//Get all the transform of the waypoint - including the the parent
private var waypoints : Transform[];
//Current waypoint index
private var int_wayIndex : int;
//Next waypoint index
private var int_nextIndex : int;
//Length of all waypoints
private var int_wayLength : int;
//Movement direction of the enemy to next waypoint
private var v3_direction : Vector3;
//Checking if the enemy hit the waypoint
private var b_isHitRadius : boolean;
Here, we just finished implementing the necessary parameters to
use for our waypoint.
```

3. Next, we will add the `Awake()` function to set up all the necessary parameters before calling the `Start()` function by adding the following code:

> The `Awake()` function is used to initialize all the variables before the game starts or before calling the `Start()` function. You can check out the following Unity scripting document for more details:
> `http://unity3d.com/support/documentation/ScriptReference/MonoBehaviour.Awake.html`.

```
//Set up all parameters before Initialize
public function Awake() : void {
   //Get all Transforms of the gameObject include the children and
the transform of this gameObject
   waypoints = gameObject.GetComponentsInChildren.<Transform>();
   //Set up the length of all transform
   int_wayLength = waypoints.Length;
   int_wayIndex = 0;
   int_nextIndex = 1;
   //Checking the orderDirection; if it's false, it means the AI
isn't moving by order, so using the random index of waypoint
   if(orderDirection == false) {
      var int_randomWay : int = Mathf.Floor(Random.value * int_
wayLength);
      //Checking to make sure that the waypoint length is more than
1
      if (int_wayLength > 1) {
         //Use Random Index
         while (int_wayIndex == int_randomWay) {
            int_randomWay = Mathf.Floor(Random.value * int_wayLength);
         }
      }
      int_nextIndex = int_randomWay;
   }
   //Set the direction to zero
   v3_direction = Vector3.zero;
   //To ignore the first waypoint at the beginning of the game
   b_isHitRadius = true;
}
```

In this function, we get the transform of each waypoint in the `gameObject` and all the children included in this `gameObject` by using the `gameObject.GetCompon entsInChildren.<Transform>()` to return the array of the `Transform` type object. Then, we set the length of this array, the start index, and next index of the waypoint. We also check to see if `orderDirection` is `false`, in which case the next index waypoint will be orderly picked. On the other hand, if it is `true`, the next index waypoint will be randomly picked.

4. Next, we add the function to set up the position of the enemy at the start position of the waypoint, which we will call from the `Start()` function of our `AIController` script in the next step. Add the following code:

```
public function StartPosition() : Vector3 {
  return waypoints[0].position;
}
```

This way, we can make sure that the enemy will always start at the waypoint index 0.

5. Then, we will create the core of this function, which will calculate and return the direction of the current position character to the waypoint position. Type the following code:

```
//Return the direction of the enemy toward the next waypoint
public function GetDirection( _AI : Transform ) : Vector3 {
  if (Vector3.Distance(_AI.position, waypoints[int_nextIndex].
position) <= radius) {
    //Only check once when the AI hit the way point
    if (!b_isHitRadius) {
      b_isHitRadius = true;
      //Update the current way index
      int_wayIndex = int_nextIndex;
      //Get Direction by order
      if (orderDirection == true) {
        //Get the next way index
        int_nextIndex = (int_nextIndex + 1) % int_wayLength;
      } else {
        var int_randomWay : int = Mathf.Floor(Random.value *
int_wayLength);
        //Checking to make sure that the waypoint length is more
than 1
        if (int_wayLength > 1) {
          //Use Random Index
          while (int_wayIndex == int_randomWay) {
            int_randomWay = Mathf.Floor(Random.value * int_
wayLength);
          }
        }
        int_nextIndex = int_randomWay;
      }
    }
  } else {
    b_isHitRadius = false;
  }
```

```
    //Get Direction from the current position of the character to
the next way point
    //Make sure that the y position equal to the waypoint y position
    var v3_currentPosition : Vector3 = new Vector3(_AI.position.x,
waypoints[int_nextIndex].position.y, _AI.position.z);
    v3_direction = (waypoints[int_nextIndex].position - v3_
currentPosition).normalized;

    return v3_direction;
}
```

6. Next, we will add two more functions to check the direction from the enemy to the player, and check to see whether the enemy is away from the target waypoint at a specific distance or not. Both of these functions will give the enemy more characteristics. Let's type both the functions as follows:

```
//To get the direction from current position of the enemy to the
player
public function GetDirectionToPlayer ( _AI : Transform, _player :
Transform ) : Vector3 {
    //Make sure that the y position equal to the waypoint y position
    var v3_currentPosition : Vector3 = new Vector3(_AI.position.x,
waypoints[int_wayIndex].position.y, _AI.position.z);
    var v3_playerPosition : Vector3 = new Vector3(_player.
position.x, waypoints[int_wayIndex].position.y, _player.
position.z);
    v3_direction = (v3_playerPosition - v3_currentPosition).
normalized;

    return v3_direction;

}

//Checking if the enemy is away from the target waypoint in the
specific distance or not
public function AwayFromWaypoint (_AI : Transform, _distance :
float) : boolean {
    if (Vector3.Distance(_AI.position, waypoints[int_nextIndex].
position) >= _distance) {
        return true;
    } else {
        return false;
    }
}
```

7. The last function of this script is the `OnDrawGizmos()` function, which will only be used in the editor or debugging process. We will use this function to draw the icon image, the radius, and the line direction between each waypoint. Let's add it as follows:

```
//Draw Gizmos and Directional line
public function OnDrawGizmos() : void {
  //Get all Transform of this game objects include the children
and the transform of this gameobject
  var waypointGizmos : Transform[] = gameObject.GetComponentsInChi
ldren.<Transform>();
  if (waypointGizmos != null) {
    if (orderDirection == true) {
      //Draw line by the order of each waypoint 0,1,2,3,...
      for (var i : int = 0; i < waypointGizmos.Length; i++) {
        Gizmos.color = Color.red;
        //Get the next way point
        var n : int = (i + 1) % waypointGizmos.Length;
        Gizmos.DrawLine(waypointGizmos[i].position,
waypointGizmos[n].position);
        Gizmos.DrawIcon(waypointGizmos[i].position, iconName);
        Gizmos.color = Color.green;
        Gizmos.DrawWireSphere(waypointGizmos[i].position, radius);
      }
    } else {
      //Draw line from one point to every points except itself
      for (var j : int = 0; j < waypointGizmos.Length; j++) {
        for (var k : int = j; k < waypointGizmos.Length; k++) {
          Gizmos.color = Color.red;
          Gizmos.DrawLine(waypointGizmos[j].position,
waypointGizmos[k].position);
        }
        Gizmos.DrawIcon(waypointGizmos[j].position, iconName);
        Gizmos.color = Color.green;
        Gizmos.DrawWireSphere(waypointGizmos[j].position, radius);
      }
    }
  }
}
```

We use `Gizmos.DrawLine()` to draw the line between each waypoint, and `Gizmos.DrawIcon()` to draw the icon image for each waypoint game object in the scene to make it easier to edit. Then, we use `Gizmos.DrawWireSphere()` to draw and calculate the area of each waypoint related to the `radius`.

Now, we are done with the `Waypoints` script. Go back to Unity editor to create the waypoint game object by going to **GameObject | Create Empty** to create the empty game object and name it `Waypoints`. Then, drag the `Waypoints` script (that we just created) to this `Waypoints` game object, and set its **Transform | Position** to **X: 0, Y: 0, Z: 0, Rotation X:0, Y: 0, Z: 0, Scale X: 1, Y: 1, Z: 1**, or we can click on the little gear in the **Inspector** view and choose **Reset** to reset all to the default positions, as shown in the following screenshot:

You will see something similar to the following screenshot:

Right now, we have the first or start position of the waypoint. We need more waypoint positions, which is very easy to achieve. You just need to create a new empty game object again and drag `Waypoints` inside. Go to **GameObject | Create Empty** to create the empty game object and name it `Waypoint`. Then, we drag the object to `Waypoints`, which we already have in the scene, and set its transform position to **X: 5.2, Y: 0, Z: 4.3**. We can also create more waypoints by pressing *Crtl + D* (in Windows) or *Command + D* (on a Mac) to duplicate another four `Waypoint` game object, and set all these objects' transform positions as follows:

- **Position X: 7.2 Y: 0 Z: 10.2**
- **Position X: 3.4 Y: 0 Z: 12.1**

- ▸ **Position X: -0.8 Y: 0 Z: 10.7**
- ▸ **Position X: -2.2 Y: 2.7 Z: 5.2**

If we take a look at the **Hierarchy** view, we will see something similar to the following screenshot:

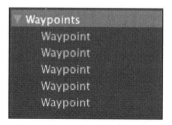

Then, if we click on **Waypoints**, and go to its **Inspector** view under the **Waypoints (Script)**, we will see the **Order Direction**. We can also toggle it **On** or **Off** to enable the movement direction of the AI, which will also show the result on the editor screen by using the `OnDrawGizmos()` function, as we can see in the following screenshot:

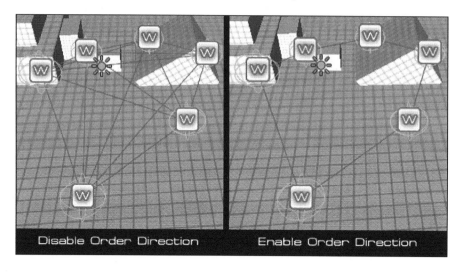

We can also move the waypoint object around to serve what we need or even increase or decrease the waypoint to fit our level.

The `waypoint` script will not work properly if we put the waypoint where the enemy can't walk through, which means that our enemy should be able to walk through and touch each waypoint (hit the green wire sphere area of each waypoint, as shown in the preceding screenshot). Otherwise, the enemy won't be able to move to the next waypoint.

We can also adjust the radius (you will see the green wire sphere change its size) in the `Waypoints` script, which will make our enemy start turning to the next waypoint faster or slower. However, we should be careful while adjusting the radius. If we set it too low, the character might not hit it and not turn to the next waypoint. So, the minimum radius should be 1.0.

In the next step, we will continue by creating the `AIController` script to make our enemy walk through each waypoint.

Objective Complete - Mini Debriefing

What we have done here is created the waypoint, which basically controls the movement of the enemy. We started by creating the `Waypoints` script, which gets the transform position of the game object and its children by using `gameObject.GetComponentsInChildren.<Transform>()`.

Then, we added the `getDirection()` function, which checked the distance between the enemy position and waypoint position, as shown in the following diagram:

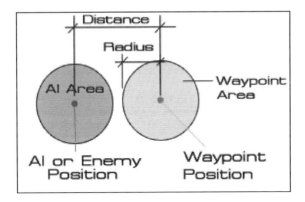

We can see from the preceding diagram that if the distance between the enemy and the waypoint position is smaller than the radius of the waypoint, it will trigger the waypoint to change the next waypoint index, which will also change the movement direction of the enemy.

Then, we added two functions: the first one is the `GetDirectionToPlayer()` function which was used to make the enemy move towards the player, and the `AwayFromWaypoint()` function was used to check the distance between the enemy and the next waypoint while the enemy is chasing the player. If it does, then we will return `true` and make our enemy go back to the next waypoint.

The `GetDirectionToPlayer()` function will make the enemy follow the player at a certain distance, and the `AwayFromWaypoint()` function will make the enemy go back to the waypoint if its position is too far away.

Next, we used the `OnDrawGizmos()` function to create the visual for the waypoint game objects to show in the editor. The `waypoint` is the empty game object, which is sometimes difficult to edit in the editor because we cannot see it in the editors.

 It is better to use gizmo than trying to use camera layers and meshes for the waypoint.

So, using gizmo is the best solution and the better way that Unity provides us to see the visual of some empty game object. We also have the `trigger` parameter in the **Inspector** view to tell our enemy to walk randomly or by the order of the waypoint index.

Classified Intel

At the beginning of the script, we use `GetComponentsInChildren.<Transform>()` function. Have a look at the Unity document at the following link:

```
http://unity3d.com/support/documentation/ScriptReference/GameObject.
GetComponentsInChildren.html.
```

You might ask—why do we call it something different than the document, and why don't we just use the `GetComponentsInChildren(Transform)` or the difference between those two function calls? Well, as is specified in the document, we will see that the `GetCompon entsInChildren(Transform)` function will return `Component[]` Or, it means that the script is attached to this game object but not the `Transform[]` type, which we need for our `Waypoints` script.

In this Unity document page, if we scroll down a little bit, we will see the following screenshot, which gives us our answer:

Functions
AddComponent
AddComponent.<T>
BroadcastMessage
CompareTag
GetComponent
GetComponent.<T>
GetComponentInChildren
GetComponentInChildren....
GetComponents
GetComponents.<T>
GetComponentsInChildren
GetComponentsInChildren...

You will see that there are two types of GetComponentsInChildren() function. So, refer to the following URL for more details:

http://unity3d.com/support/documentation/ScriptReference/GameObject.GetComponentsInChildren.ltTgt.html.

If we go to the preceding link, we will see the following function:

```
function GetComponentsInChildren.<T> () : T[]
```

We can see that the preceding function takes the type T and returns an array of type T, which we will use in this step.

In our script, we cannot use the GetComponentsInChildren.<T>() function, if we don't specify the type of our parameter as follows:

```
var waypointGizmos = gameObject.GetComponentsInChildre
n(Transform); //Correct
```

However, we will see the following error if we specify the type of our parameter:

```
var waypointGizmos : Transform[] = gameObject.GetCompo
nentsInChildren(Transform); //Error
```

The preceding code will cause the error in Unity shown in the following screenshot:

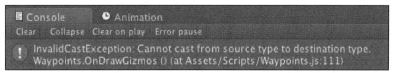

It is better to specify the type of the parameter based on its performance.

Finally, we used the `OnDrawGizmos()` function to create the visual for the waypoint game object, which will show only in the editor. We won't see anything while we are playing the real game after we build it.

However, if we want to see it while we are playing the game in the **Game** view, we can click on the **Play** button and click on the **Gizmos** button on the top-right to toggle the **Gizmos On** or **Off** as shown in the following screenshot:

Creating an enemy AI

In the last section, we created the `Waypoints` script and the `Waypoints` object, which will be used to limit the enemy movement and direction. In this section, we need to create the enemy game object, which will contain the waypoint and our AI character. We will use a prefab similar to that of the player character but remove some of it that is not necessary for the enemy.

Engage thrusters

We will start by creating the empty game object to contain the `AI` and the `Waypoints` object:

1. Go to **GameObject | Create Empty** to create the empty game object and name it `Enemy`. Then, assign its transform by clicking on this game object and go to the **Inspector** view to reset the transform to default, as follows:

   ❑ **Position X: 0 Y: 0 Z: 0**

   ❑ **Rotation X: 0 Y: 0 Z: 0**

   ❑ **Scale X: 1 Y: 1 Z: 1**

2. Next, drag the `Waypoints` game object in the **Hierarchy** view that we created in the first section inside the `Enemy` game object.

3. Then, create another empty game object by going to **GameObject | Create Empty** again and this time name it `AI`. Set the transform in the `AI` game object as follows:

   ❑ **Position X: 0 Y: 0 Z: 0**

   ❑ **Rotation X: 0 Y: 0 Z: 0**

   ❑ **Scale X: 1 Y: 1 Z: 1**

4. Drag the AI game object inside the Enemy game object in the **Hierarchy** view, and then go to the **Prefabs** folder in the **Project** view. We will see the robot_AI prefab object; drag it inside the AI game object, which is a child of the Enemy game object in the **Hierarchy** view similar to the Waypoints game object, as shown in the following screenshot:

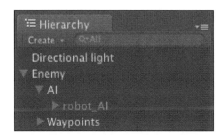

We still need one more thing inside our AI game object, which is the RocketLauncher. This is basically a similar setup as for our player character; so go to the First Person Controller game object, click on the arrow in front of it to bring down the Main Camera, and then click on the arrow in front of the Main Camera. We will see the RocketLauncher game object, which we need for our enemy. Let's press *Ctrl + D* (in Windows) or *Command + D* (on a Mac) to duplicate it, and then drag this duplicate **RocketLauncher** game object inside the **AI** game object, as shown in the following screenshot:

If we take a look at the **Hierarchy** view of the AI game and the Main Camera game object, we will see a similar structure. The only difference is that the AI game object has the AIController script and CharacterController attached to it as we can see in the preceding screenshot.

Then, we will click on **RocketLauncher** to bring up its **Inspector** view and set up the **Transform** and **Rocket Launcher (Script)** as follows:

- ▸ **Transform**:
    - ❏ **Position X: 0.28 Y: 0.31 Z: 1.55**
- ▸ **Rocket Launcher (Script)**
    - ❏ **Smoke Position: SmokePosition** (Drag the SmokePosition in the robot_ AI prefab, as shown in the following screenshot.)
    - ❏ **Ammo Count: -1**

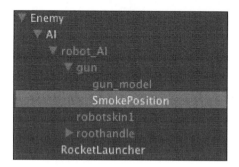

The last thing in this section—we will set up the position of our Enemy game object, which is the parent of the AI game object. So, let's click on the Enemy game object and go to its transform position, and then set the following:

- ▸ **Position X: -2.43 Y: 1.3 Z: 4.9**

Now, we are done with this section. In the next section, we will create the script to control our enemy to be able to walk, run, jump, and shoot.

Objective Complete - Mini Debriefing

In this step, we just created the Enemy and AI empty game objects, which will be the container of the Waypoints game object and AI game object. In the AI game object, we also added the robot_AI prefab and RocketLauncher prefab.

Creating the enemy movement with AIController script

From the last section, we now have our `Enemy` object, but there is no movement, yet. So, in this section, we will create the core script to control our enemy by using the similar concept used for the `CharacterControl` script in *Project 4, The Hero/Heroine Part II – Animation and Controls*, and `New3PSController` in *Project 5, Creating a Rocket Launcher*. We will mix both the scripts and create a new script to control the movements of our enemy following the waypoint and detect the player using the `Waypoints` script.

Engage Thrusters

We will start by creating the `AIController` script:

1. Go to **Assets | Create | Javascript**, name it `AIController`, and double-click on it to open **MonoDevelop**. Since we need to attach the built-in `CharacterController`, we will replace the old code with the following:

   ```
   @script RequireComponent(CharacterController)
   ```

2. Then, continue adding all necessary parameters to this script as follows:

   ```
   //Waypoint
   public var wayPoint : Waypoints;
   //Rocket Launcher
   public var rocketLauncher : RocketLauncher;
   //Get the Player
   public var player : Transform;
   //Animation Params
   public var _animation : Animation;
   public var idleAnimation : AnimationClip;
   public var walkAnimation : AnimationClip;
   public var runAnimation : AnimationClip;
   public var shotAnimation : AnimationClip;
   public var walkAnimationSpeed : float = 1.5;
   public var idleAnimationSpeed : float = 1.0;
   public var runAnimationSpeed : float = 2.0;
   public var shotAnimationSpeed : float = 0.5;
   //Character movement speed
   public var runSpeed : int = 6;
   public var walkSpeed : int = 2;
   public var jumpSpeed : float = 8.0;
   public var gravity : float = 20.0;
   //Shot Range
   ```

```
public var shotRange : float = 15.0;
//Detected the player - increase from the shot range
public var getPlayerRange : float = 5.0;
//Max distance from waypoint
public var waypointDistance : float = 10.0;
//To make the enemy walk for 4 seconds - then think
public var walkingTime : float = 4.0;
//To make the enemy stop for 2 seconds - then walk
public var thinkingTime : float = 2.0;
//Ai current HP
public var aiHP : float = 100;


//AI MAx HP
private var aiMaxHP : float;
//Character Controller
private var controller : CharacterController;
//Collision Flag return from Moving the character
private var c_collisionFlags : CollisionFlags;
//Move Params
private var f_verticalSpeed : float = 0.0;
private var f_moveSpeed : float = 0.0;
private var v3_moveDirection : Vector3 = Vector3.zero;
//Boolean
private var b_isRun : boolean;
private var b_isAiming : boolean;
private var b_isJumping : boolean;
private var b_isStop : boolean;
//Shot Params
private var b_isPrepare : boolean = false;
private var b_isShot : boolean = false;
//Rotate Params
private var q_currentRotation : Quaternion; //current rotation of
the character
private var q_rot : Quaternion; //Rotate to left or right
direction
private var f_rotateSpeed : float = 1.0; //Smooth speed of
rotation
//Stop time Counting
private var f_lastTime : float = 0;
```

With the preceding code, we basically created all the necessary parameters for our `AIController` script.

3. Now we will create the `Awake()` function to set up the necessary values for our parameter before it gets initialized in the `Start()` function, so add the following code:

```
//Using Awake to set up parameters before Initialize
public function Awake() : void {
    controller = GetComponent(CharacterController);
    b_isRun = false;
    b_isAiming = false;
    b_isJumping = false;
    f_moveSpeed = walkSpeed;
    c_collisionFlags = CollisionFlags.CollidedBelow;
    f_moveSpeed = walkSpeed;
    //To make the character stop moving at a certain time
    f_lastTime = Time.time; //Tracking the time between each
movement of the character
    b_isStop = false;
    aiMaxHP = aiHP;

    //Set up animation speed and wrapmode
    _animation[walkAnimation.name].speed = walkAnimationSpeed;
    _animation[walkAnimation.name].wrapMode = WrapMode.Loop;
    _animation[runAnimation.name].speed = runAnimationSpeed;
    _animation[runAnimation.name].wrapMode = WrapMode.Loop;
    _animation[idleAnimation.name].speed = idleAnimationSpeed;
    _animation[idleAnimation.name].wrapMode = WrapMode.Loop;
}
```

In the preceding `Awake()` function, we just assigned the value of each parameter, set up the movement speed, animation clip speed, animation wrapmode of the enemy, and the current time, which we will use to calculate the time to stop the enemy or make him walk.

4. Next, add the following `Start()` function to set the position of our enemy equal to the first waypoint position:

```
//Initialize
public function Start() : void {
    transform.position = wayPoint.StartPosition();
}
```

5. After adding the `Start()` function, we need the function to check for the `CollisionFlags` parameter of the enemy to see if our enemy hits the ground, which is very similar to the `CharacterControl` script that we used in *Project 4, The Hero/Heroine Part II – Animation and Controls*:

```
//Checking if the character hit the ground (collide Below)
public function IsGrounded () : boolean {
    return (c_collisionFlags & CollisionFlags.CollidedBelow);
}
```

6. Next, create `OnCollisionEnter()`, which is the built-in function to check whether the enemy got hit by the player, and decrease the hit-points if necessary. Also, we can add another function to get the percent of the current enemy hit-points and maximum enemy hit-points by adding the following code:

```
//Checking for the collision if the rocket hit the enemy
public function OnCollisionEnter(collision : Collision) : void {
    if (StaticVars.b_isGameOver == false) {
        if (collision.transform.tag == "Rocket") {
            var rocket : Rocket = collision.gameObject.
GetComponent (Rocket);
            var f_damage : float = rocket.getDamage();
            //Clamp down the hitpoint - not lower than 0, and not higher
than max hitpoint
            aiHP = Mathf.Clamp(aiHP-f_damage, 0, aiMaxHP);
        }
    }
}


//Get the percent of the maximum HP with the current HP
public function GetHpPercent() : float {
    return aiHP/aiMaxHP;
}
```

7. Then, we will create four functions to give the enemy a personality and make our enemy smarter:

   ❑ The first one is the `Shoot()` function, which will make the enemy shoot when the player is within shooting range of the enemy by checking the distance of the player and enemy. We will also use the `Physics.Raycast()` function to see if there is any wall blocking the direction of the shot; if there isn't, we just make the enemy shoot by adding the following code:

```
//Give the Enemy Characteristic
///////////////////////////////////////////////////////////
///
//Checking for the character is shooting
```

```
public function Shoot (_direction : Vector3) : boolean {
  var hit : RaycastHit;
  //Checking if the player hit the shooting range
  if (Vector3.Distance(transform.position, player.position)
<= shotRange) {
    // Cast ray shotRange meters in shot direction, to see
if nothing block the rocket
      if (Physics.Raycast(transform.position, _direction,
hit, shotRange)) {
        if (hit.transform.tag != "Wall") {
          b_isAiming = true;
          return b_isAiming;
          }
      }
  }
  b_isAiming = false;
  return b_isAiming;
}
```

❑ Second, we will create the `Jump()` function to make our enemy smarter by using another `Physics` class function, `Physics.CapsuleCast()`. This function will cast the capsule object from the enemy's position towards its movement direction to see if the enemy hits the wall. This will trigger the enemy to jump over the wall and continue walking towards its direction as in the following code:

```
//Make character Jump
public function Jump (_direction : Vector3) : boolean {
  //Checking for Jumping if the next y position is different
than the current y position
  var hit : RaycastHit;
    var p1 : Vector3 = transform.position + controller.
center + Vector3.up * (-controller.height*0.5);
    var p2 : Vector3 = p1 + Vector3.up * controller.height;
    // Cast character controller shape moveSpeed meters
forward, to see if it is about to hit anything
    if ((Physics.CapsuleCast (p1, p2, 0.1, _direction, hit))
&& (c_collisionFlags & CollisionFlags.Sides)) {
      if (hit.transform.tag == "Wall") {
          return true;
        }
    }
  return false;
}
```

❏ Then, we will check the distance between the player and the enemy to see if the distance is higher than the shotRange and inside the shotRange + getPlayerRange. So, let's add it as follows:

```
//Make the enemy run when the player hit certain radius
which is between the shotRange and getPlayerRange
public function Run () : boolean {
  //Checking for Running
  if ((Vector3.Distance(transform.position, player.
position) <= (getPlayerRange+shotRange)) && ((Vector3.
Distance(transform.position, player.position) > shotRange)))
  {
      b_isRun = true;
  } else {
    b_isRun = false;
  }
  return b_isRun;
}
```

❏ In the last function, to control the enemy behavior, we will make our enemy walk and stop for a certain amount of time:

```
//Calculate the time that let enemy walk and stop for the
certain time
public function IsThinking() : boolean {
  //Get the time when enemy stop walking
  if (b_isStop) {
    var f_time : float = thinkingTime;
  } else {
    //Get the time when enemy is walking
    f_time = walkingTime;
  }
  if (Time.time >= (f_lastTime + f_time)) {
    if (b_isStop) {
      b_isStop = false;
    } else {
      b_isStop = true;
    }
    f_lastTime = Time.time;
  }
  return b_isStop;
}
```

Now we are done with all the functions that give personality to our enemy.

8. The next step is the `Update()` function, which will control all the movement and animation of our enemy. So, let's type it as follows:

```
public function Update() : void {
   if (StaticVars.b_isGameOver == false) {
      var v3_rocketDirection : Vector3 = (player.position -
transform.position).normalized;
      //Checking if the enemy position is away from the waypoint in
the certain distance,
      //Make the enemy stop running, shooting, and walk back to the
target waypoint
      if (wayPoint.AwayFromWaypoint(transform, waypointDistance)) {
         b_isAiming = false;
         b_isRun = false;
      } else {
         //Checking if the enemy is not aiming - check for running
         if (!Shoot(v3_rocketDirection)) {
            //Checking if the ai is run or not aiming
            Run();
         }
      }
```

9. Continue to add the following script in the `Update()` function, which will check when the enemy isn't aiming, and then we will check for `b_isRun` to see if the enemy is running or not:

```
      if (!b_isAiming) {
         //If the ai is running don't make it think
         //Get the direction
         if (b_isRun) {
            var v3_targetDirection : Vector3 = wayPoint.
GetDirectionToPlayer(transform, player); //Move Direct to the
player
         } else {
            if (thinkingTime > 0) {
               if (!IsThinking()) {
                  v3_targetDirection = wayPoint.GetDirection(transform);
//Use random Direction
               } else {
                  v3_targetDirection = Vector3.zero;
               }
            } else {
               v3_targetDirection = wayPoint.GetDirection(transform);
//Use random Direction
            }
         }
```

10. Add the script to get the movement direction of the enemy and check for the jumping behavior as follows:

```
      //If the target direction is not zero - means there is no
button pressing
      if (v3_targetDirection != Vector3.zero) {
         //Rotate toward the target direction
         v3_moveDirection = Vector3.Slerp(v3_moveDirection, v3_
targetDirection, f_rotateSpeed * Time.deltaTime);
         //Get only direction by normalize our target vector
         v3_moveDirection = v3_moveDirection.normalized;
      } else {
         v3_moveDirection = Vector3.zero;
      }

      //Checking if character is on the ground
      if (!b_isJumping) {
         //Holding Shift to run
         if (b_isRun) {
           f_moveSpeed = runSpeed;
         } else {
           b_isRun = false;
           f_moveSpeed = walkSpeed;
         }
            //Press Space to Jump
            if (Jump(v3_moveDirection)) {
                b_isJumping = true;
                f_verticalSpeed = jumpSpeed;
            }
      }
```

11. Now we can add gravity checking, get the actual movement direction, and apply the animation clip as we did in the `CharacterControl` script in *Project 4, The Hero/Heroine Part II – Animation and Controls*. Let's add the script as follows:

```
      // Apply gravity
      if (IsGrounded()) {
         f_verticalSpeed = 0.0; //if our character is grounded
         b_isJumping = false; //Checking if our character is in the
air or not
         f_inAirTime = 0.0;
         f_inAirStartTime = Time.time;
      } else {
         f_verticalSpeed -= gravity * Time.deltaTime; //if our
character in the air
         //Count Time
```

```
        f_inAirTime = Time.time - f_inAirStartTime;
    }


    // Calculate actual motion
    var v3_movement : Vector3 = (v3_moveDirection * f_moveSpeed)
+ Vector3 (0, f_verticalSpeed, 0); // Apply the vertical speed if
character fall down
    v3_movement *= Time.deltaTime;


    //Set the prepare animation to false
    b_isPrepare = false;


    /////////////////////////////////////////////////////////
    //Checking if the character is moving or not
    if (v3_moveDirection != Vector3.zero) {
      if (f_moveSpeed == walkSpeed) {
        _animation.CrossFade(walkAnimation.name);
      } else {
        _animation.CrossFade(runAnimation.name);
      }
    } else {
      _animation.CrossFade(idleAnimation.name);
    }
    // Move the controller
        c_collisionFlags = controller.Move(v3_movement);


        //Update rotation of the character
        if ((v3_moveDirection != Vector3.zero) && (!b_isAiming)) {
          transform.rotation = Quaternion.LookRotation(v3_
moveDirection);
        }
```

12. Now we are done with the no aiming part. We will continue to add the script to check for the aiming part, which is similar to what we did in *Project 5*, *Creating a Rocket Launcher*. So, let's add the script as follows:

```
} else {//Aiming
        v3_moveDirection = Vector3.MoveTowards(v3_moveDirection,
v3_rocketDirection, 0.1);
        v3_moveDirection = v3_moveDirection.normalized;


        // Apply gravity
      if (IsGrounded()) {
        f_verticalSpeed = 0.0; //if our character is grounded
        b_isJumping = false; //Checking if our character is in the
air or not
```

```
        f_inAirTime = 0.0;
        f_inAirStartTime = Time.time;
    } else {
        f_verticalSpeed -= gravity * Time.deltaTime; //if our
character in the air
        //Count Time
        f_inAirTime = Time.time - f_inAirStartTime;
    }

    // Calculate actual motion
    v3_movement = Vector3 (0, f_verticalSpeed, 0); // Apply the
vertical speed if character fall down
    v3_movement *= Time.deltaTime;

    //Checking if the character is playing the shoot animation
    if (!b_isPrepare) {
      b_isShot = false;
      //Play the shot preparing animation function
      WaitForPrepare();
    } else {
      if (v3_rocketDirection == v3_moveDirection) {
        if (!b_isShot) {
          b_isShot = true;
          //Play the shoot animation function
          WaitForShot();
        }
      }
    }

    // Move the controller
    c_collisionFlags = controller.Move(new Vector3 (0, v3_
movement.y, 0));
    //Update rotation of the character
    transform.rotation = Quaternion.LookRotation(v3_
moveDirection);
    }
```

13. As the last step of the `Update()` function, we will add the script for the game over state and close our function as follows:

```
} else {
    //Gameover
    _animation.CrossFade(idleAnimation.name);
  }
}
```

14. Then, we will add two functions, which will be used to control the aiming and shoot animations:

```
//Wait for shoot animation
private function WaitForShot () : IEnumerator {
  _animation[shotAnimation.name].speed = shotAnimationSpeed;
  _animation[shotAnimation.name].wrapMode = WrapMode.ClampForever;
  _animation.PlayQueued(shotAnimation.name, QueueMode.PlayNow);
  BroadcastMessage("Fire", shotAnimation.length); //to enable all
the function name Fire in every MonoBehaviour Script

  yield WaitForSeconds (shotAnimation.length);
  b_isShot = false;
}

//Wait for aiming animation
private function WaitForPrepare () : IEnumerator {
  _animation[shotAnimation.name].speed = shotAnimationSpeed * 2;
  _animation[shotAnimation.name].wrapMode = WrapMode.ClampForever;
  _animation.CrossFade(shotAnimation.name, 0.6);

  yield WaitForSeconds(shotAnimation.length);
  b_isPrepare = true;
}
```

15. The last function that we add is the `OnDrawGizmos()` function, which we used in the last step to draw the line between the player position and the enemy position:

```
//Draw Gizmos and Directional line from the enemy position to the
player position
public function OnDrawGizmos() : void {
  if (player != null) {
    Gizmos.color = Color.blue;
    Gizmos.DrawLine(transform.position, player.position);
  }
}
```

With that we are done with our `AIController` script. Next, we will go back to Unity and apply the `AIController` script to the `AI` game object by dragging it from the **Project** view to the `AI` game object in the **Hierarchy** view. Then, we will go to its **Inspector** view and set the following:

- **Character Controller**
  - **Height**: 2.25
  - **Radius**: 0.4
  - **Step Offset**: 0.4
  - **Skin Width**: 0.05

- **AIController (Script)**
  - **Way Point**: **Waypoints** (Drag the `Waypoints` game object to the **Hierarchy** view here)
  - **Rocket Launcher**: **RocketLauncher** (Drag the `RocketLauncher` game object inside the `AI` game object to the **Hierarchy** view here)
  - **Player**: **robot** (Drag the `robot` game object inside the `First Person Controller` game object to the **Hierarchy** view here)
  - **Animation**: **robot_AI** (Drag the `robot_AI` game object inside this **AI** game object to the **Hierarchy** here)
  - **Idle Animation**: **idle** (Drag the `idle` animation inside the `Chapter5/Robot Artwork/robot@idle/` to the **Project** view here)
  - **Walk Animation**: **walk** (Drag the `walk` animation inside the `Chapter5/Robot Artwork/robot@walk/` to the **Project** view here)
  - **Run Animation**: **run** (Drag the `run` animation inside the `Chapter5/Robot Artwork/robot@run/` to the **Project** view here)
  - **Shot Animation**: **shoot** (Drag the `shoot` animation inside the `Chapter5/Robot Artwork/robot@shoot/` to the **Project** view here)

The enemy will also walk for 4 minutes and stop for 2 minutes, and will jump over the wall.

We can set up the walking time and thinking time by going the **AIController (Script)** component in the **Inspector** view of **AI** and set up the **Thinking Time** or **Walking Time**, as shown in the following screenshot:

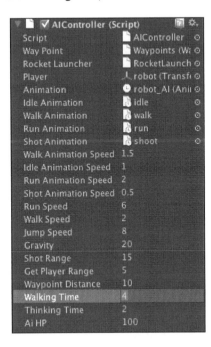

Objective Complete - Mini Debriefing

We just created our `AIController` script by mixing two scripts, the `CharacterControl` script from *Project 4*, *The Hero/Heroine Part II – Animation and Controls*, and the `New3PSController` script from *Project 5*, *Creating a Rocket Launcher*.

We also added the new code section to give our enemy some characteristics and make it smart enough to shoot the player, run towards the player, jump when it hits the wall, and to stop and walk after a certain time.

In the `Run()` function, we used the `if ((Vector3.Distance(transform.position, player.position) <= (getPlayerRange+shotRange)) && ((Vector3.Distance(transform.position, player.position) > shotRange))) {}` statement to check for the distance between the enemy and the player, which we can see from the following diagram:

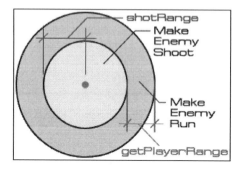

As we can see from the preceding diagram, the enemy will run towards the player if the distance between the player and the enemy is higher than the `shotRange` but lower than or equal to the `getPlayerRange`. And the enemy will shoot the player if the distance between him and the player is in the `shotRange`.

We also use both `Physics.CapsuleCast()` and `Physics.RayCast()` to check for the wall in front of the enemy.

Classified Intel

In this step, we have used both the `Physics.CapsuleCast()` and `Physics.RayCast()` functions. Both functions are very useful when one wants to check if there is anything blocking the enemy movement direction or the rocket bullet direction.

We use `Physics.CapsuleCast()` for our `Jump()` function because we want to check the area in front of the enemy and whether the capsule hits the wall or not. We also check the `CollisionFlag.Sides` for when the side of enemy collides with the wall as we use in the `Jump()` function, as shown in the following script:

```
if ((Physics.CapsuleCast (p1, p2, 0.1, _direction, hit)) && (c_
collisionFlags & CollisionFlags.Sides)) {
```

In this script, we also give the radius of the `Capsule` a value equal to `0.1` because we want to make sure that our enemy is very close to the wall or collides with the wall to make it jump, as shown in the following diagram:

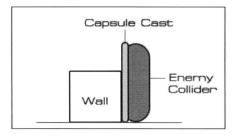

For `Physics.RayCast()`, it is very similar to the function that we used in the first chapter. It basically casts a ray from the position of the enemy's rocket launcher to the player by checking to see if there is anything blocking it, as shown in the following diagram:

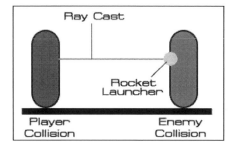

Creating a hit-point UI

Now we are at the last step of this chapter. We will add the hit-point game object for the player and enemy as well as create the `HitPointUI` script.

Engage Thrusters

Before we start creating the `HitPointUI` script, we will need to create the `HitPointUI` game object to contain it:

1. First, go to Unity and create an empty game object by going to **GameObject | Create Empty**, and name it `HitPointUI`. Then, we will reset the **Transform** to default as follows:

   □ **Position X: 0 Y: 0 Z: 0**

   □ **Rotation X: 0 Y: 0 Z: 0**

   □ **Scale X: 1 Y: 1 Z: 1**

2. Next, create a new script by going to **Assets | Create | Javascript**, name it `HitPointUI`, double-click on it to open **MonoDevelop**, and replace it with the following code:

```
public var ai : AIController;
public var player : New3PSController;

public var frameTexture : Texture2D;
public var hpTexture : Texture2D;
public var aiTexture : Texture2D;
public var textHpTexture : Texture2D;
public var textAiTexture : Texture2D;
```

Here, we just set up all the parameters needed for our `HitPointUI`.

3. Then, add the `Update()` function to check for the game over state:

```
public function Update() : void {
  //Checking if the player or AI Hit-point equal 0 or below 0
  if ((player.GetHpPercent() <= 0.0) || (ai.GetHpPercent() <=
0.0)) {
    StaticVars.b_isGameOver = true;
  }
}
```

4. We will add the `OnGUI()` function to create the hit-point UI:

```
public function OnGUI() : void {
  //Draw Text
  GUI.DrawTexture (Rect (10,10,46,32), textHpTexture);
  GUI.DrawTexture (Rect (10,42,95,32), textAiTexture);

  //Character Hp
  // Create one Group to contain both images
  // Adjust the first 2 coordinates to place it somewhere else on-
screen
  GUI.BeginGroup (Rect (110,15,156,21));
  // Draw the background image
  GUI.DrawTexture(Rect (0,0,156,21), frameTexture);
  // Create a second Group which will be clipped
  // We want to clip the image and not scale it, which is why we
need the second Group
  GUI.BeginGroup (Rect (0,0,player.GetHpPercent() * 156, 21));
  // Draw the foreground image
  GUI.DrawTexture (Rect (0,0,156,21), hpTexture);
  // End both Groups
  GUI.EndGroup ();
  GUI.EndGroup ();
```

```
//AI HP
// Create one Group to contain both images
// Adjust the first 2 coordinates to place it somewhere else on-
screen
GUI.BeginGroup (Rect (110,47,156,21));
// Draw the background image
GUI.DrawTexture(Rect (0,0,156,21), frameTexture);
// Create a second Group which will be clipped
// We want to clip the image and not scale it, which is why we
need the second Group
GUI.BeginGroup (Rect (0,0,ai.GetHpPercent() * 156, 21));
// Draw the foreground image
GUI.DrawTexture (Rect (0,0,156,21), aiTexture);
// End both Groups
GUI.EndGroup ();
GUI.EndGroup ();
}
```

In this function, we just use the new GUI function, GUI.BeginGroup(), to draw the mask for the hit-point bar.

5. Now, we will go to back to Unity and drag the HitPointUI.js script to the HitPointUI game object in the **Hierarchy** view. Then we will go to its **Inspector** view and set the following:

   ❑ **Hit Point UI (Script)**

   ❑ **Ai: AI** (Drag the AI game object inside the Enemy game object to the **Hierarchy** view here)

   ❑ **Player: First Person Controller** (Drag the First Person Controller game object to the **Hierarchy** view here)

   ❑ **Frame Texture: hitPointFrame** (Drag the hitPointFrame.png from the Chapter6/UI/ folder here)

   ❑ **Hp Texture: hitPointBarHP** (Drag the hitPointBarHP.png from the Chapter6/UI/ folder here)

   ❑ **Ai Texture: hitPointEnemy** (Drag the hitPointEnemy.png from the Chapter6/UI/ folder here)

   ❑ **Text Hp Texture: HP** (drag the HP.png from the Chapter6/UI/ folder here)

   ❑ **Text Ai Texture: Enemy** (drag the ENEMY.png from the Chapter6/UI/ folder here)

Now we have finished our game, so click on **Play** to see the result. We will see that when the player or enemy gets shot the hit-point bar will decrease.

Objective Complete - Mini Debriefing

We just created the UI game object and the script, which we use to control the hit-point UI. We also used GUI.BeginGroup() to mask the decreasing damage from either the player or enemy hitpoints.

Classified Intel

In this section, we have used GUI.BeginGroup() to mask out the texture to show how much hit points are left. The GUI.BeginGroup() function must be close to GUI.EndGroup().

In our code, we basically created the first group to contain the background texture, which is the bar frame. Then, we drew another group on top of the first group, which contains the bar texture as a clip mask. This second group's width will relate to the hit-point value left for the player or enemy, as shown in the following code:

```
//Draw the background group
GUI.BeginGroup (Rect (110,15,156,21));
  GUI.DrawTexture(Rect (0,0,156,21), frameTexture);

// Create a second Group which will be clipped
  GUI.BeginGroup (Rect (0,0, player.GetHpPercent() * 156, 21));
  GUI.DrawTexture (Rect (0,0,156,21), hpTexture);

//End both Groups
  GUI.EndGroup ();
  GUI.EndGroup ();
```

From the preceding code, we can translate to the following diagram:

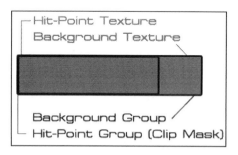

Game over-Wrapping it up

In this chapter, we just created the `Waypoints` for the enemy to follow. We also created the enemy AI that can jump, run towards the player, walk, and stop for a certain time—by creating the `AIController` script. This script used the mix of `CharacterControl` script from *Project 4, The Hero/Heroine Part II – Animation and Controls*, and `New3PSController` script from the *Project 5, Creating a Rocket Launcher*.

We also learned more about the `Gizmos()` function to display the visual of our `Waypoints` empty game object by using `Gizmo.DrawIcon()`, `Gizmo.DrawLine()`, and `Gizmo.DrawWireSphere()`.

Finally, we learned how to use the `GUI.BeginGroup()` function to mask and show the hit-point UI object for the player and the enemy.

So, let's take a look at the following screenshot to see what we have done so far:

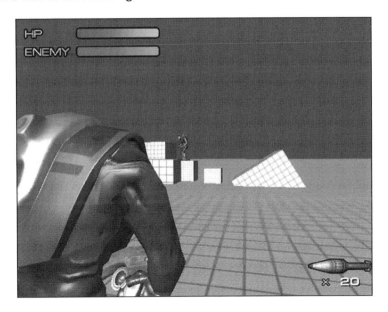

We start the game and then we get shot:

We fight back:

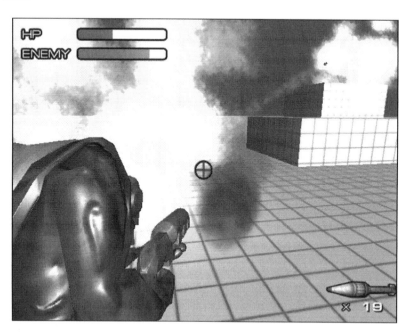

However, we lost:

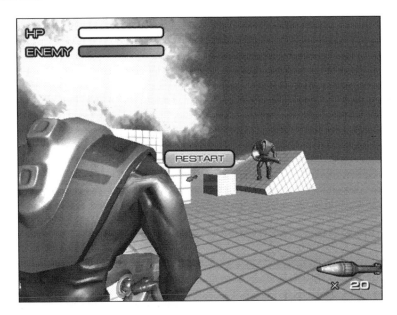

Are you ready to go gung ho?
A Hotshot challenge

Now we have an understanding of the basic concept of creating the enemy AI, but our AI script still needs a lot of improvement to make it smarter. Why don't we do something to spice it up?

- ▶ Try making a wall that the AI cannot jump over and add the ability for the enemy to avoid the wall by using `Physics.CapsuleCast` or `Physics.RayCast` and rotate the enemy rotate when it hits the wall

- ▶ Add different types of weapons for our enemy

- ▶ Try changing or adjusting the parameter of the `AIController`, such as the `shotRange` or `getPlayerRange`, to make the enemy react to the player faster

- ▶ Add more waypoints for our `Waypoints` game object to make sure our enemy has more choice to walk

- ▶ Add multiple enemies in the scene (you will need to adapt the `HitPointUI` game object to be able to track the hit points for each enemy)

- ▶ Try changing the `AIController` code for the enemy to avoid the rocket and maybe make the rocket follow the player's movement

Project 7

Forge a Destructible and Interactive Virtual World

Most games need an environment to create the feeling and experience for the players of the game's world. In games, we can also call it a level. It can interact with the player as well. The level will create the difficulty and challenges for the players to play through and finish the game. Each level will include static and non-static objects. The static objects include houses, buildings, bridges, trees, and so on, and won't be movable. On the other hand, non-static objects will interact with the player, and include rocks, doors, switches, and so on.

In many cases, we will see that games use the non-static objects to make the level much more fun to play by adding the events or triggers to the objects and making them interact with the players. For example, the players have to push the switch to open the door, or get blocked because the bridge was destroyed when the player triggered the event. We can also add physics to the non-static objects to make the objects behave realistically, such as adding physics to the rocks when they are falling down to the ground.

In this chapter, we will continue from the last chapter to optimize our `AIController` script and add the ragdoll object to replace the AI when it dies. Then, we will create a destructible rock that will trigger when the player gets close to it, and a destroyable rock that the player and AI can shoot and destroy. We will also create the ragdoll character object for the AI to behave realistically when he is killed by the player.

Mission briefing

We will start by optimizing the `AIController` script to make it run faster and attaching the ragdoll object to replace the AI with the ragdoll character object when the AI is dead.

Next, we will create simple, non-static destructible rocks, which will be triggered when the character gets close to it, and a simple destructible wall that the player can shoot the rocket to destroy. By making both of the destructible objects fall down, we will need to have a physics calculation in Unity by attaching the `rigidbody` to each object and activating it when it is triggered.

What does it do?

First, we will open our old `AIController` script (from *Project 6, Creating Smart AI Enemies*) to optimize some parameters and add the ability to replace the AI with the ragdoll object when it dies. Then, we will create the destructible wall from four multiple cube objects, which will each have a `rigidbody`. Of course, we will need to create the script to make the object break apart into `ParentRocks` and `Rock` scripts when the character's shot hits it. We will also create another destructible rock from multiple cubes, which will fall when the player gets close to it. To make this rock fall down, we will create a trigger area and a `TriggerArea` script, which will trigger and make the rock fall down when the player enters this area.

Why Is It Awesome?

Unity has the `NVIDIA PhysX physics engine` built-in, which is very powerful for creating the realistic physics simulation for our game world. In this chapter, we will learn how to apply physics to our game by applying ragdoll physics to the character as well as attaching the `rigidbody` to make the objects or environment react to the player whenever we want. This technique will add more variety to the game and will make it very challenging to play.

Your Hotshot Objectives

We will start by importing the `chapter 7` package, and then we will go to each topic as follows:

- Optimizing the `AIController` script
- Creating a ragdoll
- Creating a destructible wall
- Creating a `Rockslide` and trigger area
- Creating `ParentRocks` and rock script

Mission Checklist

First, we need the `chapter 7` package. Go to the book website—`http://www.packtpub.com/support?nid=8267`—to download the `Chapter7.zip` package. The package will contain all the necessary resources— assets, scripts, and prefabs—that we will be using in this chapter.

Import the package to Unity as you did for the previous chapters, as shown in the following screenshot:

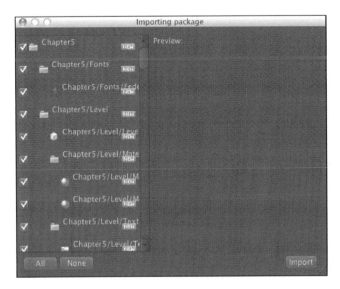

In the **Project** view, we will see the **Chapter5** folder, **Chapter6** folder, **Chapter7** folder, **Gizmos** folder, **Standard Assets**, and **VirtualWorld** scene. The **Chapter5** and **Chapter6** folders will contain the entire assets of `Chapter 5` and `Chapter 6`. The **Chapter7** folder will contain all the scripts, assets, terrain, and prefabs that will be used in this chapter. The **Gizmos** folder will contain the `wayIcon.png`. The **Standard Assets** folder contains all the necessary built-in assets that will be used in the chapter. Finally, we will use the **VirtualWorld** scene to create the destructible objects in this chapter. **VirtualWorld** scene includes the old work from `Chapter 5` and `Chapter 6`, and some new scripts to make it more suitable for this project. Let's double-click on it to open the scene.

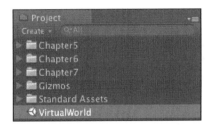

Optimizing the AIController script

In this first section, we will go back to our `AIController` script, which we had already created in the previous chapter. However, this `AIController` script needs a little more tweaking to make our game frame rate higher.

Prepare for Lift Off

Before we start tweaking the `AIController` script, we need to see the frame rate result in our game.

First, click **Play** to run the game and open the **Statistics** window by clicking on the **Stats** option on the top-right corner of the **Game** view to bring up the **Statistics** window. In this window, you can see many parameters that are very useful if you are trying to debug your game and see how much **Frame Rate**, **Draw Calls**, **Tris** (triangles), **Verts** (vertices), **Textures**, and **Memory** the game is using or running on right now.

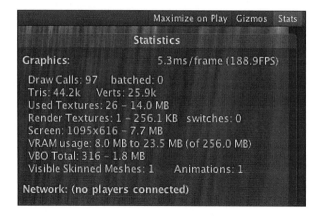

When the game is running, you will see that often the frame rate (FPS) is not stable. It will go from more than 120 FPS down to 20 FPS, which will cause the problem of lagging while we are playing the game.

You might see the different frame rates, as shown in the following screenshot, but you should be able to notice the rise and drop in the fast rate regardless of how fast or slow the FPS is:

Now, we know that the FPS is not stable and we need to fix it, but how can we know where the problem came from, what is its actual cause? You will need to play through the game and see when the FPS is going down.

First, let's think about the problem. If you look closely, you will observe that the FPS keeps fluctuating. Hence, we can assume that this is not a graphics or memory problem, as that would have caused the game to crash or the FPS to remain consistently low.

 If you are using Unity Pro, you can also use the profiling option in Unity to find the problematic code, which will be explained later in this section.

Next, let's take a look at the issue that might have caused the problem. It might be our player script or the AI script. As we haven't even controlled our character, it is likely that the problem is in our `AIController` script. In order to verify this, let's move our character to a position where we can see our AIs.

In the **Statistics** window, we see something wrong. The problem is that every time the AIs start moving, the FPS decreases. On the other hand, when the AIs stop moving, the FPS goes back to normal:

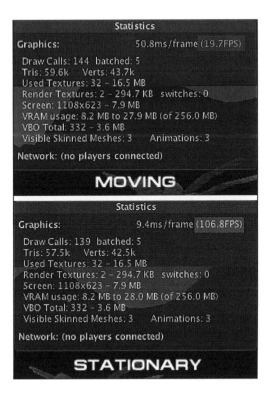

Now we know that our problem comes from something inside the `AIController` script, which should be the function that we call while the AI is moving. So, open the `AIController` script, which is located in the `Chapter7/Scripts` folder in the **Project** view, as shown in the following screenshot:

Now, double-click it, open the script and take a look at the `Update()` function, which is the core function to control our AI.

Engage Thrusters

Inside the `Update()` function, we know that the problem arises only when the character moves (which will be when the AI is not stopping or aiming).

Let's take a look inside `if (!b_isAiming) {......}`; we will see nothing different from the `CharacterControl` script, which we already used to control our character in *Project 4, The Hero/Heroine Part II – Animation and Controls*, so it shouldn't be a problem, right? However, one part of the script that we have changed to make our AI jump instead of getting the Input key is the `Jump(_direction : Vector3)` function.

In the `Jump(_direction : Vector3)` function, you will see that we have used `Physics.CapsuleCast` to check for the AI to jump if the step is in front of it. As we discussed in the last chapter, `Physics.CapsuleCast` will cast the capsule collision in the given direction (which is the `_direction` that gets passed from `Jump` function) to check if the capsule hit something.

Now, just think about it—do we really need to cast the capsule checking for the step and make the AI jump? Can't we cast only one ray to check for it?

The answer is "Yes. We can do it".

So, let's replace some old code in the Jump() function so that it looks similar to the following code:

```
//Make character Jump
public function Jump (_direction : Vector3) : boolean {
    //Checking for Jumping if the next y position is different than the
current y position
    var hit : RaycastHit;

       //Optimization
       var v3_leg : Vector3 = transform.position + controller.center +
    Vector3.up * (-controller.height*0.5);
       var f_distance : float = controller.radius * 2;
       if ((Physics.Raycast(v3_leg, _direction, hit, f_distance)) &&
    (c_collisionFlags & CollisionFlags.Sides)) {
          if (hit.transform.tag == "Wall") {
             return true;
          }
       }
    return false;
}
```

From the preceding code, we basically change the checking from the capsule cast to the ray cast by drawing the line from the bottom of our AI in the given direction, which is much faster because we only draw one line and not a whole capsule.

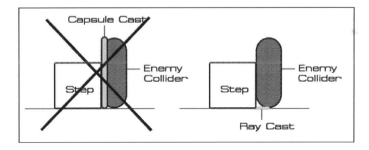

Now, we click **Play** and check our FPS to see whether the problem has been fixed by checking the **Statistics** window while the AI is moving and is stationary.

We can see that right now the FPS is a lot more stable, as shown in the following screenshot:

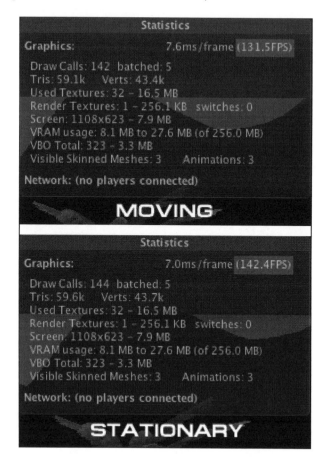

Objective Complete - Mini Debriefing

What we have done here is optimize our `AIController` script to increase the FPS by using the `Physics.Raycast` instead of `Physics.CapsuleCast` to speed up the checking process of making the AI jump.

Classified Intel

As we have seen in this chapter, we had to go through a lot of checking and coding to be able to track down and see which part of the game decreases the FPS. We were aware of the problem because we were coding it. However, if we didn't create the whole game or we use somebody else's code, it might become a nightmare to track down which section is causing the problem.

In Unity Pro, it is easier to solve or find the problem within our code by using the **Profiler** to debug our game. The way to see it is by going to **Window** | **Profiler** to open the **Profiler** view; you will see two sections in this window.

The first part is the graph for **CPU Usage**, **Rendering**, **Memory**, **Audio**, and **Physics**, as shown in the following screenshot:

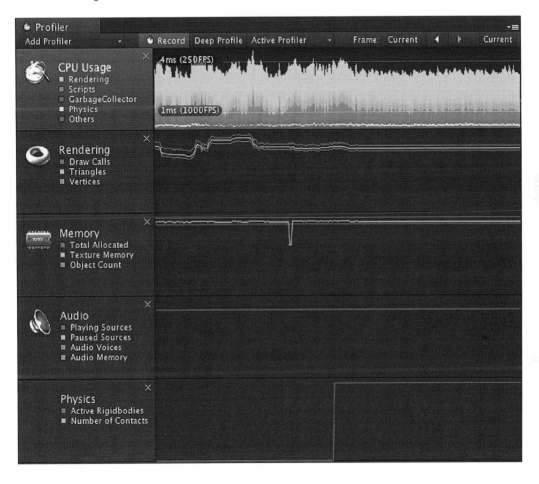

The second part will show us the functions and scripts that relate to the **CPU Usage**, **Rendering**, **Memory**, **Audio**, and **Physics**, while we are playing this scene, as shown in the following screenshot:

Hierarchy ▾					2.40 ms 415.4 FPS	
Function	**Total**	**Self**	**Calls**	**Memory**	**Time ms**	**Self ms**
▶ Camera.Render	66.6%	2.2%	1	116 B	1.60	0.05
▶ GUI.Repaint	13.8%	0.8%	1	2.0 KB	0.33	0.02
▼ AIController.Update()	6.4%	5.7%	2	180 B	0.15	0.13
Physics.Raycast	0.7%	0.7%	2	0 B	0.01	0.01
▶ MeshSkinning.Update	5.6%	0.3%	2	0 B	0.13	0.00
Overhead	2.2%	2.2%	1	0 B	0.05	0.05
NewFPSController.Update()	1.1%	1.1%	1	0.5 KB	0.02	0.02
WaterSimple.Update()	1.1%	1.1%	1	0 B	0.02	0.02
MouseLook_JS.Update()	0.9%	0.9%	2	0 B	0.02	0.02
AudioManager.Update	0.5%	0.5%	1	0 B	0.01	0.01
▶ Animation.Update	0.5%	0.0%	1	0 B	0.01	0.00
SendMouseEvents.DoSendMouseEvents()	0.2%	0.2%	1	52 B	0.00	0.00
▶ Physics.UpdateSkinnedCloth	0.0%	0.0%	2	0 B	0.00	0.00
HandleUtility.SetViewInfo()	0.0%	0.0%	1	0 B	0.00	0.00
Network.Update	0.0%	0.0%	1	0 B	0.00	0.00
CharacterMotor.Update()	0.0%	0.0%	1	0 B	0.00	0.00
Physics.Interpolation	0.0%	0.0%	1	0 B	0.00	0.00
TextureButton.Update()	0.0%	0.0%	1	0 B	0.00	0.00
HitPointUI.Update()	0.0%	0.0%	1	0 B	0.00	0.00
Application.Integrate Assets in Background	0.0%	0.0%	1	0 B	0.00	0.00
TextRendering.Cleanup	0.0%	0.0%	13	0 B	0.00	0.00

By opening the **Profiler**, we will be able to see the performance and the reason for the game to slow down. If we use the old `AIController` script and open the **Profiler** view, we will be able to see the cause that affects the performance of this game right away, as we can see in the following screenshot:

From the preceding graph, we can see that the yellow graph—which represents the **Physics**—is very high. Then, we can also see the second section, which will show the function in the script that causes the FPS issue, as shown in the following screenshot:

Hierarchy ▾					51.13 ms 19.6 FPS	
Function	Total	Self	Calls	Memory	Time ms	Self ms
▾ AIController.Update()	95.8%	0.7%	2	180 B	49.02	0.39
▸ Physics.CapsuleCast	95.0%	95.0%	2	0 B	48.62	48.62
▸ Camera.Render	2.4%	0.0%	1	116 B	1.23	0.04

From the preceding screenshot, we will see the line **Physics.CapsuleCast** inside **AIController. Update()** causes **95.0%** of the CPU usage, which is exactly what we are looking for.

 You can get more details on how to use the **Profiler** from the following URL: http://unity3d.com/support/documentation/Manual/ Profiler.html.

Creating a ragdoll

In this section, we will apply the ragdoll to the AI ragdoll game object and replace it with the current AI game object when it dies.

Prepare for Lift Off

Go to the **Project** view and open the Prefabs folder inside the Chapter7 folder. Drag the robot_AI_ragdoll prefab to the **Hierarchy** view. Then, go to the **Scene** view and press the F key to zoom into the robot_AI_ragdoll game object in the scene.

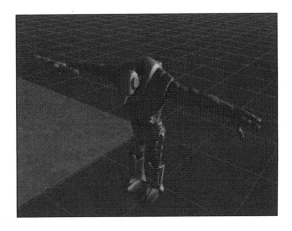

Engage Thrusters

Now, we can start applying ragdoll physics to the `robot_AI_ragdoll`:

1. Go to **GameObject | Create Other | Ragdoll...** and you will see the **Create Ragdoll** window pop up, as shown in the following screenshot:

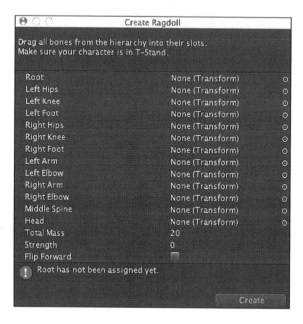

2. Go back to the **Hierarchy** view and click on the triangle in front of `robot_AI_ragdoll` to see the child names `roothandle`, then drag it to the **Root** in the **Create Ragdoll** window, as shown in the following screenshot:

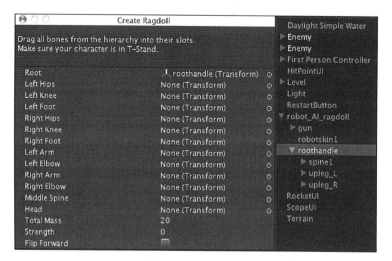

3. Drag the `upleg_L` to the **Left Hips** in the **Create Ragdoll** window and click on the **upleg_L** to bring its child names **lowleg_L**.

4. Drag the `lowleg_L` to the **Left Knee** in the **Create Ragdoll** window. Then, we will click on the **lowleg_L** to bring up its child names **heel_L** and drag it to the **Left Foot** in the **Create Ragdoll** window.

5. Do the same thing with the right side by dragging the `upleg_R` to the **Right Hips**, `lowleg_R` to the **Right Knee**, and `heel_R` and drag it to the **Right Foot** in the **Create Ragdoll** window, as shown in the following screenshot:

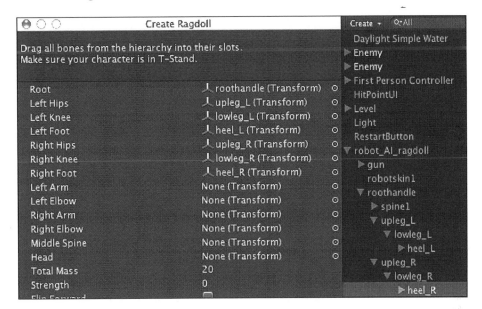

 We can hold down the _Option_ (for Mac) or _Alt_ (for Windows) key and click on the triangle in front of the object to expand or collapse the object's children.

6. We are done with the lower part of the character, so let's continue with the upper part of the body by applying everything as follows:

  - **Left Arm: uparm_L**
  - **Left Elbow: elbow_L**
  - **Right Arm: uparm_R**
  - **Right Elbow: elbow_R**
  - **Middle Spine: spine1**
  - **Head: head**

We can also see the results as shown in the following screenshot:

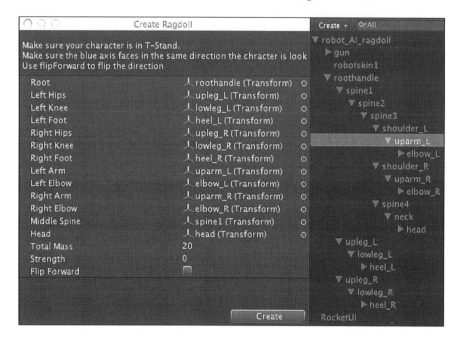

7. Click on the **Create** button to create the ragdoll for our AI object. If you click on robot_AI_ragdoll, you will see that the capsule and box colliders add on each joint, as shown in the following screenshot:

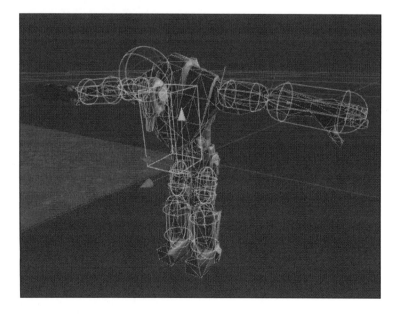

However, we are not done yet. From the preceding screenshot, we will see that we still need to adjust the colliders associated with the character shape.

8. Click on `head` in the **Hierarchy** view, go to the **Inspector** view, and set the following:

   ▸ **Sphere Collider**

       ❑ **Radius: 0.15**

       ❑ **Center: X: -0.04 Y: -0.06 Z: 0**

9. Next, click on `roothandle` in the **Hierarchy** view, go to the **Inspector** view, and set the following:

   ▸ **Box Collider**

       ❑ **Size: X: 1.3 Y: 0.5 Z: 0.35**

       ❑ **Center: X: -0.5 Y: -0.1 Z: -0.175**

10. Click on `spine1` in the **Hierarchy**, go to the **Inspector** view, and set the following:

    ▸ **Box Collider**

        ❑ **Size: X: 1.3 Y: 0.5 Z: 0.35**

        ❑ **Center: X: -0.32 Y: 0.1 Z: -0.175**

11. We just set up the ragdoll for the AI game object, but we still need to apply the collider and **Rigidbody** to the gun. So click on the **gun** game object and apply the **Rigidbody** to it by going to **Component | Physics | Rigidbody**. Go to the **Inspector** view of this game object and set the following:

    ▸ **Rigidbody**

        ❑ **Mass: 20**

12. Next, click on the triangle in front of the **gun** game object to bring up the **gun_model**, as shown in the following screenshot:

13. Apply the **Box Collider** to the **gun_model**, (which will make the gun collide with other objects when it falls down), by going to **Component | Physics | Box Collider**. We are now done with the creation of the `robot_AI_ragdoll` game object.

14. You can also click on the **robot_AI_ragdoll** game object in the **Hierarchy** view and go to the **Inspector** view, and then click on the **Apply** button to update the prefab, as shown in the following screenshot:

15. As we have already updated the robot_AI_ragdoll prefab in the **Project** view, we don't need the robot_AI_ragdoll game object in the **Hierarchy** view anymore, so we just delete it by right-clicking on it and choosing **Delete**.

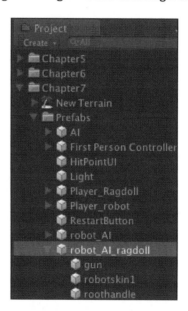

16. Now, we need to go back to the AIController script to enable the robot_AI_ragdoll game object when the AI is dead. Let's open the AIController script and add this script at the beginning, as highlighted in the following code:

```
@script RequireComponent(CharacterController)
//Ragdoll
public var aiRagdoll : GameObject;
//Waypoint
public var wayPoint : Waypoints;
```

17. Then, go to `OnCollisionEnter(collision : Collision)` and add the following highlighted lines of code:

```
//Checking for the collision if the rocket hit the AI
public function OnCollisionEnter(collision : Collision) : void {
   if (collision.transform.tag == "Rocket") {
      var rocket : Rocket = collision.gameObject.
GetComponent(Rocket);
      var f_damage : float = rocket.getDamage();
      aiHP -= f_damage;
      b_isGotHit = true;
      if (aiHP <= 0) {
         aiHP = 0;
         var obj_aiPrefab : GameObject = Instantiate(aiRagdoll,
transform.position, transform.rotation);
         GameObject.Destroy(transform.parent.gameObject);
      }
   }
}
```

18. Save the `AIController` script, and go back to the **Project** view; click on the **AI Prefab**, and go to the **Inspector** view.

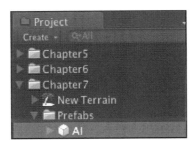

19. We will go to the **Ai Ragdoll** under the **AIController (Script)** and drag `robot_AI_ragdoll` to this **Ai Ragdoll** parameter, as shown in the following screenshot:

With that we are done with this step. We can click **Play** and see the result—when we kill the AI, we will see that the ragdoll game object (the one that we just created) replaces the AI.

Objective Complete - Mini Debriefing

We just created the ragdoll prefab game object to replace the AI when the AI is dead, which will make it look realistic. We also have used `GameObject.Destroy()` to destroy the AI game object in the scene and use the `Instantiate()` function to clone the ragdoll prefab to replace the AI game object that has already been destroyed.

Classified Intel

In this section, we created the ragdoll object to replace our `Enemy` when it dies, which looks good. However, we will see that `robot_AI_ragdoll` just fell down to the ground without any force from the rocket that was fired at it.

To make it much more fun and realistic, we can do this using two different equations.

First, we can add force (using the `AddForce()` function) to our ragdoll's `rigidbody`, which will make our ragdoll move following the rocket direction. We can do this by adding a script in the `OnCollisionEnter(collision : Collision)` in the `AIController` script, as highlighted in the following code:

```
//Checking for the collision if the rocket hit the AI
public function OnCollisionEnter(collision : Collision) : void {
  if (collision.transform.tag == "Rocket") {
    var rocket : Rocket = collision.gameObject.GetComponent(Rocket);
    var f_damage : float = rocket.getDamage();
    aiHP -= f_damage;
    b_isGotHit = true;
    if (aiHP <= 0) {
      aiHP = 0;
      var obj_aiPrefab : GameObject = Instantiate(aiRagdoll,
transform.position, transform.rotation);
      var obj_aiPrefab : GameObject = Instantiate(aiRagdoll,
transform.position, transform.rotation);
```

```
        /* Make the ragdoll react to the rocket force*/
        var f_force : float = 1000;
            //Get transform direction of the rocket
        var v3_rocketDir : Vector3 = rocket.transform.
    TransformDirection(Vector3.forward);
        //Get the rigid body of gun and the ragdoll
        var a_rigid : Rigidbody[] = obj_aiPrefab.GetComponentsInChil
    dren.<Rigidbody>();
        //Apply force to the gun rigidbody and ragdoll
        for (var r : Rigidbody in a_rigid) {
          r.AddForce(v3_rocketDir * f_force);
        }
      GameObject.Destroy(transform.parent.gameObject);
    }
  }
}
```

The second is using the explosive force (using the `AddExplosionForce()` function),
which will make our ragdoll move in a different direction depending on the distance from
the explosive position to our ragdoll's `rigidbody` object. We can do this by replacing the
following script in the same function as in the preceding code:

```
//Checking for the collision if the rocket hit the AI
public function OnCollisionEnter(collision : Collision) : void {
  if (collision.transform.tag == "Rocket") {
    var rocket : Rocket = collision.gameObject.GetComponent(Rocket);
    var f_damage : float = rocket.getDamage();
    aiHP -= f_damage;
    b_isGotHit = true;
    if (aiHP <= 0) {
      aiHP = 0;
      var obj_aiPrefab : GameObject = Instantiate(aiRagdoll,
  transform.position, transform.rotation);
        /* Make the ragdoll react to the explosion force*/
        var f_force : float = 1000;
        //Get the rigid body of gun and the ragdoll
        var a_rigid : Rigidbody[] = obj_aiPrefab.GetComponentsInChil
    dren.<Rigidbody>();
        //Apply force to the gun rigidbody and ragdoll
        for (var r : Rigidbody in a_rigid) {
          r.AddExplosionForce(f_force, rocket .transform.position,
    100.0);
        }
      GameObject.Destroy(transform.parent.gameObject);
    }
  }
}
```

> The `AddExplosionForce()` function basically applies a force to the `rigidbody`, which will simulate the explosion effects. You can see more details on the `AddExplosionForce()` function from the following Unity scripting document:
>
> `http://unity3d.com/support/documentation/ScriptReference/Rigidbody.AddExplosionForce.html`.

Creating a destructible wall

In this section, we will start creating the destructible wall with the multiple cube game objects in the Unity engine as well as adding some code to the `rocket` script to make this wall breakable when the player shoots the rocket to hit it.

Prepare for Lift Off

First, we will create the new **Tag** by going to (**Edit | Project Settings | Tags**) to bring out the Tags' **Inspector** view. In the **Inspector** view, we click on the triangle in front of the **Tags** element and at the `Element 4` type `Destructible`, as we can see in the following screenshot:

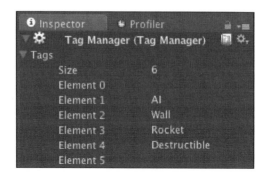

Next, we will go to **GameObject | Create Empty** to create the empty game object and name it `Wall` and reset its transform position to **X: 0, Y: 0, Z: 0**.

Engage Thrusters

Now we have set the `Destructible` tag and created an empty game object, `Wall`. Next, we will be creating the four cubes to represent each piece of the broken wall:

1. Go to **GameObject | Create Other | Cube** name it `Cube1`, and drag it inside the `Wall` game object, which we just created.

2. Add the **Rigidbody** to the **Cube** to make it fall realistically when it breaks by going to **Component | Physics | Rigidbody** and adding **Rigidbody**.

3. Next, we will go to the cube **Inspector** view to set up the parameters as follows:

   ▸ **Tag**: **Destructible**

   ▸ **Transform**

      ❏ **Position**: **X: 3 Y: 23.5 Z: 0**

      ❏ **Rotation**: **X: 0 Y: 0 Z: 0**

      ❏ **Scale**: **X: 6 Y: 6 Z: 1**

   ▸ **Box Collider**

      ❏ **Material**: **Rock** (Drag **Rock** physics material in the `Chapter7` folder to **Project** view here)

   ▸ **Mesh Renderer**

      ❏ **Materials**:

         ❏ **Size**: **1**

         ❏ **Element 0**: **Rock** (Drag **Rock** material in the `Chapter7` folder to **Project** view here)

   ▸ **Rigidbody**

      ❏ **Mass**: **100**

      ❏ **Is Kinematic**: **Check**

4. Now we have finished setting up the first cube. Let's duplicate three more cubes by pressing *Command + D* (for Mac), or *Control + D* (for Windows) and name all three `Cube2`, `Cube3`, and `Cube4`, as shown in the following screenshot:

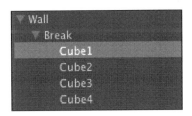

5. Then, we go to each new cube's **Inspector** view and set up its transform position as follows:

   ▸ **Transform (Cube2)**

      ❏ **Position**: **X: 3 Y: 29.5 Z: 0**

   ▸ **Transform (Cube3)**

      ❏ **Position**: **X: -3 Y: 29.5 Z: 0**

- ▸ **Transform (Cube4)**
  - ❏ **Position: X: -3 Y: 23.5 Z: 0**

6. We will click on the `Wall` game object in the **Hierarchy** view and go to the **Inspector** view and set up its **Transform** as follows:

   - ▸ **Transform**
     - ❏ **Position: X: 1037.5 Y: -16.5 Z: 693**
     - ❏ **Rotation: X: 0 Y: 36 Z: 0**
     - ❏ **Scale: X: 1 Y: 1 Z: 1**

7. Now, we will create the script that makes this wall object break apart when the character shoots at it. Let's go to the `Chapter7/Scripts` folder and double-click the `rocket` script to open this script in the script editor.

8. Inside the `rocket` script, we will add two parameters at the beginning of the script, as highlighted in the following code:

```
@script RequireComponent(ConstantForce)
//Add the explosion force and radius
public var explosionRadius : float = 50;
public var explosionForce : float = 1000;
```

9. Next, we will go to the `OnCollisionEnter (others : Collision)` function and add the following highlighted script:

```
public function OnCollisionEnter (others : Collision) : void {
  //Create the explosion on the first impact point of the rocket
and collider
  var contactPoint : ContactPoint = others.contacts[0];
  var rotation : Quaternion = Quaternion.FromToRotation(Vector3.
up, contactPoint.normal);
  GameObject.Instantiate(explosionParticle, contactPoint.point,
rotation);

  //Get the transform position of the rocket
  var v3_position : Vector3 = transform.position;
  //Get all colliders that touches or insides the explosion radius
  var a_hits : Collider[] = Physics.OverlapSphere(v3_position,
explosionRadius);
  for (var c : Collider in a_hits) {
    // Check tag
    if (c.tag == "Destructible") {
      //Get all rigidbody of the colliders
      var r : Rigidbody = c.rigidbody;
      if (r != null) {
        //Explosion
        r.isKinematic = false;
        r.AddExplosionForce(explosionForce, v3_position,
explosionRadius);
```

```
            }
          }
        }
      KillObject();
    }
```

10. Save and click on the **Play** button; if we go to the right path in the scene, we will see the `Wall` object that we have just created. We can shoot at it and it will break, as shown in the following screenshot:

Objective Complete - Mini Debriefing

In this step, we basically just created the four cube objects, and each one will have its own collider and `rigidbody`, which will make them have their direction when we apply the explosion force from the rocket that was fired at them. This will create a realistic behavior for the wall when it's breaking apart, as shown in the following diagram:

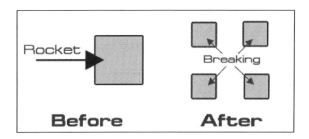

We also use the `Physics.OverlapSphere()` function to check for all the colliders that touch or get inside the explosion radius.

> For more information about the `Physics.OverlapSphere()` function, you can go to the following Unity scripting document:
>
> `http://unity3d.com/support/documentation/`
> `ScriptReference/Physics.OverlapSphere.`
> `html?from=Rigidbody.`

Classified Intel

In this step, we have used the **Rock Physics Material** apply to the Box Collider material in the cube, to which we can apply the friction and bounciness value for each object to get a realistic reaction when calculating the physics.

For the **Rock Physics Material**, we set the **Dynamic Friction** to **0.3** and **Static Friction** to **0.3**, which will make each piece have some small friction when it collides with another, because we don't want the rock too slippery or too hard to move. Since we don't want each piece of wall bouncing, we set the **Bounciness** to **0**, as shown in the following screenshot:

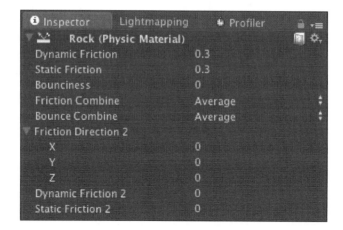

> For more details, you can go to the Unity website at:
>
> `http://unity3d.com/support/documentation/`
> `Components/class-PhysicMaterial.html.`

Creating a rockslide and trigger area

In the last section we created the destructible wall object, which contains four cubes, each with the **Rigidbody** and **Box Collider** attached to it, and we can shoot to break it.

In this last section, we will create the rockslide that the rock will fall on when the player hits the trigger area and creates the `Rocks` and `TriggerArea` script to enable and disable the `Rockslide` object.

Prepare for Lift Off

Go to **GameObject | Create Empty** to create the empty game object and name it `Rockslide` and reset its position to **X: 0, Y: 0, Z: 0**.

Then, create another empty game object by going to **GameObject | Create Empty**; name it `Break` and drag it inside the `Rockslide`, as shown in the following screenshot:

Next, create two cube objects, which will be the static object to make it look like some part of the rock is still stuck to the terrain, and the trigger area to make the rock fall down when the player hits it. Before we start, we need to reset the **Transform** of the `Break` game object to default by clicking on the little gear on the right-hand side and then choose **Reset**.

Engage Thrusters

We will start by creating eight cubes to represent the rock pieces that will fall down:

1. Let's go to **GameObject | Create Other | Cube**, name it `Cube1`, and drag it inside the `Break` game object inside `Rockslide`, which we just created.

2. Then, we will add the **Rigidbody** to the `Cube1` by going to **Component | Physics | Rigidbody**.

3. Next, we will go to the cube **Inspector** view to set up the parameters as follows:

   ▸ **Transform**

      ▫ **Position: X: -1.5 Y: 0 Z: 0**

      ▫ **Rotation: X: 0 Y: 0 Z: 0**

      ▫ **Scale: X: 3 Y: 3 Z: 5**

- ▸ **Box Collider**
    - ❑ **Material**: **Rock** (Drag **Rock** physics material in the `Chapter7` folder to **Project** view here)
- ▸ **Mesh Renderer**
    - ❑ **Materials**:
        - ❑ **Size**: **1**
        - ❑ **Element 0**: **Rock** (Drag **Rock** material in the `Chapter7` folder in **Project** view here)
- ▸ **Rigidbody**
    - ❑ **Mass**: **6000**
    - ❑ **Is Kinematic**: **Check**

4. Now, we have finished setting up the first cube. Let's duplicate seven more cubes by pressing *Command + D* (for Mac) or *Control + D* (for Windows) keys, and naming all seven cubes `Cube2`, `Cube3`, `Cube4`, `Cube5`, `Cube6`, `Cube7`, and `Cube8` similar to what we did for the `Wall` game object in the third step. Then, we go to each new cube's **Inspector** view and set up its position as follows:

- ▸ **Transform (Cube2)**
    - ❑ **Position**: **X: 1.5   Y: 0 Z: 0**
- ▸ **Transform (Cube3)**
    - ❑ **Position**: **X: -1.5 Y: 0 Z: 5**
- ▸ **Transform (Cube4)**
    - ❑ **Position**: **X: 1.5 Y: 0 Z: 5**
- ▸ **Transform (Cube5)**
    - ❑ **Position**: **X: -1.5 Y: 0 Z: 10**
- ▸ **Transform (Cube6)**
    - ❑ **Position**: **X: 1.5 Y: 0 Z: 10**
- ▸ **Transform (Cube7)**
    - ❑ **Position**: **X: -1.5 Y: 0 Z: 15**
- ▸ **Transform (Cube8)**
    - ❑ **Position**: **X: 1.5 Y: 0 Z: 15**

5. Now, we need two static objects that won't be falling down. Let's duplicate the `Cube1` object that we just created by pressing *Command + D* (for Mac) or *Control + D* (for Windows), name it `CubeBase1`, and drag it outside the `Break` game object but inside the `Rockslide` game object, as shown in the following screenshot:

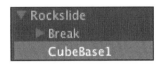

6. Go to the **CubeBase1 Inspector** view and set the parameters as follows:

  ▸ **Transform**

     ❑ **Position**: X: 0 Y: 0 Z: -5

     ❑ **Rotation**: X: 0 Y: 0 Z: 0

     ❑ **Scale**: X: 6 Y: 3 Z: 5

  ▸ **Rigidbody**: Right-click and choose **Remove Component**

7. Duplicate this object to another side by pressing *Command + D* (for Mac) or *Control + D* (for Windows), name it `CubeBase2`, and set its **Transform** as follows:

  ▸ **Transform**

     ❑ **Position**: X: 0 Y: 0 Z: 20

     ❑ **Rotation**: X: 0 Y: 0 Z: 0

     ❑ **Scale**: X: 6 Y: 3 Z: 5

8. We are almost done creating this object. The last thing is creating the trigger area to make the rock fall down when the player hits this area. So, we go to **GameObject | Create Empty**, name it `TriggerArea`, and drag it inside the `Rockslide` game object.

9. Then, add the **Box Collider** to it by going to **Component | Physics | Box Collider**, and then set the parameters as follows:

  ▸ **Transform**

     ❑ **Position**: X: -35 Y: -15 Z: -3

     ❑ **Rotation**: X: 0 Y: -25 Z: 0

     ❑ **Scale**: X: 1 Y: 1 Z: 1

  ▸ **Box Colider**

     ❑ **Is Trigger**: Check

     ❑ **Size**: X: 12 Y: 36 Z: 24

We are done with creating the `Rockslide` game object, which will look something similar to the following screenshot:

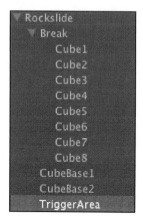

We now need to create the new script to control the **Rockslide**. Go to **Assets | Create | Javascript**, name it `Rocks`, and replace the code as follows:

```
public var downForce : float = 10;
private var a_rigid : Rigidbody[]; //Array of the children's Rigidbody
private var b_isTrigger : boolean = false;  // Is this object is
already triggered (Use for Trigger object)
private var in_count : int = 0; //Counting the number of Kinematic
Rock

//Setup Index of Children before start
public function Awake () : void {
  b_isTrigger = false;
  a_childRock = new Array();
  int_childLength = 0;
  in_count = 0;
  //Get all children's rigidbody
  a_rigid = gameObject.GetComponentsInChildren.<Rigidbody>();
}

// Use this for initialization
public function Start () : void {
  //Disable rigidbody before it triggered or hit by rocket
  DisabledRigidBody();
}
```

From the preceding code, we get the array of the children of `rigidbody` by using the `gameObject.GetComponentsInChildren.<Rigidbody>()` function. Next, we will add the code to make the rocks stop moving when they fall down and their velocity is close to zero by adding the following code:

```
//  Update every frame
public function Update () : void {
   if (b_isTrigger == true) {
     for (var r : Rigidbody in a_rigid) {
        if (r.isKinematic == false) {
           var f_sqrLen : float = (r.velocity).sqrMagnitude;
           if (f_sqrLen <= 0.0) {
              r.useGravity = false;
              r.isKinematic = true;
              in_count++;
           }
        }
     }
     //Stop updating if all the rocks stop moving
     if (in_count >= a_rigid.Length) {
       b_isTrigger = false;
     }
   }
}
```

As the last step of the script, we will add the function for getting and setting `b_isTrigger`, and also enable and disable `rigidbody`, as shown in the following script:

```
public function GetTrigger() : boolean {
   return b_isTrigger;
}

public function SetTrigger( _isTrigger : boolean) : boolean {
   b_isTrigger = _isTrigger;
}

public function EnabledRigidbody () : void {
   for (var r : Rigidbody in a_rigid) {
     r.useGravity = true;
     r.isKinematic = false;
     //Apply the velocity to the rigidbody in the -y direction to make
the object fall faster
     r.velocity = new Vector3(0, -downForce, 0);
   }
}
```

```
public function DisabledRigidBody() : void {
   for (var r : Rigidbody in a_rigid) {
      r.useGravity = false;
      r.isKinematic = true;
   }
}
```

We will use this `Rocks` script with our `Break` game object in the `Rockslide` to enable and disable `rigidbody` of its children by setting the `isKinematic` to `false` or `true`.

Next, we will need another script to control the trigger area, which will trigger the `Rockslide` falling down. Go back to Unity and go to **Assets | Create | Javascript** to create a new script and name this new script `TriggerArea`, and replace the code as follows:

```
public var rocks : Rocks;

public function OnTriggerEnter(collider : Collider) : void {
   if ((collider.transform.tag == "Player") && (rocks.GetTrigger() ==
false)) {
      rocks.EnabledRigidbody();
      rocks.SetTrigger(true);
   }
}
```

The preceding code basically tells us that if the player enters the trigger area, we will enable the `rigidbody` and make the rock fall down.

Go back to Unity and we will do the last step, which is attaching the script to the `Rockslide` game object. Let's click on the `Break` game object inside `Rockslide` and drag the `Rocks` script on it.

Then, we will click on the `TriggerArea` object inside `Rockslide` and drag the `TriggerArea` script that we just created on it. Then, we will go to the `TriggerArea` **Inspector** view and set the following:

- ▸ **Trigger Area (Script):**
  - ▫ **Rocks: Break** (Drag **Break** game object, the child of the `Rockslide` object, to the **Hierarchy** here)

Finally, we will click on the `Rockslide` game object and set its **Transform** as follows:

▶ **Transform:**

    ❏ **Position**: X: **1069** Y: **32.5** Z: **677**

    ❏ **Rotation**: X: **0** Y: **140** Z: **0**

    ❏ **Scale**: X: **1** Y: **1** Z: **1**

Now, we are finished, let's click **Play** to see our result. We will see that if we are entering the `TriggerArea` the rock will start falling down.

 We can also click on `TriggerArea` and watch our character walk into it from the **Scene** view.

Objective Complete - Mini Debriefing

We have created another destructible object, which will fall down when the player gets close to it by creating the trigger area that will be triggered when the player has entered the area. We also created the new `TriggerArea` script that was used to detect the player as well as the `Rocks` script to enable `rigidbody` and make the object destructible.

Classified Intel

In this step, we have used the `rigidbody.isKinematic = true` to disable our `rigidbody` and enable the `rigidbody` by setting it to `false`. This is the trick that we can use to check whether our object reacted with the physics or not. We can also adapt this trick when we want to play animation of this object that has the `rigidbody` attached to it by setting the `rigidbody.isKinematic` to `true`—to play the animation and disable the physics movement—or setting the `rigidbody.isKinematic` to `false`—to disable the animation and enable the physics movement.

Game over-Wrapping it up

In this chapter, we have optimized the `AIController.js` by changing from the `Physics.CapsuleCast` to `Physics.Raycast` to increase the FPS in our game. Then, we learned how to create the ragdoll object and apply it to the character when it is dead by using `Instatiate()` and `Destroy()` functions to clone the ragdoll prefab and replace the old object.

Then, we created the destructible `Wall` and destroyed it when we shot at it by adding some script to the `rocket` script.

We also created the `Rockslide` game object, the `Rocks` script to enable and disable `rigidbody` of the rocks, and the `triggerArea` game object to make the object fall down when the player hits the `triggerArea` by using another script (`TriggerArea`).

So, let's take a look at the screenshot of what we have done so far:

The rock falls down when the player hits the trigger area as shown in the previous screenshot.

The player shoots and destroys the destructible wall as shown in the previous screenshot.

The AI gets killed as shown in the previous screenshot.

The player gets killed as shown in the previous screenshot.

Are you ready to go gung ho?
A Hotshot challenge

Now we understand the concept of creating the destructible objects, but the objects that we just created are on the cube from the Unity engine. We can make it more interesting with something like the following:

> ▸ Creating your own object in any 3D software, instead of the cube, to make it much more realistic and attach the `ParentRocks.js` script to it and see how it works

> ▸ Adding some script that will make the rock damage the player and AIs when they get hit while the rock is falling down

> ▸ Adding the smoke particle to the rocks when they are falling down

> ▸ Making the ragdoll match the last AI animation post by creating the ragdoll with the AI game object and using the `isKinematic` method to enable or disable ragdoll physics instead of replacing the new object

> ▸ Creating a random rock that will fall every time the player walks by the lake

Project 8

Let the World See the Carnage! Save, Load, and Post High Scores

In this chapter, we will talk about saving and loading the high score from the local machine or web server.

Why do we need to save the high score? The advantage of the high score is to keep a record of the players and how well they progress each time they play the game. It also creates a challenge for the players to beat their record and keep playing the game again. For the online game, the high score is very important to let the players see their progress and compare with their friends or other players.

Mission briefing

We will create a simple high score table so that the players can save the score locally as well as post their score to the server database, by using the example project that is in this chapter.

This chapter is basically the extension of the project in *Project 7, Creating a Destructible and Interactive Virtual World*, and it includes the new **RESTART** button (using the OnGUI function instead of the **GUITexture** button). It also includes the time UI and score UI for the player to see the result when they complete the game.

We will start by creating the high score menu for saving and loading the score from our local machine by using the `PlayerPrefs` class in Unity, which allows us to save the parameters locally to our machine (this is very similar to `SharedObject` in ActionScript 3.0).

Then, we will create the C# `XMLParser` script that will be used to get the XML value of the return data from the provided database server. Next, we will create the Unity `Javascript`, which will handle the posting and loading of scores from the database server.

Finally, we need to encrypt our high score by using the MD5 encryption class written by *Matthew Wegner*. For more details please refer to the following website:

`http://www.unifycommunity.com/wiki/index.php?title=MD5.`

The MD5 encryption script will allow us to encrypt the hash key, which will prevent submission of fake high scores.

What Does It Do?

When we finish this chapter, we will have the **GAME OVER** menu, which has four buttons to allow the players to submit their score on their local machine and server database, to load the high score data from the player's local machine, to load the high score from the server database, and a **RESTART** button to replay the game.

Why Is It Awesome?

What we will get from this chapter is the way to use `PlayerPrefs` to save high score. This `PlayerPrefs` also allows us to save game data, such as the location of the player, current stage, or current hit points. We will learn how to set up the basic database server by using MySQL and PHP script to return the high score data in the XML format to the game. We will also look at how to create the C# script to parse our XML data for using our high score table. Lastly, we will get to know how to use MD5 script to encrypt the user data before sending to the server database.

Your Hotshot Objectives

We will start by importing the `chapter8` package, which we will download in the next section, and then begin creating the high score table with the following topics:

- ▶ Creating a high score menu
- ▶ Saving and loading local high score
- ▶ Getting XML data from server
- ▶ Posting and loading high score to server

Mission Checklist

First, we need the `chapter8` package. We can start by going to this URL: `http://www.packtpub.com/support?nid=8267` to download the `Chapter8.zip` package. The package will contain all the necessary resources such as assets, scripts, and prefabs that we will be using for this project.

Then, we import the package to Unity as we did for the other chapters, as shown in the following screenshot:

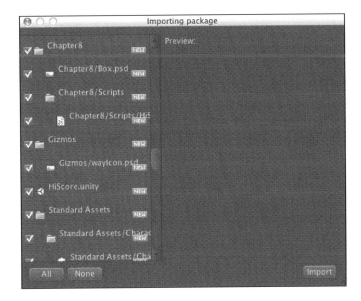

In the **Project** view, we will see the **Chapter5**, **Chapter6**, **Chapter7**, **Chapter8**, **Gizmos** folders, the **HiScore** scene, and **Standard Assets**. The **Chapter5**, **Chapter6**, and **Chapter7** folders will contain all the scripts, assets, terrain, and prefabs, which we will use from the previous chapters. The **Chapter8** folder will have the `Box.psd` file, `HiScore.php` script, and a `scripts` folder that contains the `HiScore.js` script, which we will use in this chapters. The **Gizmos** folder will contain the `wayIcon.png` file. **Standard Assets** contains all the necessary built-in assets that will be used in the chapter. Finally, **HiScore** is the scene we will use for this chapter.

Double-click on the **HI-SCORE** scene to open the scene for **Chapter8**.

Creating a high score menu

In this section, we will create three menu pages.

First is the game over menu, which will contain the following:

- The final score of the player
- The text field for the player to enter his/her name
- The **SUBMIT** button to save the player's score
- The **LOCAL HI-SCORE** button to see the scores from the player's local machine
- The **SERVER HI-SCORE** button to see the scores from the database server
- The **RESTART** button to replay the game

Second is the local high score table menu, which will contain the high score data in the scrolled area that loads the local high score data from the player machine when the player clicks on the **LOCAL HI-SCORE** button on the first page.

Also, the server high score table page will be similar to the local high score page except that the score data in this table will load from the database on the server, which allows the duplicate names.

Prepare for Lift Off

Double-click the `HiScore` script to open **MonoDevelop** and start adapting in `HiScore` script. Now we are ready to roll.

Engage Thrusters

We will start creating the **GAMEOVER** menu by using the `OnGUI()` function, similar to what we did in *Project 2, Creating a Menu in an RPG*:

1. At the beginning of this script, type the highlighted code in the `HiScore.js` after the line `public var customSkin : GUISkin;`, as shown next:

```
public var customSkin : GUISkin;

//Setting the default string on the submit text field
public static var userName : String = "Player 1";

//Setting the maximum number of users displayed on the scoreboard
public var maxUsers : int = 10;
```

```
//Creating the enum parameter for the menu page
enum Page { GAMEOVER, LOCALSCORE, SERVERSCORE };

//Creating the enum parameter for the menu page
private var e_page : Page = Page.GAMEOVER;

//Creating the scroll position for the local high score scroller
area
private var scrollPositionL : Vector2 = Vector2.zero;

//Creating the scroll position for the server high score scroller
area
private var scrollPositionS : Vector2 = Vector2.zero;

//Checking if the restart button is clicked by the user
private var b_isClickRestart : boolean = false;

//Checking if the submit button is clicked by the user
private var b_isClickSubmit : boolean = false;
```

2. Next, set up the default value for our parameters by adding the following script to the `Start()` function:

```
public function Start() : void {
  //Initializing
  e_page = Page.GAMEOVER;
  scrollPosition = Vector2.zero;
  b_isClickRestart = false;
  b_isClickSubmit = false;
}
```

3. Continue to the next function `OnGUI()`; we will add more script here to create our **GAMEOVER** menu page. So let us add the highlighted script as follows:

```
public function OnGUI() : void {
  if (StaticVars.b_isGameOver) {
    GUI.skin = customSkin;
    //Checking if we didn't click on the restart button
    if (b_isClickRestart == false) {
      //Checking for the current page
      switch (e_page) {
        case Page.GAMEOVER:
          GameoverPage(); //Creating game over page
          break;
        case Page.LOCALSCORE:
          LocalScorePage(); //Creating local score page
```

```
            break;
          case Page.SERVERSCORE:
            ServerScorePage(); //Creating server score page
            break;
        }
        //Creating the Restart Button
        if (GUI.Button(new Rect((Screen.width - 240)*0.5, (Screen.
height*0.1) + 320, 240, 30), "RESTART")) {
            b_isClickRestart = true;
            Restart();
        }
      } else {
        //If we clicked on the restart button - just put the
Loading... text here
        GUI.Box(new Rect(Screen.width*0.1, Screen.height*0.1,
Screen.width * 0.8, Screen.height * 0.8), "", GUI.skin.
GetStyle("Box2"));
        GUI.Label(new Rect((Screen.width-150)*0.5, (Screen.
height-50)*0.5, 150, 50), "LOADING...", GUI.skin.
GetStyle("Text1"));
      }
    }
}
```

4. Then, create the new GameoverPage() function:

```
//Creating Gameover Page GUI
private function GameoverPage() : void {
  //Creating the background box
  GUI.Box(new Rect(Screen.width*0.1, Screen.height*0.1, Screen.
width * 0.8, Screen.height * 0.8), "GAMEOVER", GUI.skin.
GetStyle("Box2"));
  //Creating Text Label to show the final score of the player
  GUI.Label(new Rect((Screen.width - 400)*0.5, (Screen.height*0.1)
+ 50, 400, 25), "Final Score: " + TimeScoreUI.int_currentScore.
ToString(), GUI.skin.GetStyle("Text1"));
  //If the user didn't click submit, we create the submit button
and text field for the player to submit the score
  if (b_isClickSubmit == false) {
    GUI.Label(new Rect((Screen.width - 300)*0.5, (Screen.
height*0.1) + 80, 300, 25), "Enter Your Name", GUI.skin.
GetStyle("Text1"));
    //Creating the input text field to get the player name
    userName = GUI.TextField(new Rect((Screen.width - 240)*0.5,
(Screen.height*0.1) + 120, 240, 40), userName, 8);
    //Submit button
```

```
    if (GUI.Button(new Rect((Screen.width - 240)*0.5, (Screen.
height*0.1) + 200, 240, 30), "SUBMIT")) {
        b_isClickSubmit = true;
        //TODO: Submitting both local and server high score here
    }
}
//Creating the Local Hi-Score page button
if (GUI.Button(new Rect((Screen.width - 240)*0.5, (Screen.
height*0.1) + 240, 240, 30), "LOCAL HI-SCORE")) {
    e_page = Page.LOCALSCORE;
}
//Creating the Server Hi-Score page button
if (GUI.Button(new Rect((Screen.width - 240)*0.5, (Screen.
height*0.1) + 280, 240, 30), "SERVER HI-SCORE")) {
    //TODO: Loading the score data from server here
    e_page = Page.SERVERSCORE;
}
}
```

5. Next, we will create the `LocalScorePage()` function. This function will load the high score from the player's local machine and display it on the menu. This menu will include the scrolled area and scroll bar to show the player's score data. Let's create the `LocalScorePage()` function as follows:

```
//Loading the local scores
private function LocalScorePage() : void {
    //Creating the background box
    GUI.Box(new Rect(Screen.width*0.1, Screen.height*0.1, Screen.
width * 0.8, Screen.height * 0.8), "LOCAL HI-SCORE", GUI.skin.
GetStyle("Box2"));
    //Creating the scrolled area and scrollbar to view the player
scores
    scrollPositionL = GUI.BeginScrollView (new Rect ((Screen.width
- 320)*0.5, (Screen.height*0.1) + 80, 320, 180), scrollPositionL,
new Rect (0, 0, 300, 30*maxUsers));
    for (var i: int = 0; i < maxUsers; i++) {
        //Setting the number of the user
        GUI.Label(new Rect(0, i * 30, 35, 30), (i+1).ToString() +
".");
        //TODO: Showing the user name and score here
    }
    GUI.EndScrollView (); //End Scroll Area
    if (GUI.Button(new Rect((Screen.width - 240)*0.5, (Screen.
height*0.1) + 280, 240, 30), "BACK")) {
        e_page = Page.GAMEOVER;
    }
}
```

6. This function will create the **LOCAL HI-SCORE** menu that includes the background box, the scrolled area to display the user's scores, and the **Back** button to go back to the **GAMEOVER** page.

7. Finally, we will create the last function for the `HiScore` script, the `ServerScorePage()` function. This function is very similar to the `LocalScorePage()` function that we created earlier, except that this function will load the score data from the server (we will have to wait until it is loaded). We will talk about this in a later step. So right now, we will create the `ServerScorePage()` function as follows:

```
//Loading score from server
private function ServerScorePage() : void {
  //Creating the background box
  GUI.Box(new Rect(Screen.width*0.1, Screen.height*0.1, Screen.
width * 0.8, Screen.height * 0.8), "SERVER HI-SCORE", GUI.skin.
GetStyle("Box2"));
  //TODO: Checking is the loader completed
  scrollPositionS = GUI.BeginScrollView (new Rect ((Screen.width
- 320)*0.5, (Screen.height*0.1) + 80, 320, 180), scrollPositionS,
new Rect (0, 0, 300, 30*maxUsers));
    for (var i: int = 0; i < maxUsers; i++) {
      //Setting the number of the user
        GUI.Label(new Rect(0, i * 30, 35, 30), (i+1).ToString() +
".");
        //TODO: Showing the user name and score here
      }
  GUI.EndScrollView (); //End Scroll Area
  //TODO: If the loader doesn't complete display Loading... text
    if (GUI.Button(new Rect((Screen.width - 240)*0.5, (Screen.
height*0.1) + 280, 240, 30), "BACK")) {
      e_page = Page.GAMEOVER;
    }
}
```

8. Now, we can go back to Unity and click **Play** to see our result by letting the character die or killing all enemies in the scene. We will see something similar to the following screenshot:

We can also include `StaticVars.b_isGameOver = true;` in the `Start()` function to see our **GAMEOVER** menu, right away.

We can click on the **LOCAL HI-SCORE** button or **SERVER HI-SCORE** button to go to another page, click on the **RESTART** button to replay the game, enter the name or the text field and click on the **SUBMIT** button, even though it won't save or send any score right now. At the **LOCAL HI-SCORE** or **SERVER HI-SCORE** page, you can also see the **BACK** button to go back to the **GAMAEOVER** menu, and the **RESTART** button to restart the game.

In the next step, we will be creating the script to save the local high score for the user, which will check whether the player's final score is saved or not. This script will automatically sort the score order from the maximum to minimum, and display it to the scoreboard.

Objective Complete - Mini Debriefing

We just finished creating the **GAMEOVER** menu that will display the player's final score, has the option for the player to submit his/her score, and a button to see the local scoreboard as well as the server scoreboard.

First, we created the `userName` parameter to set the default username on the **Submit** text field, and `maxUsers` to limit the maximum number of users that will display on our scoreboard.

Then, we created the `enum` variable to check for the current page of our menu, which contains the **GAMEOVER** page, local score page, and server score page. We also have the `scrollPosition` parameter to create the scrolled area for the high score table. Then, we have two `boolean` parameters to check whether the **RESTART** and **SUBMIT** buttons have been clicked by the user or not.

In the `OnGui()` function, we first checked if the **RESTART** button is clicked by using the `if` statement to check it. If the **RESTART** button has been clicked, the `Restart()` function will be called and the loading menu will be displayed for the user to wait for the game to restart. On the other hand, if the player doesn't click on the **RESTART** button, the game will show that the menu page depends on the current stage of the page by using the `switch` statement to check for the `e_page` parameters, which are `Page.GAMEOVER`, `Page.LOCALSCORE` and `Page.SERVERSCORE`. Each case will call the function to draw the UI of its menu, which are the `GameoverPage()`, `LocalScorePage()`, and `ServerScorePage()`.

Next, we created the `GameoverPage()` function, which we can divide into three sections. First, we created the background, then the label for our menu, and then we displayed the final score, which is `TimeScoreUI.int_currentScore`. Then, we checked if the player clicked the **SUBMIT** button. If not, we will have the **SUBMIT** button and the text field for the players to enter their names and post their scores. In the last step, we created the **LOCAL HI-SCORE** and **SERVER HI-SCORE** button, which will set the `e_page` parameter to `Page.LOCALSCORE` and `Page.SERVERSCORE`.

Finally, we created the other two functions. The `LocalScorePage()` function will show the result of the high-score table from the local machine, and `ServerScorePage()` will show the result of the high-score table from the server.

Classified Intel

In this chapter, we created the `enum` parameter to check for the menu page.

The `enum` parameter is very similar to the object class that only contains the `Integer` type or we can say that only `int` type in the Unityscript. In Unity JavaScript or C#, we create `enum` by using the same syntax, which is `enum Page { OBJECT1, OBJECT2, OBJECT3 };` or `enum Page { OBJECT1=1, OBJECT2, OBJECT3 };`.

From those scripts, if we don't assign the integer value to any object, the value of each object will automatically be assigned, starting from `0` and so on. If we assign the integer `1` to the first value, then that object value will be `1` instead of `0` and the rest will continue from `1` and so on. We can also assign the number for each object manually, such as `enum Page { OBJECT1=2, OBJECT2=7, OBJECT3=0 };`. This will assign each object to have its own value.

For more details on `enum`, we can go to the following website:

`http://msdn.microsoft.com/en-us/library/sbbt4032%28v=vs.80%29.aspx.`

What is the advantage of using `enum` in Unity? If we take a look at our code at the line `private var e_page : Page = Page.GAMEOVER;` and change the word `private` to `public`, then go back to the Unity and click on the `HiScore` game object to see the **Inspector** view, we will see the new editable parameter names **E_page**, which is the drop-down button. If we click on it, we will see that we can choose only three values, which are **GAMEOVER**, **LOCALSCORE**, and **SERVERSCORE**:

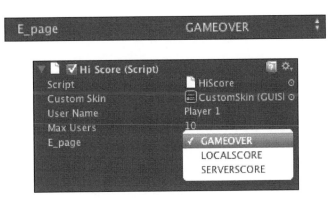

Those names are from the `enum` objects that we assigned in the `HiScore.js` script. The advantage of using `enum` parameter is that we will be able to create the editable value that limits the number of choices and protects an invalid input data, which will save us from having to write an extra code to check for the invalid input data. For example, if we were using integers, having a page value of 500—which is an invalid page number—would not make any sense.

This is very useful when we work with other people or when we are testing the game because we can make it readable for everyone; they can just basically set up the `enum` parameter and then adjust it in the editor while they are testing the game.

Saving and loading the local high score

In this section, we will be creating two scripts for saving and loading the high score from our local machine. The first script will be the `UsersData` script, which will contain all the functions to save and load the score to our local machine by using the `PlayerPrefs` class. Then, we will create the `LocalHiScore` script, which will contain the function to sort user scores and check for the final score submission. Finally, we will go back to the `HiScore` script to create a `LocalHiscore` object to save and load high scores locally.

Prepare for Lift Off

Before we start, we need to know the basic parameters we need to include in the high-score table. We will need the order number, username, and the user score, as shown in the following screenshot:

Engage Thrusters

We will start by creating the `UsersData` class to contain the user data and functions, which will load and save the user data to the local machine using `PlayerPref`:

1. In Unity, go to **Assets | Create | Javascript**, name it **UsersData** and double-click to open **MonoDevelop**, and then replace the script as follows (you should remove all the existing script that is automatically created with Unity):

```
class UsersData {
  //Game Key - to make sure that each object has different key set
  public var keylocal : String = "ShooterLocal";
  private var s_keyScore : String = "Score";
  private var s_keyName : String = "Name";

  private var s_name : String;
  private var int_score : int;
  private var as_randomNames : String[] = ["Antony", "John",
"Will", "Kate", "Jill"]; //To get a random name

  //Setting the user name and score
  public function Init(name : String, score : int) : void {
    int_score = score;
    s_name = name;
  }
```

```
   public function GetName() : String {
     return s_name;
   }

   public function GetScore() : int {
     return int_score;
   }
```

2. We just created the `Init()` function to set up the score and name from this object. Next, we will create the `SaveLocal()` function, which will get the index and save the name and score to our local machine by using `PlayerPref`:

```
//Saving Data
   public function SaveLocal (index : int) : void {
     //Saving user score
     PlayerPrefs.SetInt(keylocal + s_keyScore + index.ToString(),
int_score);
     //Saving user name
     PlayerPrefs.SetString(keylocal + s_keyName + index.ToString(),
s_name);
   }
```

3. Then, we will create the `LoadLocal()`, `LoadScore()`, and `LoadName()` functions, which will load the user's score and name from the index:

```
//Loading Data
   public function LoadLocal (index : int) : void {
     int_score = LoadScore(index);
     s_name = LoadName(index);
   }

   private function LoadScore (index : int) : int {
     //Checking to see if the value already exists
     var s_newKey : String = keylocal + s_keyScore + index.
ToString();
     if (PlayerPrefs.HasKey(s_newKey)) {
       return PlayerPrefs.GetInt(keylocal + s_keyScore + index.
ToString());
     } else {
       //If no key exist return 0 score
       return 0;
     }
   }

   private function LoadName (index : int) : String {
```

```
//Checking to see if the value already exist
var s_newKey : String = keylocal + s_keyName + index.
ToString();
if (PlayerPrefs.HasKey(s_newKey)) {
    return PlayerPrefs.GetString(keylocal + s_keyName + index.
ToString());
} else {
    //If no key exist return random name;
    var int_random : int = Random.Range(0, as_randomNames.
length);
    return as_randomNames[int_random];
}
}
}
```

4. Next, we will continue creating the next script, so let's create the `LocalHiScore` script and replace it as follows:

```
class LocalHiScore {
    private var int_maxUser : int;
    private var int_minScore : int;
    private var as_users : UsersData[]; //To get all loader data
name

}
```

5. Here, we set up the `LocalHiScore` script to have `class` keyword, which is similar to the `UsersData` script, because we don't need this class to inherit from `MonoBehaviour`. We also set up all necessary parameters for this class. Next, we will add the setup function and load function to this class. Let's add the following highlighted code:

```
class LocalHiScore {
    private var int_maxUser : int;
    private var int_minScore : int;
    private var as_users : UsersData[]; //To get all loader data
name

    //Setting the maximum user to display on the menu
    //Loading the user data and store it in here
    public function SetMaxUser (maxUser : int ) : void
        int_maxUser = maxUser;
        //Loading all the users data from the local machine
        LoadGameLocal();
    }

    public function LoadGameLocal () : void {
```

```
         //Creating the array of UsersData object
         as_users = new UsersData[int_maxUser];
         //Creating the array of int to store all the user scores data
         var a_scores : int[] = new int[int_maxUser];
         for (var i: int = 0; i < int_maxUser; i++) {
            //Creating the user data object, load data, and store it to
      the UsersData array
            var obj_user : UsersData = new UsersData();
            obj_user.LoadLocal(i);
            as_users[i] = obj_user;
            a_scores[i] = as_users[i].GetScore();
         }
         //Getting the minimum score for the save data purpose
         int_minScore = Mathf.Min(a_scores);
      }
   }
```

6. Then, we will add the SaveGame (scores : int, name : String) and SortUser (array : UsersData[]) functions to sort the user data and save it to the local machine after the LoadGameLocal() function, as shown highlighted in the following code:

```
class LocalHiScore {
 //Above Script
 /////////////////////////////

 public function LoadGameLocal () : void {
    //Creating the array of UsersData object
    as_users = new UsersData[int_maxUser];
    //Creating the array of int to store all the user scores data
    var a_scores : int[] = new int[int_maxUser];
    for (var i: int = 0; i < int_maxUser; i++) {
       //Creating the user data object, load data, and store it to
   the UsersData array
       var obj_user : UsersData = new UsersData();
       obj_user.LoadLocal(i);
       as_users[i] = obj_user;
       a_scores[i] = as_users[i].GetScore();
    }
    //Getting the minimum score for the save data purpose
    int_minScore = Mathf.Min(a_scores);
 }

 public function SaveGame (scores : int, name : String) : void {
```

```
        //Submitting the score if the score is higher than the minimum
score of the database
        if (scores >= int_minScore) {
            var a_newData : Array = new Array(as_users);
            //Removing the last Array
            a_newData.Pop();
            //Create new user and save it to array
            var obj_user : UsersData = new UsersData();
            obj_user.Init(name, scores);
            a_newData.Add(obj_user);
            //Setting JS Array back to Builtin
            as_users = a_newData.ToBuiltin(UsersData);
            //Sorting Data
            SortUser(as_users);
        }
        for (var i: int = 0; i < int_maxUser; i++) {
            as_users[i].SaveLocal(i);
        }
    }


    //Sorting the score from the maximum to minimum
    private function SortUser (array : UsersData[]) : void {
        for (var i : int = 0; i < array.length-1; i++) {
            for (var j : int = i+1; j < array.length; j++) {
                //If the first score is lower than second score swap the
position
                if (array[i].GetScore() <= array[j].GetScore()) {
                    var obj_temp : UsersData = array[i];
                    array[i] = array[j];
                    array[j] = obj_temp;
                }
            }
        }
    }
}
```

7. We will add two more functions for getting the user score and name from the index to use it to display on the menu after the `SortUser (array : UsersData[])` function, as shown in the following code:

```
class LocalHiScore {
  //Above Script
  ////////////////////////////

  //Sort the score from the maximum to minimum
```

```
private function SortUser (array : UsersData[]) : void {
    for (var i : int = 0; i < array.length-1; i++) {
        for (var j : int = i+1; j < array.length; j++) {
            //If the first score is lower than the second score swap
the position
            if (_array[i].GetScore() <= array[j].GetScore()) {
                var obj_temp : UsersData = array[i];
                array[i] = array[j];
                array[j] = obj_temp;
            }
        }
    }
}

public function GetNameData(index : int) : String {
    return as_users[index].GetName();
}

public function GetScoreData(index : int) : int {
    return as_users[index].GetScore();
}
}
```

8. We are almost done. Finally, we will go back to the `HiScore` script to add some scripts and enable the game to save and load the high score locally. Let's go back to the `HiScore` script, at the line before the `Start()` function, and add the following highlighted code:

```
private var b_isClickSubmit : boolean = false; //Checking if the
submit button is clicked by the user

private var obj_localHiScore : LocalHiScore; //Creating the
LocalHiScore Object

public function Start() : void {
    //Initializing
```

9. Then, we will go to the `Start()` function and create the `LocalHiScore` object, as shown highlighted in the following code:

```
public function Start() : void {
    //Initializing
    e_page = Page.GAMEOVER;
    scrollPosition = Vector2.zero;
    b_isClickRestart = false;
    b_isClickSubmit = false;
```

```
//Creating a Local Hiscore Object
obj_localHiScore = new LocalHiScore();
//Setting the maximum scores to show on the table & loading the
local high score data here
    obj_localHiScore.SetMaxUser(maxUsers);
}
```

In this `Start()` function, we created the new `LocalHiScore` object, and set the max user display and load the user data from the local machine.

10. We already have the user data object, and now we need to save the score by going to the `GameoverPage()` function inside the `Submit` button function and type the following highlighted code:

```
//Submit button
    if (GUI.Button(new Rect((Screen.width - 240)*0.5, (Screen.
height*0.1) + 200, 240, 30), "SUBMIT")) {
        b_isClickSubmit = true;
        //TODO: Submitting both local and server high score here
    obj_localHiScore.SaveGame(TimeScoreUI.int_currentScore,
userName); //Submitting to the local score
    }
```

11. This is the code for saving the score locally after the player clicks on the **SUBMIT** button. Then, we save the score to our local machine. Now we need to load the user score data and display it on the menu in the scrolled area by going to the `LocalScorePage()` function and adding the highlighted code as follows:

```
//Loading the local scores
private function LocalScorePage() : void {
    //Creating the background box
    GUI.Box(new Rect(Screen.width*0.1, Screen.height*0.1, Screen.
width * 0.8, Screen.height * 0.8), "LOCAL HI-SCORES", GUI.skin.
GetStyle("Box2"));
    //Creating the scrolled area and scrollbar to view the player
scores
    scrollPosition = GUI.BeginScrollView (new Rect ((Screen.width -
320)*0.5, (Screen.height*0.1) + 80, 320, 180), scrollPosition, new
Rect (0, 0, 300, 30*maxUsers));
    for (var i: int = 0; i < maxUsers; i++) {
        //Set the number of the user
        GUI.Label(new Rect(0, i * 30, 35, 30), (i+1).ToString() +
".");
        //TODO: Showing the user name and score here

        GUI.Label(new Rect(35, i * 30, 120, 30), obj_localHiScore.
GetNameData(i));
```

```
       GUI.Label(new Rect(155, i * 30, 145, 30), GlobalFunction.
    addCommasInt(obj_localHiScore.GetScoreData(i)), GUI.skin.
    GetStyle("Score"));
        }
    GUI.EndScrollView (); //End Scroll Area
    if (GUI.Button(new Rect((Screen.width - 240)*0.5, (Screen.
    height*0.1) + 280, 240, 30), "BACK")) {
        e_page = Page.GAMEOVER;
    }
}
```

These two lines will load the username and score, and display it on the scrolled area in the
LOCAL HI_SCORE menu page.

Next, we can go back to Unity, click **Play**, and try to complete the game by killing all the
enemies to bring up the **GAMEOVER** menu. Right now, we will be able to enter our name,
submit the score, and see the high score board if we click on the **LOCAL HI-SCORE** button:

We typed our name and clicked to submit the score.

If we clicked on the **LOCAL HI-SCORE** button, we will see that our name and score appears on the scoreboard, as shown in the following screenshot:

Objective Complete - Mini Debriefing

We just created two classes, UsersData and LocalHiScore, for saving and loading the user's local high score data and displayed it on the **LOCAL HI-SCORE** page by using the PlayerPrefs to save and load the array of UsersData objects. We also checked for the user submission score and sorted the score before saving it to the local object.

In the UsersData script, we started by creating the class UsersData {. This is because this class only contains the data and doesn't want to use any Start() or Update() function that inherits from the MonoBehaviour class. If we don't put the class keyword, Unity will automatically inherit this class from MonoBehaviour, which is the default setting for Unity Javascript, so it means that we can run this script without adding the class keyword.

We can also inherit the class from MonoBehaviour in Javascript by using the class keyword, as shown in the following script:

```
class MyClass extends MonoBehaviour { }
```

The preceding script will also inherit MyClass from MonoBehaviour.

However, it will be too expensive to use. To make it easy to understand, all scripts that inherit from MonoBehaviour will have the Start(), Update() classes, and all the MonoBehaviour functions run in the Unity background.

The classes that aren't derived from MonoBehaviour objects, Start(), Update(), and so on, won't be called on MonoBehaviour unless they are connected to the game objects.

Next, we set up the necessary parameters for this class. Then, we save the score in the `SaveLocal(index : int)` function, which will take the `index` number of each user included with the local key and put in the `PlayerPrefs` key. This will allow us to save multiple users without having any problems.

In the `SaveLocal()` function, we use `PlayerPrefs.SetInt(KeyString, int_score);` to save the score and `PlayerPrefs.SetString(KeyString, s_name);` to save the username.

Next, we have the `LoadLocal(index : int)` function, which will take the index number of the users and load the username and score from the `PlayerPrefs`.

The `LoadLocal()` function will contain two functions. The first is `LoadScore(index : int)`, which will load the user's score by using `PlayerPrefs.HasKey(KeyString)` to check for the similar key saved on this local machine. If it has, we will load the score by using the `PlayerPrefs.GetInt(KeyString)` function, and if not, we will return 0 for the score. The next function is `LoadName(index : int)`, which is very similar to the `LoadScore(index : int)` function, but this time we will use `PlayerPrefs.GetString(KeyString)` to get the username. Also, if we can't find the key, we will return the random name in the `as_randomNames` array of string.

Then, we created the `LocalHiScore` script to load and save our user data. In this script, we created `SetMaxUser(maxUser : int)` to get the maximum number of users to display on the menu, and called the `LoadGameLocal()` function. This function will load the user data, and then store the data to the array. The function also gets the minimum score from the user data and stores this score for comparing when the player submits the score.

In the `LocalHiScore` script, we also created `SaveGame(scores : int, name : String)` to save the player's final score to the local machine and the `SortUser(array : UsersData[])` function to sort the user data before saving. In the `SaveGame(scores : int, _name : String)` function, first we checked whether the player's submitted score is higher than the minimum score from the user data or not. If it isn't, we don't add the new score to the user data. On the other hand, if the submitted score is higher than the minimum score, the old minimum score will be removed, and the new score will be added to the new user data. Then, we call the `SortUser(array : UsersData[])` function. This function will sort the array of the `UsersData` from the highest to lowest user score.

Finally, we go back to the `HiScore` script to add the script that will display our local high score.

Classified Intel

In this section, we have used the `PlayerPrefs` to load and save the user data (name and score) to our local machine. The `PlayerPrefs` class is basically used for saving or loading the data by using the key string to identify each piece of data. We can set the value that we want to store and load to `string`, `float`, or `int` type.

For storing or saving the data, we can use `PlayerPrefs.SetInt(Key, Value)`, `PlayerPrefs.SetFloat(Key, Value)`, or `PlayerPrefs.SetString(Key, Value)`. We can create the new data by giving a different `Key` for each saving data. On the other hand, if we want to replace the old data with the new data, we just have to set the same `Key` to the new data that we will save.

For loading the data, we will use `PlayerPrefs.GetInt(Key)`, `PlayerPrefs.GetFloat(Key)`, or `PlayerPrefs.GetString(Key)` to get value that we have stored. We can also check whether the data is already stored in this machine or not by using `PlayerPrefs.HasKey(Key)`.

We already talked about how to save and load the data from `PlayerPref`, but we didn't talk about how to remove it. We can use `PlayerPrefs.Delete(Key)` to remove the data that we don't want by specifying the `Key`. Also, if we want to remove all the data that we have saved, we can use `PlayerPrefs.DeleteAll()`.

> We can also go to the following website for more details on the `PlayerPrefs` class:
>
> `http://unity3d.com/support/documentation/ScriptReference/PlayerPrefs.html`.

Getting XML data from the server

In this section, we will create the C# script that will parse the XML data from the server to use in the next step. We will create the C# script because it is much easier to use the `XmlDocument` from `.Net` framework in C#.

Prepare for Lift Off

Let's go to **Assets | Create | C Sharp Script** and name it `XMLParser` and put it inside the `Standard Assets` folder, as shown in the following screenshot:

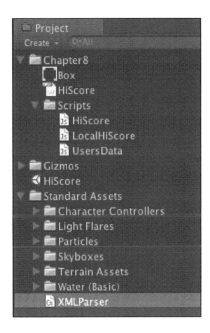

Before we begin to code the C#, we should know that the way to write the script in C# is different from Unity JavaScript (we can see more details in *Appendix C, Major Differences Between C# and Unity JavaScript*), which we already know from the previous chapter. However, we will have a quick refresh of the idea for writing C#. First of all, when we declare the variable in C#, we will use `Type varName = value;` instead of `var varName : Type = value;` in Unityscript. Second, when we create the function in C#, the syntax is very similar to when we create the variable. We will use something like `public void functionName () { ... }` instead of `public function functionName () : void { ... }` that we used in Unityscript. Also, if we want the function to return the type, we will just replace the word `void` with the type that we want. For example, if we want this function to return the `string` type, we will write the code like `public string functionName () { ... }`. It's just a small switch of the syntax. Also, if we take a look at the C# syntax, we will see that in C# we don't use the words `function` or `var` to declare either the variable or function. It only uses the type to declare.

Engage Thrusters

We will double-click the `XMLParser` script that we just created to open it in **MonoDevelop**:

1. First, we will start coding at the beginning of the `XMLParser` script, as shown in the following highlighted code:

```
using UnityEngine;
using System.Collections;
using System.Xml;
```

The using System.Xml allows us to access the System.
Xml library in the .NET Framework. If you have any experience with
ActionScript, this is similar to import flash.something. The
using System.Xml will include the XmlDocument and XmlNode
object, which we will use in our XMLParser script.

2. Then, we will replace all the rest with the following script:

```
public static class XMLParser {
   private static XmlDocument doc;
   private static static XmlNode root;

   private string[] names;
   private static int[] scores;
   private static int userLength;
```

3. Next, we will add the Parse() function to parse the XML string. Let's type it
    as follows:

```
public static void Parse( string xml) {
   doc = new XmlDocument();
   doc.LoadXml(xml); // Loading from String
   //Using doc.Load("HiScore.xml"); When load from an xml file

   //Using Last Child to Skip the <?xml version="1.0"
encoding="UTF-8"?>
   //If we load from the xml file we will use the FirstChild
instead
   root = doc.LastChild;
   if (root.HasChildNodes) {
     //Getting the Node Length
     userLength = root.ChildNodes.Count;
     names = new string[userLength];
     scores = new int[userLength];
     for (int i = 0; i < userLength; i++) {
       //Getting the user name and score XmlAttribute
       XmlAttribute nameAtt = root.ChildNodes[i].
Attributes["name"];
       XmlAttribute scoreAtt = root.ChildNodes[i].
Attributes["score"];
       //Assigning the user name data to array
       names[i] = (string)nameAtt.Value;
       //Assigning the user score data to array
       scores[i] = ConvertStringtoInt((string)scoreAtt.Value);
     }
   }
}
```

4. Then, we will create the `ConvertStringtoInt()` function, which will convert the string type to integer type as well as create the `Name()`, `Score()`, and `UserLength()` functions as follows:

```
//Converting string to int
private static int ConvertStringtoInt( string s) {
    int j;
    bool result = System.Int32.TryParse(s, out j);
    if (true == result) {
        return j;
    } else {
        Debug.Log("Error...");
        return 0;
    }
}


//Getting user name from index
public static string Name ( int index) {
    return names[index];
}
//Getting user score from index
public static int Score ( int index) {
    return scores[index];
}
//Getting user length
public static int UserLength () {
    return userLength;
}
}
```

Objective Complete - Mini Debriefing

In this section, we basically just created the C# `XMLParser` script, to parse the XML string that we loaded from the server, and then we stored the user's data in this class to use it at a later stage.

First, we used the `static` keyword for this class, because we want it to be accessible from the entire project. Then, we created the `XmlDocument` and `XmlNode` parameters to hold the XML data that we want to parse. Then, we have one array of `string` and one array of `int` to store the users' name and score. And the last parameter is to store the length of the users that we got from the XML data.

Next, we created the `Parse(string xml)` function. This function will create the `XmlDocument` and we use `LoadXml(xml)` to load the string XML that we pass to this function. Then, we get the `XmlNode` from the last child of the `XmlDocument`:

```
root = doc.LastChild;
```

We used `LastChild()` because we want to skip the first node, which is the headline of the XML file `<?xml version="1.0" encoding="UTF-8"?>`. After we got the `root` `XmlNode`, we checked for the child in this node, assigned the number of its children, and created the array to store username and score data from this node:

```
            //Getting the Node Length
            userLength = root.ChildNodes.Count;
            names = new string[userLength];
            scores = new int[userLength];
    Then, we loop to all the children, get the attribute of each child,
    and store it to names[] and scores[] array by using the script below:
            for (int i = 0; i < userLength; i++) {
                //Getting the user name and score XmlAttribute
                XmlAttribute nameAtt = root.ChildNodes[i].Attributes["name"];
                XmlAttribute scoreAtt = root.ChildNodes[i].
    Attributes["score"];
                //Assigning the user name data to array
                names[i] = (string)nameAtt.Value;
                //Assigning the user score data to array
                scores[i] = ConvertStringtoInt((string)scoreAtt.Value);
            }
```

Since `scoreAtt.Value` is a string and we want to store it as an integer, we need to convert the string data to an integer by creating the function that will convert the `string` type to `int` type, which we call `ConvertStringtoInt( string s)`.

```
        private int ConvertStringtoInt( string s) {
            int j;
            bool result = System.Int32.TryParse(s, out j);
            if (true == result) {
              return j;
            } else {
              Debug.Log("Error...");
                return 0;
            }
        }
```

From the preceding function, first we create the `int` variable `j`, and then we use `System.Int32.TryParse(s, out j);` to convert the string to an integer. This function will return the result `true` or `false`; if `true`, it means that the result got converted to an integer, and then we return `j`, which is the output from the `System.Int32.TryParse(s, out j);` function. On the other hand, if the result is not an integer, we trace out the error and return `0`.

 The `out` keyword in C# will cause the arguments to be passed by reference, which means that we can use the `out` keyword to return the values in the same variable as a parameter of the method.

For example, if we created the C# script named `Test`, as shown in the following script, and attach this script to the game object in Unity, we will see the trace result display `i = 5` and `j = 0`:

```
using UnityEngine;
using System.Collections;

public class Test : MonoBehaviour {
  // Use this for initialization
  public void Start() {
    int i;
    int j = Testout(out i);
    Debug.Log("i = " + i);  //Will show the result  i = 5
    Debug.Log("j = " + j);  //Will show the result  j = 0
  }

  public int Testout(out int i) {
    i = 5;
    return 0;
  }
}
```

Then, the rest of the `XMLParser` script is to get the value for the length of user, the username, and score. We create this function because we only want to get the data from this XML class, we don't need to set it. This is just some protection to make sure that our user's data that loaded from the XML doesn't change.

Classified Intel

At the beginning of this section, we added the `XMLParser` script to the `Standard Assets` folder. Why did we do that? Is it really important to add the script in the `Standard Assets` folder? The answer is "Yes". We need to put this script in the `Standard Assets` folder. This is because of the way Unity builds the script. In Unity, the JavaScript is built first and then the C# script, so if we want to call a C# script from our JavaScript, we will get the error, as shown in the following screenshot (you can see more details in *Appendix C, Major Differences between C# and Unity JavaScript*):

> ⓘ Assets/Chapter8/Scripts/ServerHiScore.js(45,9): BCE0005: Unknown identifier: 'XMLParser'.

So, the best way to do it is to code our entire project either in JavaScript or C#. However, there is a way to call the C# script function or class from Unity JavaScript, which is the way we just did in this chapter. As we know JavaScript is complied before the C# script. Also, all the code or scripts in the `Standard Assets` folder will be compiled before the rest of the code in the project is compiled. So, we just reordered the code complier to compile `XMLParser` first and then the rest of our code later.

>
>
> We can read more details of the compiler order from the following Unity website:
>
> ```
> http://unity3d.com/support/documentation/
> ScriptReference/index.Script_
> compilation_28Advanced29.html.
> ```

Posting and loading high scores to the server

In this section, we will create the `ServerHiScore` script to post and load the high score data from the server, which we will use in the `WWWForm` class to communicate with the PHP file on the website, which I already set up. We will also create a hash key and encrypt it with the MD5 encryption to protect and check for the user before posting the score to the database.

Prepare for Lift Off

Before we create the `ServerHiScore` script, we will need to get the MD5 encryption script to encrypt our data. Let's create the new Unity JavaScript and name it `MD5.js` in **MonoDevelop**. Then, browse to the following link:

```
http://www.unifycommunity.com/wiki/index.php?title=MD5.
```

On this page, you will see the MD5 class for C# script and JavaScript that is written by Matthew Wegner. Go to **JavaScript** and copy the code and paste it in the MD5.js script that we just created:

```
#pragma strict

static function Md5Sum(strToEncrypt: String)
{
    var encoding = System.Text.UTF8Encoding();
    var bytes = encoding.GetBytes(strToEncrypt);

    // encrypt bytes
    var md5 = System.Security.Cryptography.MD5CryptoServiceProvider();
    var hashBytes:byte[] = md5.ComputeHash(bytes);

    // Convert the encrypted bytes back to a string (base 16)
    var hashString = "";

    for (var i = 0; i < hashBytes.Length; i++)
    {
        hashString += System.Convert.ToString(hashBytes[i], 16).
PadLeft(2, "0"[0]);
    }

    return hashString.PadLeft(32, "0"[0]);
}
```

This script will allow us to encrypt our string with the MD5 encryption.

We can use #pragma strict in the Unity JavaScript to tell Unity to disable the dynamics typing var name = 5 and force us to use the static typing var name : int = 5. This will also make it easy for us to debug because if we forgot to use the static typing, Unity will give us an error when the script is being compiled.

Engage Thrusters

We will create the `ServerHiScore` script to send and load the user data to the server, which is also encrypted with the MD5.

1. Let's go to **Assets | Create | JavaScript** and name it `ServerHiScore`. Then, we will double-click it to open **MonoDevelop** and add the following code:

    ```
    //Setting the PHP url here
    public var PHPUrl : String = "http://www.jatewit.com/Packt/
    HiScore.php";
    //Setting the hash key id
    public var hashKey : String = "UNITYGAMEDEVELOPMENTHOTSHOT";

    private var obj_WWW : WWWForm;
    private var b_loaded : boolean;

    public function Start() : void {
      // Empty Check for Inspector values
      if( PHPUrl == "" ) {
        Debug.LogError( "PHP Url cannot be null." );
      }
      if( hashKey == "" ) {
        Debug.LogError( "Hash Key cannot be null." );
      }
    }
    ```

    In the preceding script, we created the parameter to set the PHP URL that we will be connected to (we won't see anything if we try to view the link in our browser), set the hash key to check for the user, and create the `WWWFrom` and `boolean` objects to use in this script. In the `Start()` function, we just checked to make sure that the `PUPUrl` and `hashKey` are not null.

2. Then, create the `SendScore(score : int, name :String)` function, which will take two parameters `score` and `name`. This function will create the `WWWFrom`, set the parameter, and send it to the URL that we just assigned. Let's type the function as follows:

    ```
    //Creating the function to send
    public function SendScore( score : int, name : String) : void {
      var w_form : WWWForm = new WWWForm();
      //Telling PHP that the user is submitting the data
      w_form.AddField("action", "PostScore");
      //Sending hash code key to prevent unwanted user
      w_form.AddField("hash", MD5.Md5Sum(name + "-" + score.ToString()
    + "-" + hashKey)); //Encrypt with MD5
      //Sending the user score
    ```

```
   w_form.AddField("score", score);
   //Sending the user name
   w_form.AddField("name", name);
   //Start waiting for the response back from the server
   StartCoroutine(WaitingForResponse(new WWW(PHPUrl, w_form),
null));
}
```

3. Create the `WaitingForResponse( www : WWW, callback : Function)` `: IEnumerator` function as mentioned previously. Let's continue from after the `SendScore()` function and type it as follows:

```
//Waiting for the response back from the server
public function WaitingForResponse( www : WWW, callback :
Function) : IEnumerator {
   yield www;

   if (www.error == null) {
      Debug.Log("Successful.");
   } else {
      Debug.Log("Failed.");
   }

   if (callback != null) {
      callback(www.text);
      callback = null;
   }

   //Clears data
   www.Dispose();
}
```

4. We already have the function to send; now we need to load the data from the server, so we will create the `GetScores()` function to load the user's score data from the server. Let's type it as follows:

```
//Getting the score from the server
public function GetScores() : void {
   b_loaded = false;
   var w_form : WWWForm = new WWWForm();
   //Telling PHP that the user is loading the data
   w_form.AddField("action", "GetScore");
   //Start waiting for the response back from the server
   StartCoroutine(WaitingForResponse(new WWW(PHPUrl, w_form),
LoadXMLData));
}
```

5. Next, we create the `LoadXMLData(string : String)` function, which will parse the XML string data that returns from the server. We will type this script after the `GetScores()` function as follows:

```
//Parse the XML data from the server
public function LoadXMLData(string : String) : void {
  XMLParser.Parse(string);
  b_loaded = true;
  Debug.Log(string);
}
```

6. Next, type the rest of the code as follows:

```
//Getting User length
public function GetUserLength() : int {
  if (XMLParser != null) {
    return XMLParser.UserLength();
  } else {
    return 0;
  }
}
//Getting User Name by index
public function GetNameData(index : int) : String {
  if (XMLParser != null) {
    return XMLParser.Name(index);
  } else {
    return "";
  }
}
//Getting User Score by index
public function GetScoreData(index : int) : int {
  if (XMLParser != null) {
    return XMLParser.Score(index);
  } else {
    return 0;
  }
}
//Loaded XML
public function IsLoaded() : boolean {
  return b_loaded;
}
```

The preceding functions get the server data from the `XMLParser` (where we stored users' data that returns from the server).

7. Now, we will go back to the `HiScore.js` script to add some code in it and make it work. In the `HiScore.js` script before the `Awake()` function, add the highlighted code as follows:

```
private var obj_localHiScore : LocalHiScore; //Creating the
LocalHiScore Object
private var obj_serverHiScore : ServerHiScore; //Creating the
ServerHiScore Object

public function Start() : void {
    //Initializing
```

8. Go inside the `Start()` function and type the highlighted code:

```
public function Start() : void {
    //Initializing
    e_page = Page.GAMEOVER;
    int_items = 10;
    scrollPosition = Vector2.zero;
    b_isClickRestart = false;
    b_isClickSubmit = false;

    //Creating a Local Hiscore Object
    obj_localHiScore = new LocalHiScore();
    //Setting the maximum scores to show on the table & loading the
local high score data here
    obj_localHiScore.SetMaxUser(int_items);
    //Creating a Server Hiscore Object
    obj_serverHiScore = GetComponent.<ServerHiScore>();
}
```

9. Now we have the `ServerHiScore` object created, we need to go to the `GameoverPage()` function inside the **SERVER HI-SCORE** button page code, and type the following highlighted code:

```
if (b_isClickSubmit == false) {
    GUI.Label(new Rect((Screen.width - 300)*0.5, (Screen.
height*0.1) + 80, 300, 25), "Enter Your Name", GUI.skin.
GetStyle("Text1"));
    //Creating the input text field to get the player name
    userName = GUI.TextField(new Rect((Screen.width - 240)*0.5,
(Screen.height*0.1) + 120, 240, 40), userName, 8);
    //Submit button
    if (GUI.Button(new Rect((Screen.width - 240)*0.5, (Screen.
height*0.1) + 200, 240, 30), "SUBMIT")) {
        b_isClickSubmit = true;
        //TODO: Submitting both local and server high score here
```

```
obj_localHiScore.SaveGame(TimeScoreUI.int_currentScore,
userName); //Submitting to the local score
    //Submitting to server
    obj_serverHiScore.SendScore(TimeScoreUI.int_currentScore,
userName);
    }
}
//Creating the Local Hi-Score page button
if (GUI.Button(new Rect((Screen.width - 240)*0.5, (Screen.
height*0.1) + 240, 240, 30), "LOCAL HI-SCORE")) {
    e_page = Page.LOCALSCORE;
}
//Creating the Server Hi-Score page button
if (GUI.Button(new Rect((Screen.width - 240)*0.5, (Screen.
height*0.1) + 280, 240, 30), "SERVER HI-SCORE")) {
    //TODO: Loading the score data from server here
    obj_serverHiScore.GetScores();
    e_page = Page.SERVERSCORE;
}
```

10. This will submit and load the score from the server. Then, we go to the
    ServerScorePage() function and replace the code as follows:

```
//Loading score from server

private function ServerScorePage() : void {
    //Creating the background box
    GUI.Box(new Rect(Screen.width*0.1, Screen.height*0.1, Screen.
width * 0.8, Screen.height * 0.8), "SERVER HI-SCORE", GUI.skin.
GetStyle("Box2"));
    //TODO: Checking is the loader completed
    if (obj_serverHiScore.IsLoaded()) {
        var int_numUsers : int = obj_serverHiScore.GetUserLength();
        if (int_numUsers >= maxUsers) {
            int_numUsers = maxUsers;
        }
        scrollPositionS = GUI.BeginScrollView (new Rect ((Screen.width
- 320)*0.5, (Screen.height*0.1) + 80, 320, 180), scrollPositionS,
new Rect (0, 0, 300, 30*int_numUsers));
        for (var i: int = 0; i < int_numUsers; i++) {
            //Setting the number of the user
            GUI.Label(new Rect(0, i * 30, 35, 30), (i+1).ToString() +
".");
            //TODO: Showing the user name and score here
            GUI.Label(new Rect(35, i * 30, 120, 30), obj_
serverHiScore.GetNameData(i));
            GUI.Label(new Rect(155, i * 30, 145, 30), GlobalFunction.
addCommasInt(obj_serverHiScore.GetScoreData(i)), GUI.skin.
GetStyle("Score"));
```

```
    }
    GUI.EndScrollView (); //End Scroll Area
  } else {
    //TODO: If the loader doesn't complete display Loading... text
    GUI.Label(new Rect((Screen.width-150)*0.5, (Screen.
height*0.1)+120, 150, 50), "LOADING...", GUI.skin.
GetStyle("Text1"));
  }
  if (GUI.Button(new Rect((Screen.width - 240)*0.5, (Screen.
height*0.1) + 280, 240, 30), "BACK")) {
    e_page = Page.GAMEOVER;
  }
}
```

The preceding code will wait for the server to finish loading and display the users'
scoreboard. If the loading didn't finish, the menu will show only the **Loading...** text;
otherwise, it will display the users' names and scores that were returned from the
server database.

11. Finally, go back to Unity editor, click on the **HiScore** game object in the **Hierarchy**
to bring up the **Inspector**, then drag-and-drop the `ServerHiScore` script in the
HiScore game object and click **Play**. When we die or kill all the enemies in the scene,
we will be able to load the **SERVER HI-SCORE** board by clicking on the **SERVER HI-
SCORE** button, and the **SUBMIT** button will now submit the score to the server and
save the score to our local machine at the same time.

 We might not get the same image as shown in the preceding screenshot
because the server database will be updated with different users.

Objective Complete - Mini Debriefing

We learned how to use the `WWWForm` and `WWW` object to post and load the high score from the server. We also used the MD5 encryption to encrypt the key before posting the data to protect it from unwanted users. Then, we used the `StartCoroutine()` function to wait for the response from the server.

First, we created the `ServerHiScore` script to send and receive the user data from the server database. In the `Start()` function, we checked to make sure that we have the server URL and encryption key.

Next, in the `SendScore()` function, we first created `WWWForm`. Then we used `AddField("action", "Posting");`, which will tell PHP that we want to send the score by setting the `action` to `Posting`. (The `action` parameter and `Posting` value are set in the PHP code, which you can see in the `HiScore.php` that I have attached with this code). Then, we set the `hash` with the MD5 encryption value of `hashKey`, set the `score`, and `name` to the `WWWForm` object. In the last line, we use `StartCoroutine(WaitingForRe sponse(new WWW(PHPUrl, w_form), null))` function to wait for the response from the server. The `StartCoroutine()` function basically takes the `IEnumerator`, which we pass to the `WaitingForResponse(new WWW(PHPUrl, w_form), null)` function here. This function basically creates the `WWW` object that sends our `WWWForm` object to the specific `PHPUrl`. It also takes the `Function` to callback when it is finished.

Then, we have the `WaitingForResponse()` function, which will wait for the response from the server, and check if the sending request succeeds. Then we check if there is any callback function to call. If there is a callback function, we will call it. Finally, we just clear all data by using `www.Dispose()`.

Next, we created the `GetScore()` function, which is very similar to the `SendScore()` function except that we only send one parameter to PHP, which is `action` to tell PHP that we want `GetScore`. Also, in the `StartCoroutine()` function, we put the callback function in the `WaitingForResponse()` function, which is `LoadXMLData`. This will be called after the loading is finished.

Then, we have the `LoadXMLData()` function, which will call the `XMLParser. Parse()` function to parse the XML string data that returns from the server, then store it in the `XMLParser` class. We also created `GetUserLength()`, `GetNameData()`, `GetScoreData()`, and `IsLoaded()` to get the user data from index and check if the data has been loaded.

Then, we go back to the `HiScore` script to add the function that will save and load the user data to the server database.

Finally, we applied the `ServerHiScore` script to the **HiScore** game object in **Hierarchy** view to get the result we want.

Classified Intel

In this step, we use `AddField("fieldname", "value");` in `WWWForm` to add the value and pass it to the server. In this function, the `fieldname` mostly depends on the PHP script on the server.

We can open the `HiScore.php` file that we have in this project package and take a look at the following line:

```
$action = $_POST[ 'action' ]; //Get request action from Unity
```

We will see that the word `action` is the same keyword that we assigned in the `AddField()` function at the beginning of the `SendScore()` function:

```
w_form.AddField("action", "PostScore");
```

It is basically the keyword that we use to communicate the value between Unity and PHP. In this PHP file, we used MySQL to set up the database on my website, so if you have your website and the database set up with MySQL, you can adjust this PHP to point to your database and put it to your website.

>
> For more information on how to set up MySQL database on your website, you can go to the following link and download the file:
>
> `http://www.webwisesage.com/addons/free_ebook.html`.
>
> There is also a video tutorial of *How to set up MySQL database, PHP, and flash*, from *Lee Brimelow*. You can find it from the following link:
>
> `http://www.gotoandlearn.com/play.php?id=20`.

Game over-Wrapping it up

In this chapter, we have created the scripts that help us to be able to save, load, and post the high score locally and to the server database. We also created the C# script to use for parsing the XML string format to the value that we want as well as the using of mixing script between the C# and JavaScript.

Finally, I want to thank all of you for reading this book. I hope you got some useful information from it.

Are you ready to go gung ho? A Hotshot challenge

We have learned many things from this chapter, such as save and load the value locally by using `PlayerPrefs`, using the `WWWForm` to post and load the high score from the server, encrypt the key code with `MD5`, and load the XML string by using `XmlDocument`. However, those aren't the things that we can do. Let's try something out and see how much we learned from this chapter:

- Create the save game position for our game by using `PlayerPrefs` to save the current position of our character in the game and load it as well

- Try adapting the `XMLParser` script to load the XML file by using `xml.Load(filename.xml)` to load the XML file to your game

- Create your database and PHP on your website by using `HiScore.php` and changing the `PHPUrl` to your website; you can also change the hash key to the one that you prefer

- Make the game prompt the user to enter their name only if they actually qualify for the new high score

Appendix A

Important Functions

The purpose of this appendix is to explain the meaning of some important methods used in Unity, referenced from the Unity Scripting Documentation.

Awake

The `Awake` function is called when the script instance is being loaded.

`Awake` is used to initialize any variable or game state before the game starts. It is called only once during the lifetime of the script instance. It is also called after all the objects are initialized, so you can safely speak to other objects or query them using, for example, `GameObject.FindWithTag`. Each `Awake` function of the `GameObject` is called in a random order between objects. Because of this, you should use `Awake` to set up references between scripts, and use `Start` to pass any information back and forth. `Awake` is always called before any `Start` functions. This allows you to order initialization of scripts.

For C# and Boo, users use `Awake` instead of the constructor for initialization, as the serialized state of the component is undefined at construction time. `Awake` is called once, just like the constructor.

`Awake` cannot be a coroutine.

Example

```
private var myTarget : GameObject;
function Awake() {
  myTarget = GameObject.FindWithTag("Target");
}
```

Start

Start is called just before any of the Update methods are called.

Start is only called once in the lifetime of the behavior. The difference between Awake and Start is that Start is only called if the script instance is enabled. This allows you to delay any initialization code, until it is really needed.

The Start function is called after all Awake functions on all script instances have been called.

Example

```
private var myLife : int;
function Start() {
  myLife = 5;
}
```

Update

Update is called for every frame, if MonoBehaviour is enabled.

Update is the most commonly used function to implement any kind of game behavior.

Example

```
// Moves the object forward 1 meter per second
function Update () {
  transform.Translate(0, 0, Time.deltaTime*1);
}
```

FixedUpdate

FixedUpdate is called for every fixed framerate frame, if MonoBehavior is enabled.

FixedUpdate should be used instead of Update when dealing with Rigidbody. For example, when adding a force to a rigidbody, you have to apply the force for every fixed frame inside FixedUpdate instead of every frame inside Update, because the physics simulation is carried out in discrete timesteps. The FixedUpdate function is called immediately before each step.

Example

```
// Apply an upward force to the rigidbody every frame
function FixedUpdate () {
  rigidBody.AddForce(Vector3.up);
}
```

LateUpdate

LateUpdate is called for every frame, if MonoBehaviour is enabled.

LateUpdate is called after all Update functions have been called. This is useful to order script execution. For example, a follow camera should always be implemented in LateUpdate because it tracks objects that might have moved inside Update.

Example

```
// Moves the object forward 1 meter per second
function LateUpdate () {
  transform.Translate(0, 0, Time.deltaTime*1);
}
```

OnGUI

OnGUI is called for rendering and handling GUI events, such as GUI.Button, GUI.Label, GUI.Box, and so on.

This means that your OnGUI implementation might be called several times per frame (one call per event). If the enabled property of MonoBehaviour is set to false, OnGUI will not be called.

Example

```
// Draw the Button (width = 150, height = 50) at the position x = 10,
y = 10.
function OnGUI () {
  if (GUI.Button(Rect(10, 10, 150, 50), "My Button")) {
    Debug.Log("Hello World");
  }
}
```

OnDrawGizmos

Implement OnDrawGizmos if you want to draw gizmos that are also pickable and always drawn. This allows you to quickly pick important objects in your scene. You can also use OnDrawGizmos to draw the line or different types of Gizmos, such as Gizmos.DrawRay, Gizmos.DrawLine, Gizmos.DrawWireSphere, and so on, which will make it easier for you to debug.

 OnDrawGizmos will use a mouse position that is relative to the **Scene** view.

Example

```
var target : Transform;
// Draw the blue line from this object to the target
function OnDrawGizmos () {
  if (target != null) {
    Gizmos.color = Color.Blue;
    Gizmos.DrawLine(transform.position, target.position);
  }
}
```

Reference

The methods mentioned earlier can be referenced from the following Unity Scripting Reference:

http://unity3d.com/support/documentation/ScriptReference/
MonoBehaviour.Awake.html

http://unity3d.com/support/documentation/ScriptReference/
MonoBehaviour.Start.html

http://unity3d.com/support/documentation/ScriptReference/
MonoBehaviour.Update.html

http://unity3d.com/support/documentation/ScriptReference/
MonoBehaviour.FixedUpdate.html

http://unity3d.com/support/documentation/ScriptReference/
MonoBehaviour.LateUpdate.html

http://unity3d.com/support/documentation/ScriptReference/
MonoBehaviour.OnGUI.html

http://unity3d.com/support/documentation/ScriptReference/
MonoBehaviour.OnDrawGizmos.html

http://unity3d.com/support/documentation/ScriptReference/Gizmos.
DrawLine.html

Appendix B

Coroutines and Yield

This appendix presents a brief review of `coroutines` and `yield`, referenced from the Unity Scripting Reference.

YieldInstruction

When writing game code, one often ends up needing to script a sequence of events. This could result in a code similar to the following.

Example

```
private var state = 0;
function Update() {
  if (state == 0) {
    // do step 0
    Debug.Log("Do step 0");
    state = 1;
    return;
  }
  if (state == 1) {
    // do step 1
    Debug.Log("Do step 1");
    state = 0;
    return;
  }
}
```

The preceding code basically does `step0` and `step1`, then goes back to `step 0` (as a loop), and then if there are more events that will happen after `step1`, and so on. Too many `if` statements can make the code look ugly in the long run.

In this case, it's more convenient to use the `yield` statement. The `yield` statement is a special kind of return that ensures that the function will continue from the line after the `yield` statement the next time it is called. The result would be something similar to the following code.

Example

```
function Start() {
  while (true) { //Use this line instead of Update()
    //do step 0
    Debug.Log("Do step 0");
    yield;  //wait for one frame
    //do step 1
    Debug.Log("Do step 1");
    yield;  //wait for one frame
  }
}
```

The preceding code will have a similar result without having a new variable and an extra `if` statement to check for each step event.

You can also pass special values to the `yield` statement to delay the execution of the `Update` function until a certain event has occurred, such as `WaitForSeconds`, `WaitForFixedUpdate`, `Coroutine`, and `StartCoroutine`.

 You can't use `yield` from within `Update` or `FixedUpdate`, but you can use `StartCoroutine` to start a function that can use `yield`.

WaitForSeconds

Suspends the `coroutine` execution for the given amount of seconds.

`WaitForSeconds` can only be used with an `yield` statement in `coroutines`.

Example

```
function Start() {
  // Prints 0
  Debug.Log (Time.time);
  // Waits 5 seconds
  yield WaitForSeconds (5);
  // Prints 5.0
```

```
   Debug.Log (Time.time);
}
```

You can both stack and chain `coroutines`.

The following example will execute `Do` but will continue after calling `Do` immediately:

```
function Start() {
  Do();
  Debug.Log ("This is printed immediately");
}

function Do() {
  Debug.Log ("Do now");
  yield WaitForSeconds (5); //Wait for 5 seconds
  Debug.Log ("Do 5 seconds later");
}
```

The following example will execute `Do` and `wait` until it is finished before continuing its own execution:

```
//Chain Coroutine
function Start() {

  //The below line is similar to the yield Do(); only if you
are using Unity JavaScript. However, if you use C#, you must use
StartCoroutine. (For more details in the Appendix C)
  yield StartCoroutine(Do());

  Debug.Log ("This is printed after 5 seconds");
  Debug.Log ("This is after the Do coroutine has finished execution");
}

function Do() {
  Debug.Log ("Do now");
  yield WaitForSeconds (5); //Wait for 5 seconds
  Debug.Log ("Do 5 seconds later");
}
```

WaitForFixedUpdate

Waits until the next frame rate of `FixedUpdate` function. (For more details have a look at *Appendix A, Important Functions.*)

`WaitForFixedUpdate` can only be used with a `yield` statement in `coroutines`.

Example

```
function Start() {
  // Wait for FixedUpdate to finished
  yield new WaitForFixedUpdate();
  // Call After FixedUpdate
  Debug.Log ("Call after FixedUpdate");
}

function FixedUpdate() {
  Debug.Log ("FixedUpdate");
}
```

Coroutine

StartCoroutine returns a coroutine. Instances of this class are only used to reference these coroutines and do not hold any exposed properties or functions.

A coroutine is a function that can suspend its execution of yield until the given YieldInstruction finishes.

Example

```
function Start() {
  // Starting = 0.0
  Debug.Log ("Starting = " + Time.time);

  // Start function WaitAndPrint as a Coroutine
  yield WaitAndPrint();

  // Done WaitAndPrint = 5.0
  Debug.Log ("Done WaitAndPrint = " + Time.time);
}

function WaitAndPrint() {
  //Suspend execution for 5 seconds
  yield WaitForSeconds(5);

  // WaitAndPrint = 5.0
  Debug.Log ("WaitAndPrint = " + Time.time);
}
```

StartCoroutine

Starts a coroutine.

The execution of a coroutine can be paused at any point using the `yield` statement. The `yield` return value specifies when the coroutine is resumed. Coroutines are excellent when modeling behavior over several frames. Coroutines have virtually no performance overhead. `StartCoroutine` function always returns immediately, however you can yield the result. This will wait until the coroutine has finished execution.

 When using JavaScript it is not necessary to use `StartCoroutine`, as the compiler will do this for you. When writing C# code you must call `StartCoroutine`. (For more details, refer to *Appendix C, Major differences Between C# and Unity JavaScript*.)

In the following example, we show how to invoke a `coroutine` and continue executing the function in parallel:

```
function Start() {
   // Starting = 0.0
   Debug.Log ("Starting = " + Time.time);

   // StartCoroutine WaitAndPrint (In JavaScript, you can also use
WaitAndPrint(5.0) which will get the same result.
   StartCoroutine(WaitAndPrint(5.0));

   // Before WaitAndPrint = 5.0
   Debug.Log ("Before WaitAndPrint = " + Time.time);
}

function WaitAndPrint(waitTime : float) {
   //Suspend execution for 5 seconds
   yield WaitForSeconds(waitTime);

   // WaitAndPrint = 5.0
   Debug.Log ("WaitAndPrint = " + Time.time);
}
```

The following example will wait until the `WaitAndPrint` function is finished and then continues executing the rest of the code in the `Start` function:

```
function Start() {
   // Starting = 0.0
   Debug.Log ("Starting = " + Time.time);

   // StartCoroutine WaitAndPrint (In JavaScript, you can also use
yield WaitAndPrint(5.0) which will get the same result.
   yield StartCoroutine(WaitAndPrint(5.0));

   // Done WaitAndPrint = 5.0
   Debug.Log ("Done WaitAndPrint = " + Time.time);
}

function WaitAndPrint(waitTime : float) {
   //Suspend execution for 5 seconds
   yield WaitForSeconds(waitTime);

   // WaitAndPrint = 5.0
   Debug.Log ("WaitAndPrint = " + Time.time);
}
```

Using StartCoroutine with method name (string)

In most cases, you would want to use the preceding `StartCoroutine` variation. However, `StartCoroutine` using a string method name allows you to use `StopCoroutine` with a specific method name.

 The downside is that the string version has a higher runtime overhead to start the coroutine and you can pass only one parameter.

In the following example, we show how to invoke a coroutine using a string name and how to stop it:

```
function Start() {
   // Start Coroutine DoSomething
   StartCoroutine("DoSomething", 5.0);

   //  Wait for 2 seconds
   yield WaitForSeconds(2.0);
```

```
  // Stop Coroutine DoSomething
  StopCoroutine ("DoSomething");
}

function DoSomething (someParameter : float) {
  while (true) {
    // DoSomething Loop
    Debug.Log ("DoSomething Loop = " + Time.time);
    // Yield execution of this coroutine and return to the main loop
until next frame
    yield;
  }
}
```

StopCoroutine

Stops all coroutines for the specific method name running on this behavior.

 Only StartCoroutine using a string method name can be stopped using StopCoroutine.

Example

```
function Start() {
/  / Start Coroutine DoSomething
  StartCoroutine ("DoSomething", 5.0);

  //  Wait for 2 seconds
  yield WaitForSeconds (2.0);

  // Stop Coroutine DoSomething
  StopCoroutine ("DoSomething");
}

function DoSomething (someParameter : float) {
  while (true) {
    // DoSomething Loop
    Debug.Log ("DoSomething Loop = " + Time.time);
    // Yield execution of this coroutine and return to the main loop
until next frame
    yield;
  }
}
```

StopAllCoroutines

Stops all coroutines running on this behavior.

Example

```
    function Start() {
// Start Coroutine DoSomething
    StartCoroutine("DoSomething", 5.0);

//  Wait for 1 seconds
    yield WaitForSeconds(1.0);

    // Stop All Coroutine
    StopAllCoroutines();
}

function DoSomething (someParameter : float) {
    while (true) {
      // DoSomething Loop
      Debug.Log ("DoSomething Loop = " + Time.time);
      // Yield execution of this coroutine and return to the main loop
until next frame
      yield;
    }
}
```

Reference

The methods discussed earlier are referenced from the following pages:

http://unity3d.com/support/documentation/ScriptReference/index.
Corouines_26_Yield.html

http://unity3d.com/support/documentation/ScriptReference/
aitForSeconds.html

http://unity3d.com/support/documentation/ScriptReference/
WaitorFixedUpdate.html

http://unity3d.com/support/documentation/ScriptRefernce/Coroutine.
html

http://unity3d.com/support/documentation/ScriptReference/
MonoBehaviour.StartCoroutne.html?from=index

```
http://unity3d.com/support/documentation/ScriptReference/
MonoBehaviour.StoCoroutine.html
```

```
http://unity3d.com/support/documentation/ScriptReference/
MonoBehaviour.StopAllCoroutines.html
```

More details

The following link provides a good explanation and tutorial of how to use `coroutine`:

```
http://marvelopermedia.com/tutorial-coroutines-pt-1-waiting-for-
input/.
```

Appendix C

Major Differences between C# and Unity JavaScript

This appendix will provide a brief reference of the syntactical differences between C# and JavaScript in Unity. This section references from the Unity answer forum:

```
http://answers.unity3d.com/questions/12911/what-are-the-syntax-
differences-in-c-and-javascrip.html.
```

Unity Script Directives

Unity has a number of **Script Directives**, and we can find them at this URL: `http://unity3d.com/support/documentation/ScriptReference/20_class_hierarchy.Attributes.html`, for example `RequireComponent`.

JavaScript:

```
@script RequireComponent(Rigidbody)
```

C#:

```
[RequireComponent(typeof(Rigidbody))]
```

Type names

A couple of the basic types are spelt differently in pure Unity C#. In JavaScript, we use `Boolean` and `String`, but in pure Unity C#, we use `bool` and `string`.

JavaScript:

```
var isHit : Boolean;
var myName : String;
```

C#:

```
bool isHit;
string myName;
```

However, there is an exception. If you include `System` in your C# script, you will be able to use `String` and `Boolean` classes (the upper-case) of **.NET**, similar to the following script:

C#:

```
using System;

Boolean isHit;
String myName;
```

Variable declaration

Variable declaration is different, including access and type specification.

JavaScript: The type specification is not necessary.

```
public var playerLife = 1;      // a public var
int playerLife = 2;         // **private** access is default
public GameObject myObj;       // a type is specified (no value
assigned)
```

C#: The type is always stated when declaring a variable.

```
var playerLife = 1;         // **public** access is default
private var playerLife = 2;      // a private var
var myObj : GameObject;       // a type is specified (no value
assigned)
```

Variable with Dynamic Type Resolution

Only in JavaScript, variables can have an unspecified type. This only occurs if you don't assign a value or specify a type while declaring the variable.

JavaScript: The type specification is not necessary.

```
var playerLife : int;  // statically typed (because type specified)
var playerLife = 2;  // statically typed (because type is inferred
from value
assigned)
var playerLife;  // dynamically typed (because neither a type or value
is specified)
```

The dynamically typed variables will cause slower performance, and you can run into casting problems. You can use `#pragma strict`, including it at the top of a script, to tell Unity to disable the dynamic typing in the script and report compile errors when this is a dynamic type in the script.

Multi-dimensional array declaration

JavaScript:

```
var myArray = new int[8,8];     // 8x8 2d int array
```

C#:

```
int[,] myArray = new int[8,8];     // 8x8 2d int array
```

Character literals not supported

Unity's JavaScript seems to be missing the syntax to declare character literals. This means you need to get them implicitly by referencing a character index from a string.

JavaScript:

```
var myChar = "a"[0];     // implicitly retrieves the first character
of the string "a"
```

C#:

```
char myChar = 'a';     // character 'a'
```

Class declarations

You can define classes in JavaScript, in a similar way as you do it in C#. The following example is a class that inherits from MonoBehaviour.

JavaScript:

```
class MyClass extends MonoBehaviour {
  var myVar = 1;
  function Start() {
    Debug.Log("Hello World!");
  }
}
```

C#:

```
class MyClass : MonoBehaviour {
  public int myVar = 1;
  void Start() {
    Debug.Log("Hello World!");
  }
}
```

However in JavaScript, if you're inheriting from MonoBehaviour, you don't need to write a class body at all. You can also write the following script in JavaScript, which will get a similar result as the preceding JavaScript:

```
var myVar = 1;
function Start() {
  Debug.Log("Hello World!");
}
```

Unity will automatically implement an explicit class body for you.

You can also write classes that do not inherit from anything; however, you can't place these scripts on the game objects—you have to instantiate them with the new keyword.

JavaScript:

```
class MyClass {
  var myVar = 1;
  function MyClass() {
    Debug.Log("Hello World!");
  }
}
```

C#:

```
class MyClass {
  public int myVar = 1;
  void MyClass() {
    Debug.Log("Hello World!");
  }
}
```

 If you are inheriting from MonoBehaviour, you should not use constructors or destructors. Instead, use the event handler functions Start, Awake, and OnEnabled.

Limited interface support

While Unity's JavaScript does support inheritance and interfaces, it has very limiting caveat that you can either inherit your class from an existing class, or declare one interface.

JavaScript (only one allowed):

```
class MyClass extends MyObject {...}
```

C#:

```
class MyClass : MonoBehaviour, IMyObject, IMyItem {...}
```

Generics

The C# syntax supports generics that allows you to use classes and methods, which do not specifically declare a type. Instead, the type is passed as a parameter when calling the method or instantiating the class at runtime.

.Net comes with some useful generic classes, such as the List and Dictionary, and Unity's own API has some generic functions, which remove the need for some of the verbose casting that would otherwise be necessary in C#.

JavaScript:

```
//Automatically cast the correct type
var someScript : MyScript = GetComponent(MyScript);

//or using the Generic version in Javascript
var someScript : MyScript = GetComponent.<MyScript>();
```

C#:

```
//with out Generic
var someScript : MyScript = (MyScript)GetComponent(typeof(MyScript));
//or using the Generic version in C#
var someScript : MyScript = GetComponent<MyScript>();
```

The foreach keyword

C# iterators use `foreach` instead of `for`. Also, notice the variable declaration within the `for`/`foreach` statement. C# requires the type of the item contained in the list to be explicitly declared.

JavaScript:

```
for (var item in itemList) {
   item.DoSomething();
}
```

C#:

```
foreach (ItemType item in itemList) {
   item.DoSomething();
}
```

 Although the JavaScript version uses inefficient dynamic typing (since you can't declare the type), the static-typed alternative is as follows.

JavaScript:

```
for (var item = itemList.GetEnumerator(); item.MoveNext();) {
   item.DoSomething();
}
```

The new keyword

In JavaScript, you can create a new instance of an object or `struct` without using the `new` keyword. In C#, using `new` is mandatory.

JavaScript:

```
var myPosition = Vector3(0,0,0);
var myInstance = MyClass();
//We can also use new keyword in JavaScript
var myInstance = new MyClass();
```

C#:

```
Vector3 myPosition = new Vector3(0,0,0);
MyClass myInstance = new MyClass();
```

YieldInstruction and coroutine

There are differences in the syntax of C# and JavaScript as follows:

JavaScript:

```
yield WaitForSeconds(3);          //pauses for 3 seconds
yield WaitForMyFunction();         //start coroutine

function WaitForMyFunction() {…}     //coroutine function
```

C#:

```
yield return new WaitForSeconds(3);   //pauses for 3 seconds
yield return WaitForMyFunction();    //start coroutine

IEnumerator WaitForMyFunction() {…}    //coroutine function
```

 In JavaScript, it will automatically generate the return type to `IEnumerator` if you put `yield` instruction inside the function. On the other hand, in C# you will need to specify the return type to `IEnumerator`.

However, if we want to wait for the user input in C#, which might be over several frames, we will have to use `StartCoroutine`. In JavaScript, the compilers will automatically do it for us.

JavaScript:

```
yield WaitForMyFunction(5);
//This is similar with
yield StartCoroutine(WaitForMyFunction(5));

function WaitForMyFunction(waitTime : float) {…}
//coroutine function
```

C#:

```
//Need to put StartCoroutine
yield return StartCoroutine(WaitForMyFunction(5));

IEnumerator WaitForMyFunction(waitTime : float) {…}
//coroutine function
```

Casting

JavaScript automatically casts from one type to another, wherever possible. For example, the `Instantiate` command returns a type of `Object`:

JavaScript:

```
//There's no need to cast the result of "Instantiate" provided the
variable's type is declared.
var newObject : GameObject = Instantiate(sourceObject);
```

C#:

```
// in C#, both the variable and the result of instantiate must be
declared.
// C# first version
GameObject foo = (GameObject) Instantiate(sourceObject);
// C# second version
GameObject foo = Instantiate(sourceObject) as GameObject;
```

There are two different ways of casting in C#. For the first line in the preceding code, if the object can't be instantiated, it will throw an exception. You would need to use a `try/catch` to properly handle it. The second line, if it fails, will set `foo` to `null`, and not throw an exception. Then you would just need to test, if the returned object was `null`.

Properties with getters/setters

In C#, it is possible to define special functions that can be accessed as if they were variables. For instance, we could say `foo.someVar = "testing";`, and under the hood, there are `get` and `set` functions, which process the argument testing and store it internally. However, they could also do any other processing on it, for instance, capitalizing the first letter before storing it. So you're not just doing a variable assignment, you're calling a function that sets the variable, and it can do whatever the functions do.

C#:

```
public class MyClass {
private int foo = 8;   //"backing store"
public int Foo {
    get {
        return foo;
    }
    set {
      foo = value;
    }
}
}
```

However, in Unity JavaScript, we can also use `get` and `set` functions similar to the C# version, but we need to write the class body whenever you want to use the `get` or `set` function.

JavaScript:

```
public class MyClass {
private var foo = 8;   //"backing store"
function get Foo () : int {
  return foo;
}
function set Foo (value) {
  foo = value;
}
}
```

Changing Struct properties by value VS by reference

Structures are passed by value in C#, so you cannot change the x or y value of a `Vector3` and you need to create a new `Vector3` and assign it to the `Vector3` that you want. However, in JavaScript, you can write it as follows.

JavaScript:

```
transform.position.x = 1;
```

C#:

```
transform.position = new Vector3(1, transform.position.y, transform.
position.z);
```

Function/method definitions

First of all, terminology – JavaScript uses the term function, while C# calls these methods. They mean the same thing, and most C# coders understand the term function.

JavaScript functions are declared with the keyword `function` before the function name. C# method declarations just use the return type, and the method name. The return type is often `void` for common Unity events. JavaScript functions are `public` by default, and you can specify them as private if required. C# methods are `private` by default, and you can specify that they should be public if required.

In JavaScript, you can omit the parameter types and the return type from the declaration, but it's also possible to explicitly specify these (which is sometimes necessary if you run into type ambiguity problems).

JavaScript:

```
// a common Unity Monobehaviour event handler:
function Start () { ...function body here... }

// a private function:
private function TakeDamage (amount) {
energy -= amount;
}

// a public function with a return type.
// the parameter type is "Transform", and the return type is "int"
```

```
function GetHitPoint (hp : int) : int {
   return (maxHp - hp);
}
```

C#:

```
// a common Unity monobehaviour event handler:
void Start() { ...function body here... }

// a private function:
void TakeDamage(int amount) {
energy -= amount;
}

// a public function with a return type.
// the parameter type is "Transform", and the return type is "int"

public int GetHitPoint (int hp) {
   return (maxHp - hp);
}
```

Reference

The methods mentioned earlier can be referenced from the following websites:

```
http://answers.unity3d.com/questions/12911/what-are-the-syntax-
differences-in-c-and-javascrip.html
```

```
http://www.unifycommunity.com/wiki/index.php?title=Csharp_
Differences_from_JS
```

```
http://unity3d.com/support/documentation/ScriptReference/index.
Writing_Scripts_in_Csharp.html
```

```
http://www.unifycommunity.com/wiki/index.php?title=Csharp_
Differences_from_JS.
```

Appendix D
Shaders and Cg/HLSL Programming

This appendix presents a brief overview of the structure of surface shaders and Cg/HLSL programming.

Shaders in Unity can be written in one of the following three different ways:

- Surface shaders will probably be your best bet. Write your shader as a surface shader if it needs to interact properly with lighting, shadows, projectors, and so on. Surface shaders also make it easy to write complex shaders in a compact way—it's a higher level of abstraction. Lighting for most surface shaders can be calculated in a deferred manner (except for some custom lighting models), which allows your shader to efficiently interact with many real-time lights. You write surface shaders in a couple of lines of Cg/HLSL and a lot more code gets autogenerated from that.

- Vertex and fragment shaders will be required, if you need some very exotic effects that the surface shaders can't handle, if your shader doesn't need to interact with lighting, or if it's an image effect. Shader programs written this way are the most flexible way to create the effect you need (even surface shaders are automatically converted to a bunch of vertex and fragment shaders), but that comes at a price— you have to write more code and it's harder to make it interact with lighting. These shaders are written in Cg/HLSL as well.

- Fixed function shaders need to be written for old hardware that doesn't support programmable shaders. You will probably want to write fixed function shaders as an nth fallback to your fancy fragment or surface shaders, to make sure your game still renders something sensible when run on old hardware or simpler mobile platforms. Fixed function shaders are entirely written in a language called ShaderLab, which is similar to Microsoft's .FX files or NVIDIA's CgFX.

Regardless of which type you choose, the actual meat of the shader code will always be wrapped in ShaderLab, which is used to organize the shader structure. It looks similar to the following code:

```
Shader "MyShader" {
  Properties {
    // All properties go here
    _MyTexture ("My Texture", 2D) = "white" { }
  }

  SubShader {
      //  Choose your written style
      //  - surface shader or
      //  - vertex and fragment shader or
      //  - fixed function shader
  }

  SubShader {
      // Optional - A simpler version of the SubShader above that can run
  on older graphics cards
  }
  }
```

However, we will only talk about the surface shaders, which we used in *Project 3, The Hero/ Heroine Part I – Models and Shaders*.

ShaderLab properties

From the preceding example code, in the `Properties` block, we can define the type of properties, as shown in the following table:

Type	Description
name ("display name", Range (min, max)) = number	Defines a float property, represented as a slider from min to max in the Inspector view.
name ("display name", Color) = (number,number,number,number)	Defines a float property, represented as a slider from min to max in the Inspector view.
name ("display name", Color) = (number,number,number,number)	Defines a color property.
name ("display name", 2D) = "name" { options }	Defines a 2D texture property.

Type	Description
`name ("display name", Rect) = "name" { options }`	Defines a rectangle (non power of 2) texture property.
`name ("display name", Cube) = "name" { options }`	Defines a cubemap texture property.
`name ("display name", Float) = number`	Defines a float property.
`name ("display name", Vector) = (number,number,number,number)`	Defines a four-component vector property.

Each property inside the shader is referenced by `name` (in Unity, it's common to start shader property names with underscore). The property will show up in material inspector as **Display name**. For each property a default value is given after the equals sign:

- ▸ For `Range` and `Float` properties: It's just a single number
- ▸ For `Color` and `Vector` properties: It's four numbers in parentheses
- ▸ For texture (`2D`, `Rect`, `Cube`): The default value is either an empty string, or one of the built-in default textures—`white`, `black`, `gray`, or `bump`.

Example

```
Properties {
  _MainTex ("Texture ", 2D) = "white" {} // textures

  _SpecColor ("Specular color", Color) = (0.30, 0.85, 0.90, 1.0) //
color

  _Gloss ("Shininess", Range (1.0,512)) = 80.0 // sliders
}
```

Surface shaders

To use the surface shaders, you need to define a surface function (`void surf(Input IN, inout SurfaceOutput o)`) that takes any UVs or data you need as input, and fills in the output structure `SurfaceOutput`. The `SurfaceOutput` structure basically describes properties of the surface (that is albedo color, normal, emission, specularity, and so on). Then, you write this code in Cg/HLSL.

Surface shader compiler then figures out the inputs that are needed, the outputs that are filled, and so on, and generates actual vertex and pixel shaders as well as rendering passes to handle forward and deferred rendering.

The surface shaders placed inside CGPROGRAM. . .ENDCG block, must be placed inside the SubShader block, and uses the #pragma surface ... directive to indicate that it's a surface shader. You will see that the surface shaders placed inside CGPROGRAM and ENDCG block in the following example:

```
Shader "My Lambert" {
   Properties {
      _MainTex ("Texture", 2D) = "white" {}
   }
   SubShader {
      Tags { "RenderType"="Opaque" }
      LOD 200 //Optional that allows the script to turned the shader on
or off when the player's hardware didn't support your shader.
      CGPROGRAM
      #pragma surface surf Lambert
      sampler2D _MainTex;

      struct Input {
         float2 uv_MainTex;
      };

      void surf (Input IN, inout SurfaceOutput o) {
         fixed4 c = tex2D (_MainTex, IN.uv_MainTex);
         o.Albedo = c.rgb;
         o.Alpha = c.a;
      }
      ENDCG
   }
   FallBack "Diffuse"
}
```

#pragma surface

The #pragma surface directive is:

```
#pragma surface surfaceFunction lightModel [optionalparams]
```

Required parameters

The following are the required parameters for the #pragma surface directive:

▶ surfaceFunction—the Cg function that has surface shader code. The function should have the form void surf (Input IN, inout SurfaceOutput o), where Input is a structure you have defined. Input should contain any texture coordinates and extra automatic variables needed by the surface function.

▶ lightModel—lighting model to use. Built-in ones are Lambert (diffuse) and BlinnPhong (specular). You can also write your own by using the following custom lighting models:

- ❑ half4 LightingName (SurfaceOutput s, half3 lightDir, half atten);: This is used in a forward rendering path for light models that are not view direction dependent (for example, diffuse).

- ❑ half4 LightingName (SurfaceOutput s, half3 lightDir, half3 viewDir, half atten);: This is used in a forward rendering path for light models that are view direction dependent.

- ❑ half4 LightingName_PrePass (SurfaceOutput s, half4 light);: This is used in a deferred lighting path.

> Note that you don't need to declare all functions. A lighting model either uses view direction or it does not. Similarly, if the lighting model will not work in deferred lighting, you just do not declare the _PrePass function. All the shaders that use it will compile to forward rendering only, such as the shader that we did in *Chapter 3, The Hero/ Heroine Part I – Models and Shaders*. We don't need the _PrePass function because our shader needs the view direction(viewDir) and the light direction(lightDir) for our custom lighting function to calculate the ramp effect for the cartoon style shader (Toon Shader/ Cel Shader), which is only available in forward rendering.

▶ Optional parameters [optionalparams]:

Type	Description
alpha	Alpha blending mode. Use this for semitransparent shaders.
alphatest:VariableName	Alpha testing mode. Use this for transparent-cutout shaders. Cutoff value is in float variable with VariableName.
vertex:VertexFunction	Custom vertex modification function. See the Tree Bark shader, for example.
exclude_path:prepass or exclude_path:forward	Do not generate passes for given rendering path.
addshadow	Add shadow caster and collector passes. Commonly used with custom vertex modification, so that shadow casting also gets any procedural vertex animation.
dualforward	Use dual lightmaps in forward path.
fullforwardshadows	Support all shadow types in forward rendering path.
decal:add	Additive decal shader (for example, terrain AddPass).
decal:blend	Semitransparent decal shader.

Type	Description
softvegetation	Makes the surface shader only be rendered when Soft Vegetation is on.
Noambient	Do not apply any ambient lighting or spherical harmonics lights.
novertexlights	Do not apply any spherical harmonics or per-vertex lights in forward rendering.
nolightmap	Disables lightmap support in this shader (makes a shader smaller).
Noforwardadd	Disables forward rendering additive pass. This makes the shader support one full directional light, with all other lights computed per-vertex/SH. Makes shaders smaller as well.
approxview	Computes normalized view direction per-vertex instead of per-pixel, for shaders that need it. This is faster, but view direction is not entirely correct when camera gets close to the surface.
halfasview	Pass half-direction vector into the lighting function instead of view-direction. Half-direction will be computed and normalized per vertex. This is faster, but not entirely correct.

Additionally, you can write #pragma debug inside the CGPROGRAM block, and then the surface compiler will spit out a lot of comments of the generated code. You can view that using Open Compiled Shader in shader inspector.

Surface shaders input structure

The input structure Input generally has any texture coordinates needed by the shader. Texture coordinates must be named uv followed by a texture name (or start it with uv2 to use the second texture coordinate set).

Example:

```
Properties {
    _MainTex ("Texture", 2D) = "white" {}
}
......

    sampler2D _MainTex;
  ......
    struct Input {
       float2 uv_MainTex;
    };
```

We can also have the additional values that can be put into the input structure:

Type	Description
`float3 viewDir`	Contains view direction, for computing parallax effects, rim lighting, and so on.
`float4` with `COLOR` semantic	Contains interpolated per-vertex color.
`float4 screenPos`	Contains screen space position for reflection effects. Used by WetStreet shader in Dark Unity, for example.
`float3 worldPos`	Contains world space position.
`float3 worldRefl`	Contains world reflection vector if surface shader does not write to o.Normal. See Reflect-Diffuse shader, for example.
`float3 worldNormal`	Contains world normal vector if surface shader does not write to o.Normal.
`float3 worldRefl;` `INTERNAL_DATA`	Contains world reflection vector if surface shader writes to o.Normal. To get the reflection vector based on per-pixel normal map, use WorldReflectionVector (IN, o.Normal). See Reflect-Bumped shader, for example.
`float3 worldNormal;` `INTERNAL_DATA`	Contains world normal vector if surface shader writes to o.Normal. To get the normal vector based on per-pixel normal map, use WorldNormalVector (IN, o.Normal).

SurfaceOutput structure

The standard output structure of surface shaders is as follows:

```
struct SurfaceOutput {
   fixed3 Albedo;
   fixed3 Normal;
   fixed3 Emission;
   half Specular;
   fixed Gloss;
   fixed Alpha;
};
```

You can also find it in the `Lighting.cginc` file inside Unity in `{unity install path}/Data/CGIncludes/Lighting.cginc` on Windows, and in `/Applications/Unity/Unity.app/Contents/CGIncludes/Lighting.cginc` on a Mac.

Cg/HLSL programming

This section presents a brief description of how to access the shader `Properties` in Cg/HLSL programming, and the data types and common methods used in Cg/HLSL programming.

Accessing shader properties in Cg/HLSL

Shader can be declared with properties in a `Properties` block. If you want to access some of those properties in a Cg/HLSL shader program, you need to declare a Cg/HLSL variable with the same name and a matching type.

Example:

```
Properties {
    _MainTex ("Texture", 2D) = "white" {}
}

SubShader {

    ......

    CGPROGRAM
    sampler2D _MainTex;

    ...
```

Property types to Cg/HLSL variable types are as follows:

- `Color` and `Vector` properties map to `float4` variables.

- `Range` and `Float` properties map to `float` variables.

- `Texture` properties map to `sampler2D` variables for regular (2D) textures. `CUBE` and `RECT` textures map to `samplerCUBE` and `samplerRECT` variables, respectively.

Data type

Cg/HLSL has six basic data types. Some of them are the same as in C, while others are especially added for GPU programming. These types are:

Date type	Description
float	A 32-bit floating point number (high precision floating point. Generally 32 bits, just like float type in regular programming languages).
half	A 16-bit floating point number (medium-precision floating point. Generally 16 bits, with a range of -60000 to +60000 and 3.3 decimal digits of precision)
int	A 32-bit integer.

Date type	Description
`fixed`	A 12-bit fixed point number (low-precision fixed point. Generally 11 bits, with a range of -2.0 to +2.0 and 1/256th precision).
`bool`	A Boolean variable (FALSE = 0, TRUE = 1).
`sampler*`	Represents a texture object (sampler1D, sampler2D, sampler3D, samplerCUBE, samplerRECT).

Cg/HLSL also features `vector` and `matrix` data types that are based on the basic data types, such as `float3` and `float4x4`. Such data types are quite common when dealing with 3D graphics programming. Cg/HLSL also has `struct` and `array` data types, which work in a similar way to their C equivalents.

Common methods to create shaders

Method	Description
`dot( a, b )`	Dot product of two vectors.
`cross( A , B )`	Cross product of vectors A and B; A and B must be three-component vectors.
`max( a, b )`	Maximum of a and b.
`min( a , b )`	Minimum of a and b.
`floor( x )`	Get largest integer not greater than x.
`round( x )`	Get closest integer to x.
`ceil( x )`	Get smallest integer not less than x.
`pow( x , y )`	Computes x raised to the power y.
`normalize( v )`	Returns a vector of length 1 that points in the same direction as vector v.
`saturate( x )`	Clamps x to the [0, 1] range.
`tex2D(sampler, x )`	2D texture lookup (sampled data at the location indicated by the texture coordinate set in the sampler object).

The preceding methods are the common methods that you can use to create your shader with Cg/HLSL. There are a lot of methods that you can also use in Cg/HLSL.

For more details, you can refer to the following site:

`http://http.developer.nvidia.com/CgTutorial/cg_tutorial_appendix_e.html`.

Note that `UnpackNormal( x )` is the method that is provided by Unity to unpack the normal or bump texture, which you can find in the `UnityCG.cginc` file inside Unity `{unity install path}/Data/CGIncludes/UnityCG.cginc` on **Windows**, and in `/Applications/Unity/Unity.app/Contents/CGIncludes/UnityCG.cginc` on **Mac**.

Reference

The preceding content is referenced from the following websites:

`http://unity3d.com/support/documentation/Manual/Shaders.html`

`http://unity3d.com/support/documentation/Components/SL-SurfaceShaders.html`

`http://unity3d.com/support/documentation/Components/SL-PropertiesInPrograms.html`

`http://unity3d.cba.pl/Documentation/Documentation/Components/SL-Properties.html`

`http://unity3d.com/support/documentation/Components/SL-ShaderPerformance.html`

`http://en.wikipedia.org/wiki/Cg_%28programming_language%29`

`http://http.developer.nvidia.com/CgTutorial/cg_tutorial_frontmatter.html`

Index

trigger parameter 224
type names 340

U

unitypackage 180
Unity Script Directives 339
Unity ShaderLab forum
  URL 136
Unity Shader Reference
  URL 136
Unity website
  URL 141
update
  about 324
  example 324
Update() function 27, 28, 31, 46, 159, 168, 170,
      186, 189, 193, 194, 235, 244, 256, 304
Update functions 168
upleg_R 263
UserLength() function 309
userName parameter 293

V

variable declaration 340
Vector3.Slerp() 160
Vector3.Slerp() function 160
vertex$VertexFunction parameter 355
vertex shaders 351

W

WaitForFixedUpdate
  example 331
WaitForSeconds
  example 330, 331
WaitingForResponse() function 320

Wall game object 276
WarpMode parameter 143
waypoint
  AIController script 218, 223
  Awake() function 217
  AwayFromWaypoint() function 224
  creating 215
  GetComponentsInChildren() function 225
  GetComponentsInChildren.<T>() function 225
  GetComponentsInChildren.<Transform>()
      function 224
  GetComponentsInChildren(Transform) function
      224
  getDirection() function 223
  GetDirectionToPlayer() function 224
  lift off, preparing for 215, 216
  OnDrawGizmos() function 220, 222, 224, 226
  Start() function 217
  trigger parameter 224
  Waypoint game object 221
  waypoint script 223
Waypoint game object 221
Waypoints object 226
Waypoints script 221, 223, 229

X

XML data
  getting, from server 306-312
  lift off, preparing for 306, 307
XMLParser script 286, 307

Y

YieldInstruction
  about 329
  example 329, 330
yield statement 330

Thank you for buying
**Unity 3 Game
Development HOTSHOT**

About Packt Publishing

Packt, pronounced 'packed', published its first book "*Mastering phpMyAdmin for Effective MySQL Management*" in April 2004 and subsequently continued to specialize in publishing highly focused books on specific technologies and solutions.

Our books and publications share the experiences of your fellow IT professionals in adapting and customizing today's systems, applications, and frameworks. Our solution based books give you the knowledge and power to customize the software and technologies you're using to get the job done. Packt books are more specific and less general than the IT books you have seen in the past. Our unique business model allows us to bring you more focused information, giving you more of what you need to know, and less of what you don't.

Packt is a modern, yet unique publishing company, which focuses on producing quality, cutting-edge books for communities of developers, administrators, and newbies alike. For more information, please visit our website: www.packtpub.com.

Writing for Packt

We welcome all inquiries from people who are interested in authoring. Book proposals should be sent to author@packtpub.com. If your book idea is still at an early stage and you would like to discuss it first before writing a formal book proposal, contact us; one of our commissioning editors will get in touch with you.

We're not just looking for published authors; if you have strong technical skills but no writing experience, our experienced editors can help you develop a writing career, or simply get some additional reward for your expertise.

Unity 3D Game Development by Example Beginner's Guide

ISBN: 978-1-849690-54-6   Paperback: 384 pages

A seat-of-your-pants manual for building fun, groovy little games quickly

1. uild fun games using the free Unity 3D game engine even if you've never coded before

2. Learn how to "skin" projects to make totally different games from the same file – more games, less effort!

3. Deploy your games to the Internet so that your friends and family can play them

4. Packed with ideas, inspiration, and advice for your own game design and development

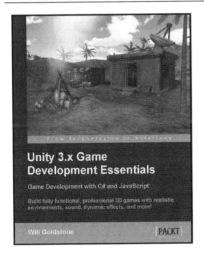

Unity 3.x Game Development Essentials

ISBN: 978-1-849691-44-4   Paperback: 420 pages

Build fully functional, professional 3D games with realistic environments, sound, dynamic effects, and more!

1. Kick start your game development, and build ready-to-play 3D games with ease.

2. Understand key concepts in game design including scripting, physics, instantiation, particle effects, and more.

3. Test & optimize your game to perfection with essential tips-and-tricks.

4. Written in clear, plain English, this book takes you from a simple prototype through to a complete 3D game with concepts you'll reuse throughout your new career as a game developer.

Please check **www.PacktPub.com** for information on our titles